翻译专业经典系列教材

English-Chinese Translation in Interaction

英汉互动翻译教程

李　明　编著

清华大学出版社
北京

版权所有，侵权必究。举报：010-62782989，beiqinquan@tup.tsinghua.edu.cn。

图书在版编目（CIP）数据

英汉互动翻译教程 / 李明编著. —北京：清华大学出版社，2016（2021.12重印）
翻译专业经典系列教材
ISBN 978-7-302-43408-5

Ⅰ. ①英… Ⅱ. ①李… Ⅲ. ①英语—翻译—教材 Ⅳ. ①H315.9

中国版本图书馆 CIP 数据核字（2016）第075244号

责任编辑：田　园
封面设计：平　原
责任校对：王凤芝
责任印制：沈　露

出版发行：清华大学出版社
　　　　网　　址：http://www.tup.com.cn, http://www.wqbook.com
　　　　地　　址：北京清华大学学研大厦A座　邮　编：100084
　　　　社 总 机：010-62770175　邮　购：010-62786544
　　　　投稿与读者服务：010-62776969, c-service@tup.tsinghua.edu.cn
　　　　质量反馈：010-62772015, zhiliang@tup.tsinghua.edu.cn
印 装 者：大厂回族自治县彩虹印刷有限公司
经　　销：全国新华书店
开　　本：185mm×230mm　　印　张：18.75　　字　数：295 千字
版　　次：2016 年 5 月第 1 版　　印　次：2021 年 12 月第 6 次印刷
定　　价：69.00元

产品编号：068659-03

前　言

　　翻译是跨语言、跨文化的交际活动。它在中国历史上起过非常重要的作用，在 21 世纪的今天，随着中国同世界各国之间在政治、经济、文化、外交、教育、科技等各个领域中的交往与合作越来越密切，越来越频繁，作为在这种交往与合作中的媒介——翻译，更是起着举足轻重的作用。正是因为翻译之重要，上海市政府于 20 世纪 90 年代中期就推出了上海市中、高级口译资格证书考试，并将其作为上海市 90 年代"十大紧缺人才培训工程"之一进行推广。顺应社会经济发展需要，国家人事部也于 2003 年开始，试行全国翻译专业资格（水平）考试。在今天新的时代语境下，翻译学科与专业建设在我国已经取得了前所未有的发展，已有许多高等外语院校或外语院系成立了翻译学院或翻译系，开始招收翻译专业本科生、翻译硕士专业研究生。目前，我国具有翻译专业本科教育培养资质的高校达 152 所（截至 2015 年），具有翻译硕士专业学位培养资质的高校达 206 所（截至 2014 年 7 月）。除此之外，我国各高校的英语专业、商务英语专业以及硕士研究生阶段，甚至是博士研究生阶段，开设翻译方向或翻译课程的高校更是难计其数。

　　在此背景下，我国的翻译教学呈现出一派欣欣向荣的景象。各个高校开设的翻译课程类型众多，有英汉翻译、汉英翻译、商务英汉翻译、商务汉英翻译、基础笔译、笔译初阶、笔译中阶、笔译高阶、翻译批评与赏析、翻译工作坊、文体与翻译、科技翻译、旅游翻译、法律翻译、传媒翻译等等。这些课程的开设为繁荣我国翻译教学，培养我国各行各业所需的翻译人才提供了前提条件。翻译教学成败的一个重要因素便是翻译教材是否适用。十几年来，许多翻译界专家学者和有识之士，投入大量精力编写了各种各具特色的翻译教材，为我国翻译人才的培养作出了重要贡献。笔者自 1995 年硕士研究生毕业以来，一直在高校教学第一线从事翻译教学工作，为本科生开设过英汉翻译、汉英翻译、译作赏析、商务英汉翻译、商务汉英翻译等课程。所有这些课程的教学使我充分认识到，翻译教材必须具有较强的可操作性，只有这样，翻译课

教师在课堂上才能够讲解自如，使学生从中获益。

何为具有较强的可操作性？目前市面上的翻译教材可谓汗牛充栋，但教材的编写基本上都没有脱离从翻译概论、翻译基础理论、英汉语言文化对比、词语翻译、翻译技巧等到各种文体翻译的这种思路和模式。而且，有些翻译教材中的许多例句内容较为单薄且略显陈旧，时代感不强，缺乏一定的思想性和趣味性。教师上课时，如果使用这些句子作为例句，往往难以从中挖掘出较为深刻的思想内涵，对翻译技巧的阐释力不够强。另外，许多教材的编著者在编写翻译教材的过程中，多喜欢不加分析地直接引用他人的译文作为译例（殊不知许多译文是需要仔细斟酌推敲，并有大的改进之余地的），这样就导致许多译例以讹传讹。作为翻译教材，所引用的原文例子应该经典，所给出的译文应该准确、通顺、有韵味，只有这样，才能够为翻译学习者提供一个示范，将他们引入正确的翻译之途。

笔者自1995年开始翻译教学时起即着手收集资料，2003年初动笔编写，2006年完成并出版了这本《英汉互动翻译教程》。该教材融入了笔者翻译教学的理念和思路，也融入了笔者对翻译的感悟和理解，旨在让翻译教师在课堂内外以与学生分享心得体会的交流及互动方式传授翻译技艺。

该教材于2006年首次出版后每年重印3 000册，多年来一直畅销不衰，受到广大高校青年学子和从事翻译教学的老师们的热烈欢迎。书中融入的作为译者最为真切感受的译文点评，是广大翻译教师、高校青年学子以及各届热衷于翻译研究和翻译实践的仁人志士最为欣赏和喜欢的真材实料，再加上书中的例句选择精当，课后练习生动有趣且有译文对照及篇章练习译文点评，使得这本教材成为英语语言文学专业翻译方向本科生、商务英语专业商务翻译方向本科生、翻译专业本科生和热爱翻译的仁人志士不可多得的案头必备。

本教材共分二十章，每一章包括理论探讨、译例举隅及翻译点评、翻译比较与欣赏和翻译练习四个部分。在第二十章之后还根据本教材需要增加了一些附录，作为对本教材的补充和完善。每一章第一部分的"理论探讨"，以深入浅出的方式，讲解与本章所涉翻译技巧有关的理论，但理论的陈述均和译例紧密结合，避免空洞讲解理论。第二部分的"译例举隅及翻译点评"，主要用例句来阐明第一部分所陈述的内容，并在【点评】中作一些鞭辟入里的分析，必要时还增加更多例句予以佐证。第三部分为"翻

前　言

译比较与欣赏"，该部分内容可以作为学生课外研读和赏析的内容，一般提供四个译例，每个译例都提供两到三个或三个以上的译文，供学习者比较、研读、分析、欣赏之用。本教材编著者对其中许多译例都给出了自己的译文。尽管译文没有最好，但本人所给出的译文是在本人的知识和能力范围内所能给出的自认为最好的译文。第四部分为"翻译练习"。翻译练习包括句子翻译和篇章翻译两项内容，其中篇章翻译包含篇章翻译 1 和篇章翻译 2 两个部分。句子翻译在 10 到 20 句之间，篇章翻译 1 提供了一个参考译文，篇章翻译 2 则提供了两个译文（一个是参考译文，一个是本人给出的译文）和译文点评，译文点评主要由我曾经的翻译学硕士研究生、现为我校英语语言文化学院的青年教师卢立程老师撰写，他对两个译文进行了客观、中肯的评价，供翻译学习者学习参考。*

　　读者从笔者对本教材的编写不难看出，笔者非常关注句子和句子以上语言单位（即语篇）的翻译。应该说，句子和语篇是笔者所认为的不同层面的翻译单位。前者为微观层面的翻译单位，后者为宏观层面的翻译单位。另外，笔者始终认为，从大的方面讲，翻译能丰富人类文化、促进文化交流，为建设一个国家的富强、民主、文明作出贡献；从小的方面即个人方面来讲，翻译能提高个人语言文化素养，也能增强个人身心修养。从事翻译实践活动其乐无穷，质疑他人的译文并尽自己所能提供令自己心仪的译文，会不断增加我们的智慧，让我们不断地享受美味的精神食粮。再者，我很注重翻译技巧的训练。对待翻译技巧，我很同意霍桂桓在其论文《翻译的技巧、理想、标准及其形成过程——兼析作为〈论不可译性〉之理论前提的康德先验哲学观》中所持的看法：

　　虽然表面看来，"翻译技巧"似乎仅仅处于没有理论色彩的"技术"层次之上，但从作为社会个体的翻译者的生成过程角度来看，情况就大不相同了——首先，作为这种个体的具体生成过程的结果，它是翻译者以往的成功经验的总结和结晶，因而完全可以说是一定的翻译理想和翻译标准得到某种程度上的实现之后的结晶；尽管迄今为止的翻译理论研究并没有从这种角度对它加以充分的重视。其次，在翻译和翻译教学过程中，它既是使翻译者、翻译学习者避免走弯路、从而事半功倍的方便法门，同时也从具体操作角度

---

* 翻译练习答案及译文点评请登录清华大学出版社网站 www.tup.tsinghua.edu.cn 下载，或联系编辑邮箱 tianyuan_tup@qq.com。

体现了某种"翻译理想"和"翻译标准",因而是实现和达到后者的有效手段。不过,只有把它与某种"翻译理想"和"翻译标准"实际联系起来,我们才能真正看到这一点并加以认真的研究。最后,同时也最重要的是,无论"写作技巧"还是"翻译技巧",都是与作者、翻译者特定的人生经历、知识素养和精神境界紧密联系在一起的,是这种生成过程、素养和境界的积淀结果。

本教材所选译例均来自本人从事翻译教学过程中的精心积累以及各种翻译教科书。所有译例均具有较强的时代感、思想性、趣味性,不管是教师讲解还是学生欣赏,均可对它们细细品味、细细回味,领略其中无限的妙处。

本教材出版已经十年。历经十年检验,仍然深受广大读者欢迎,这对笔者来说无疑是极大的鼓励。今天,在清华大学出版社伯乐相马,拟将该教材作为"翻译专业经典系列教材"之一予以出版之际,笔者对其中的部分内容进行了修订,还增加了一些新的内容。相信在清华大学出版社的努力之下,该教材一定会成为名副其实的经典。在此,我要衷心感谢清华大学出版社外语分社的郝建华社长对本教材的出版所给予的充分认可和大力支持,感谢该出版社的编辑田园女士为本教材的策划所作的辛勤付出。

本教材适合英语语言文学专业翻译方向本科生、商务英语专业商务翻译方向本科生、翻译专业本科生和各界热爱翻译的仁人志士作为教材或辅助材料之用,也可作为广大高校英语教师和其他英语爱好者学习翻译的教材。因笔者的精力和水平有限,艺海无涯,译海无涯,书中谬误之处在所难免,恳请广大译界专家学者和读者批评指正。

编　者
二〇一六年一月于广东外语外贸大学高级翻译学院

目 录

第一章　翻译概论
一、理论探讨 1
二、译例举隅及翻译点评 5
三、翻译比较与欣赏 9
四、翻译练习 11

第二章　翻译的过程
一、理论探讨 14
二、译例举隅及翻译点评 17
三、翻译比较与欣赏 24
四、翻译练习 26

第三章　直译与意译
一、理论探讨 29
二、译例举隅及翻译点评 31
三、翻译比较与欣赏 35
四、翻译练习 37

第四章　词义的选择
一、理论探讨 39
二、译例举隅及翻译点评 41
三、翻译比较与欣赏 48
四、翻译练习 51

第五章　语境对词义选择的作用
一、理论探讨 54
二、译例举隅及翻译点评 57
三、翻译比较与欣赏 63

四、翻译练习 66

第六章　省词翻译法
　　一、理论探讨 69
　　二、译例举隅及翻译点评 70
　　三、翻译比较与欣赏 75
　　四、翻译练习 78

第七章　增词翻译法
　　一、理论探讨 81
　　二、译例举隅及翻译点评 81
　　三、翻译比较与欣赏 91
　　四、翻译练习 94

第八章　翻译中重复的运用
　　一、理论探讨 98
　　二、译例举隅及翻译点评 101
　　三、翻译比较与欣赏 107
　　四、翻译练习 109

第九章　翻译中文字的简练
　　一、理论探讨 112
　　二、译例举隅及翻译点评 114
　　三、翻译比较与欣赏 119
　　四、翻译练习 122

第十章　词类转换翻译法
　　一、理论探讨 125
　　二、译例举隅及翻译点评 126

三、翻译比较与欣赏 131
四、翻译练习 133

第十一章　引申翻译法
一、理论探讨 137
二、译例举隅及翻译点评 138
三、翻译比较与欣赏 143
四、翻译练习 145

第十二章　被动语态的汉译
一、理论探讨 149
二、译例举隅及翻译点评 150
三、翻译比较与欣赏 155
四、翻译练习 157

第十三章　翻译中句子结构的调整
一、理论探讨 160
二、译例举隅及翻译点评 161
三、翻译比较与欣赏 168
四、翻译练习 171

第十四章　英语主语的汉译法
一、理论探讨 174
二、译例举隅及翻译点评 175
三、翻译比较与欣赏 181
四、翻译练习 183

第十五章　正说反译、反说正译法
一、理论探讨 186

二、译例举隅及翻译点评 188
　　三、翻译比较与欣赏 194
　　四、翻译练习 197

第十六章　定语从句的翻译法
　　一、理论探讨 200
　　二、译例举隅及翻译点评 202
　　三、翻译比较与欣赏 207
　　四、翻译练习 209

第十七章　英语特殊句式的翻译
　　一、理论探讨 214
　　二、译例举隅及翻译点评 214
　　三、翻译比较与欣赏 219
　　四、翻译练习 221

第十八章　隐喻的翻译
　　一、理论探讨 224
　　二、译例举隅及翻译点评 226
　　三、翻译比较与欣赏 231
　　四、翻译练习 234

第十九章　英语长句的翻译（一）
　　一、理论探讨 237
　　二、译例举隅及翻译点评 240
　　三、翻译比较与欣赏 246
　　四、翻译练习 249

第二十章　英语长句的翻译（二）

一、理论探讨...252
二、译例举隅及翻译点评.......................................255
三、翻译比较与欣赏...263
四、翻译练习...265

附录

附录一：中国翻译简史...269
附录二：翻译标准的新思考.....................................275
附录三：金隄建议的翻译的步骤.................................279

参考文献..281

第一章 翻译概论

> 不愿付诸努力、不愿忍受挫折者永远成不了翻译家。
>
> ——兰德斯

一、理论探讨

翻译的性质

翻译是人类精神文明中最富活力、最敏锐的领域之一。(刘宓庆,1999:Ⅱ)说它最富活力,是因为只要世界上不同民族的人们之间有交流,翻译活动便永远不会停止;不同民族的人们之间交流得越频繁,翻译活动也就越频繁。说它最敏锐,是因为"翻译,无论是作为文化现象、思想运动,还是作为一项职业、一种知识技能,总与所处的时代背景密不可分。翻译的观念、方法、样式、标准、风格,无不与时俱进"(刘宓庆,1999:Ⅱ)。因此,翻译最敏锐地反映着时代特征。

什么是翻译?翻译有广义和狭义之分。

广义的翻译包括语际翻译(interlingual translation),即语言与语言之间的转换、语内翻译(intralingual translation),即同一语言文化系统内部语言变体与语言变体之间的转换、符际翻译(intersemiotic translation),即语言同非语言符号之间的代码转换和基本信息传达。语言与语言之间的翻译指的是不同语言,如英语与汉语、汉语与法语、俄语与德语等之间的代码转换与信息传达。同一语言文化系统内部语言变体与语言变体之间的翻译指的是同一种语言的变体,比如古今语言(如汉语的文言文与白话文,古英语与现代英语等)之间、不同方言(如粤语与普通话,客家话与闽南话等)

之间的语码转换与信息传达。语言同非语言符号之间的翻译指的是自然语言（如英语、汉语等）与其他交际符号（如手语、交通标志、计算机语言等）之间的语码转换与信息传达，如，把一条交通规则画成一个交通标志，人机对话等。可见，广义的翻译可谓包罗万象。

狭义的翻译主要指语际翻译，它是指运用一种语言（目的语，target language）把另一种语言（源语，source language）所表达的思维内容准确、通顺地重新表达出来，使译文读者能得到原作者所表达的思想，得到与原文读者大致相同的感受（范仲英，1994：13）。本书我们所谈论的翻译主要是狭义的翻译。

美国翻译理论家尤金·奈达（Nida, 1959: 19）认为，所谓翻译就是首先在意义方面，其次在风格方面用最切近的、自然的对等语将源语信息在目的语当中再现出来[1]。

从以上中西译论对翻译的定义可以看出，翻译是一种语言之间的转换活动，是一种精神产品的再生产过程，这种过程通过翻译者的创造性思维活动来完成。这种转换活动由于涉及两种语言的内在规律和相互联系，因而具有其独特的科学的规律性，对这种科学的规律性，翻译工作者要能够进行科学的认识和把握。与此同时，在翻译者对原文进行再创造的过程中，不是机械地对原文照搬、模仿和假借，而是采用各种独特的翻译方法，灵活地、创造性地对原文进行移植、重塑、再造和复归，因而翻译是一种艺术性的重构活动与再现活动（张泽乾，1994：249-250）。因此，翻译既是科学，又是艺术。但正如许多其他艺术形式一样，艺术的成型要靠具体的技能来完成。对于翻译而言，要想使译文成为一种创造性艺术，除了要科学地掌握所涉及的两种语言之间的转换规律之外，还要运用诸如增词、减词、引申、转换词类、调整结构、转换视角等翻译技巧，以便达到艺术地再现原文信息的目的。这些翻译技巧是可以通过课堂讲授和翻译实践来掌握的。因此，翻译又可以说是一种技能。

翻译的目的和功能

翻译是一种跨语言（cross-linguistic）、跨文化（cross-cultural）、跨社会（cross-social）的交际活动。它是不同民族之间思想交流的桥梁和接力（范仲英，1994：12）。

---

[1] 奈达的原文为：Translating consists in reproducing in the receptor language the closest natural equivalent of the source language message, first in terms of meaning, and secondly in terms of style.

说它是桥梁，是因为：正是有了翻译，不同民族的人们之间才得以沟通思想感情、传播文化知识、促进文明进步；正是有了翻译，才能使得不懂原语的人们能够通过译文而轻松地获取原文作者所传递的信息、思想、情感、观点和意图等。

说它是接力，是因为：正是有了译文，才使得译者将原文作者的信息、思想、情感、观点和意图等像接力赛中的接力棒那样，从一个民族传递到另一个民族，从而将原文信息的传播范围扩大。

翻译的标准和原则

翻译标准是衡量翻译工作效果的标尺和检验翻译成果质量的准绳，翻译原则是从事翻译活动所应遵循的指导思想和应服从的基本法则（张泽乾，1994：260）。什么是翻译标准？我国最著名和讨论得最多的要数清代翻译家严复于1898年提出的"信、达、雅"（faithfulness, expressiveness and elegance）三字标准，该三字标准对后世翻译界产生了深远影响。严复认为，"信"即"忠实"，指译文要抓住原文要旨，不偏离原文思想、情感、观点和意图。"达"即"通顺"，指译文词句可以有所颠倒或增删，"取明深义，故词句之间，时有所颠倒附益，不斤斤于字比句次"。"达"与"信"同等重要，顾"信"而不"达"，"虽译犹不译也"。要使译文"达"，译者必须认真通读原文，并"融会于心"，再用地道的目的语再现原文信息。碰到"原文词理本深，难于共喻"之处，"则当前后引衬，以显其意"。"雅"就是指译文要古雅，要采用汉代以前使用的古典文字。

严复之后，许多人对"雅"字颇有异议，于是提出了各自的翻译标准。如林语堂提出了"忠实、通顺、美"（faithfulness, smoothness, beauty），瞿秋白提出了"忠实、精确"，曾虚白提出了"意似"等翻译标准；当代翻译家刘重德提出了"信、达、切"（faithfulness, expressiveness and closeness），台湾翻译理论家思果提出了"信、达、贴"（faithfulness, expressiveness and fitness），翻译理论家金隄提出了"信、达、神韵"（faithfulness, expressiveness and charm），傅雷提出了"神似说"（transference of soul or spirit），钱钟书提出了"化境说"（sublimed adaptation）等等。

当代翻译理论和实践家庄绎传先生对严复的"信、达、雅"三字标准作了这样的阐释："如果一篇译文在内容上是忠实的，在语言上是通顺的，在风格上是得体的，那的确就是一篇很好的译文了。"也就是说，"信、达、雅"三字标准的意思是"忠实准确（faithfulness）"、"通顺流畅（smoothness）"、"风格得体"（appropriateness in style）。

我们既可以在评判别人的译文时，用这三个字作为尺度进行评判，在进行翻译时，我们也可以这三个字作为翻译原则予以遵循。

在西方，第一个较为全面地对"信"（faithfulness）、"达"（perspicuity）、"雅"（gracefulness）进行探讨的翻译理论家为John Dryden。他在1680年的一篇翻译奥维德（Ovid）作品的"译例言"中谈及了这三个问题；又在1697年翻译维吉尔（Virgil）作品的"译例言"中再次提到，要用自己的语言去再现原文的"雅"（elegance）（王东风，2002：67）。第一个对翻译原则进行探讨的翻译理论家为泰特勒（Alexander Fraser Tytler, 1747-1813）。他认为：第一，翻译应该完全再现原作的思想；第二，译文的写作风格和行文方式应该同原文如出一辙；第三，译文读来应该同原作一样如行云流水。[2]（转引自仲伟合，2001：77）泰特勒的翻译三原则同"信、达、雅"三字翻译标准完全一样，只是第二条原则同第三条原则与"达"和"雅"在次序上颠倒了过来，即泰特勒的第二条原则相当于"雅"，第三条原则相当于"达"。

从以上观之，中西翻译标准和翻译原则可谓不谋而合。我们在评判译文时可以使用该翻译标准进行评判；在从事翻译时，可以使用该翻译原则来指导我们的翻译实践和翻译活动。

➡ 翻译的种类

翻译按照所涉及的语言，可分为语内翻译和语际翻译两类。按照其工作方式，翻译可分为口译（interpreting）、笔译（translation）和机器翻译（machine translation）三种。口译分为连续翻译（consecutive interpreting）和同声传译（simultaneous interpreting），前者指口译人员等讲话人讲完一部分内容或全部讲完内容之后，再翻译给听众。后者是指口译人员在讲话人发言的同时，边听边译。按照所翻译的材料划分，有科技翻译、

---

[2] 泰特勒的翻译三原则原文为：I. That the translation should give a complete transcription of the ideas of the original work. II. That the style and manner of writing should be of the same character with that of the original. III. That the translation should have all the ease of the original composition.

文学翻译、新闻翻译、政论文翻译、应用文翻译等等。按照具体的处理方式，可分为全译（full-text translation）、摘译（abridged translation）和编译（adapted translation）等。

二、译例举隅及翻译点评

【例1】

原　　文：子曰："学而时习之，不亦说乎！有朋自远方来，不亦乐乎！人不知而不愠，不亦君子乎！"

译文一：孔子说："学习了而时常温习，不也高兴吗！有朋友从远方来，不也快乐吗！别人不了解我，我并不怨恨，不也是君子吗？"（徐志刚 译）

译文二：The Master said, To learn and at due times to repeat what one has learnt, is that not after all a pleasure? That friends should come to one from afar, is this not after all delightful? To remain unsoured even though one's merits are unrecognized by others, is that not after all what is expected of a gentleman?（Waley 译）

【点评】原文同译文一之间的转换属于语内翻译（intralingual translation），即使用同一语言的其他语言符号对原文进行阐释或者重述（rewording）。原文同译文二之间的转换属于语际翻译（interlingual translation），即两个不同语言之间所进行的转换。

【例2】

原　　文：A: What does your watch say?

B: It says "five past three".

【点评】在这一话轮中，B 实际上是在进行一种翻译，这种翻译叫做符际翻译（intersemiotic translation），即语言同非语言符号之间的代码转换。当 A 询问 B 几点钟的时候，B 只能看钟或者手表，而钟或者手表并不能说话，B 只能根据钟表的时针和分针来确定具体几点钟了。而 B 所言实际上是

5

言语传达一个非言语信息（non-linguistic message）。将非言语信息用言语传达出来是翻译的一种方式，这不是从一种语言到另一种语言的转换过程，而是从非语言交际系统到语言交际系统的过程。非语言交际系统和语言交际系统的共同特征是两者都属于"符号系统"（即用于交际的系统）。雅可布逊（Jakobson）将这种由非语言交际系统到语言交际系统的转换过程称为符际翻译是恰当的。其实，我们每个人每一天、每一刻都在进行着符际翻译而不自知。从这个意义上说，我们每个人都是某种意义上的译者。(Hervey et al., 1995: 8-9)

【例3】

原　文：Zhou came through to Kissinger as subtle, brilliant, and indirect, a politician of vision who refused to get bogged down in petty details.

译文一：周恩来让基辛格感到自己很敏感、有才气、委婉，是一个拒绝过分关注细微末节的有眼力的政治家。

译文二：在基辛格眼里，周恩来敏锐、聪慧而含蓄，是一位目光远大，不斤斤于细节的政治家。（王宏印，2002：24）

译文三：基辛格感觉到，周恩来敏锐、聪慧、含蓄，具有政治家的远见卓识而不斤斤计较任何细节。（李明 译）

【点评】译文一相对于原文，"信"是"信"，但没有进入到语义的深层次，因而这种"信"只是表面层次上的"信"；在语言的表达上，译文一不是通顺的汉语，带有欧化语言的味道。译文二相对于译文一要略胜一筹，语言很通顺，取得了"达"的效果，但在风韵和美学价值上没有达到最佳境界，故仍有可改进的地方，尤其是，采用了"是……的政治家"这样非常没有力度的一种句式。译文三可谓完全达到了"信、达、雅"三字标准，在语言的"雅"方面，达到了刘宓庆先生（1999：160）所说的准确、精炼、隽秀，所选择的"具有政治家的远见卓识而不斤斤计较任何细节"这样的表达很有力度。

【例4】

原　文：我干了一天活，累得连炕都上不去，浑身疼得要命，睡也睡不着。

译文一：I was so fatigued after a day's drudgery that I found it very hard to mount the *kang*. My whole frame aching acutely, I could not go to sleep, however hard I tried.

译文二：I was so tired after a day's work that I could hardly get on to the *kang*. As my body ached all over, I simply couldn't get to sleep even if I tried to.（朱佩芬，1995：6）

【点评】两种译文均很好地传达出了原文的意义，但风格迥异。译文一在用词方面可谓精雕细琢，使用了诸如 fatigued、drudgery、mount、frame、acutely 以及 however hard 之类的非常书面化的语言。译文二则使用常用词语，完全没有文绉绉的书面语言。译文一属于笔译，译文二属于口译。笔译同口译之区别可以通过用词来体现，也可以通过句法来体现。这里是通过用词来体现两者之间的区别的。因此，翻译时，在选词过程中，把握词语的正式程度和语体非常重要。再如：

原　文：I am very glad to hear that the contract has been signed only after two rounds of discussions.

译文一：欣闻只进行两轮谈判就订立了合同，甚为高兴。

译文二：听说才经过两轮谈判就签了合同，我很高兴。

【例5】

原　文：I would like to conclude with the hope that all of you will have a chance to come to the United States soon, not only to continue our common pursuits of professional interest, but to partake of our hospitality as well.

译文一：最后，我衷心希望在座各位不久能有机会来到美国，同我们一道继续探讨专业方面我们共同感兴趣的问题，同时也让各位亲自领略我们的盛情款待。

译文二：在结束致词之前，我要表达一个愿望，希望在座诸位不久能有机会访问

美国。我们将在那里尽我们的地主之谊,双方将继续进行专业方面的探讨。

【点评】 译文一和译文二在句法上有区别:译文一用词比较考究,使用的句子是比较复杂的长句,而译文二使用的则是简单句。使用简单句符合说话的习惯,同时也可以避免句法上的差错。因此,译文一属于笔译的行文方式,译文二则属于口译的行文方式。

由例4和例5观之,口译和笔译思路截然不同,做法相距甚远。对于同一个人来说,要成为口译和笔译都精通的通才,是非常困难的。

【例6】

原　文:The research work is being done by a group of dedicated and imaginative scientists who specialize in extracting from various sea animals substances that may improve the health of the human race.

译文一:这项研究工作正在被一小组专心致志、具有想象力的科学家进行着。这些科学家专门研究从各种各样的海洋动物中提取一些可能改进人类健康的物质。

译文二:一群(为数不多的)科学家正在专心致志地从事这项研究(工作),他们以丰富的想象力专门钻研从各种海洋动物身上提取增进人类健康的物质。（李明 译）

【点评】 读罢译文一,没有人能够说该译文没有再现源语信息,也没有人能够说译文有语法错误,但读起来就是生硬、单调、乏味,具有很强的翻译腔。作为译文,读起来不应该一听上去就是译文。如果一听上去就是译文,说明译文不符合目的语表达规范,因而不通顺、不流畅、不地道。作为译文,一方面要忠实于原文,另一方面又要通顺地道,没有斧凿的痕迹,那样的译文才算是上佳的译文。在仔细斟酌、修改、润色之后,我们有了译文二。译文二没有斧凿的痕迹,读来通顺流畅、符合汉语表达习惯。

【例7】

原　文:In secret we met; In silence I grieve.

译文一：我们暗中相会；我暗自悲伤。（穆凤良，2009：226）

译文二：当年你我偷偷幽会，今天唯我暗自伤悲。（穆凤良，2009：226）

译文三：秘密地，当时我俩约会；默默地，如今我独自伤悲。（李明 译）

【点评】译文一为什么不恰当？因为该译文没有体现动词"相会"和"悲伤"各自的时态。译文二中出现了原文中似乎没有明确表示出来的"当年"和"今天"，那么，它们分别从何而来呢？仔细分析不难看出，译者如此翻译的理据是：动词met使用的是一般过去时，动词grieve使用的是一般现在时。根据原文句子所表达的意思，译者分别将这两种动词定位在"当年"和"今天"发生，基本上符合实际，也符合逻辑。译文三则使用"当时"和"如今"进行表达。"当时"比"当年"所指的时间似乎更宽泛一些，同样，"如今"比"今天"所指的时间也更宽泛一些。

英语句子中的限定动词体现时态，而汉语里的动词则不体现时态，英汉翻译时，一定要注意英语原文句子中限定动词的时态在汉语译文中的再现。再如：1) Many strange new means of transport **have been developed** in our century, the strangest of them being perhaps the hovercraft. 在我们这个世纪，很多新奇的交通工具都已研制出来了，其中最为奇特的交通工具也许要数气垫船了。2) **Had** Senator Jeremy **had** eyes **for** his daughter, he **would have seen** that, in place of the young girl of 15 he had brought in Hawaii a short month ago, he was now taking away with him a woman. 参议员杰里米要是**留意到了自己女儿**，他**早就会注意到**，他现在带走的，不是他在短短一个月之前带来的那个15岁的少女，而是一个成熟的女人。

三、翻译比较与欣赏

【例1】

原　文：It was an old woman, tall and shapely still, though withered by time, on whom

his eyes fell when he stopped and turned.

译文一：当他站住并转身时，目光落在一个老年妇女的身上，她身材高，而且模样好，虽然时光使她变得干枯了。

译文二：他站住了，转过身来，定睛一看，是个年迈的妇女，她身材很高，而且仍然匀称；虽然受了时间的折磨而有点憔悴。

译文三：他站住了，转过身来，定睛一看，是个年迈的妇女。她身材修长，虽受岁月的折磨而显憔悴，但风韵犹存。

译文四：他停住脚步，转过身来，目光落在一位年迈妇女的身上。她身材高挑，虽然经受岁月的磨难而憔悴，但风韵仍不减当年。（李明 译）

【例 2】

原　文：And I do not mistrust the future; I do not fear what is ahead. For our problems are large, but our heart is larger. Our challenges are great, but our will is greater. And if our flaws are endless, God's love is truly boundless.

译文一：而我不是不相信未来；我不害怕即将来临的事情。因为我们的问题是大的，但是我们的信心更大。我们的挑战是大的，但是我们的决心更大。如果我们的缺点是没完没了的，上帝的爱是真正的无穷无尽的。

译文二：我并不信任未来；我并不害怕我们面临的问题。我们的问题很多，但我们的心胸更宽广。我们面临的挑战很严峻，但我们的决心更坚定无比。如果说我们的弊病层出不穷的话，那么上帝的爱更是真正的广袤无边。

译文三：我深信未来，但不害怕我们要面对的一切。我们要面对的问题很多很多，但我们的心怀要更加博大宽广；我们要面对的挑战非常严峻，但我们的意志会更加坚定。如果说我们有着数不清的缺点，那么上帝的爱一定会博大无边。（李明 译）

【例 3】

原　文："I'm an orphan myself," she answered, "and whoever tries to twist you up, may the end of his nose take a twist. But don't let them think they can take advantage of me. I want a dowry of fifty guilders, and let them take up a collection besides.

Otherwise they can kiss my you-know-what."（摘自"Gimpel the fool"，参见周方珠《英汉翻译原理》, pp. 16-23）

译文一："我自己不也是孤儿"。她答道，"谁要是捉弄你，谁的鼻子尖就会被弄歪。不过，别让他们以为他们可占我的便宜，我要价值50盾的嫁妆，还要他们拿一份彩礼。否则，让他们来吻我的那个玩意儿。"

译文二："我不也是孤儿"。她答道，"谁要是捉弄你，就要谁的鼻子尖歪了。不过，别老以为他们能占本人的便宜，我要50盾的嫁妆，还要他们凑一份彩礼，不然的话，就让他们来吻我的那个吧。"

译文三："人家不也是孤儿"。她答道，"谁骗你，谁就不得好死。不过，他们要是认为能占我的便宜（他们要是想占我的便宜），没门儿，我要的是50盾的嫁妆，外加一份彩礼，要是没有这些，就让他们来舔本姑娘（姑奶奶）的屁股。"

【例4】

原　文：He was slightly disturbed by the cashier, a young and giggling Wisconsin school-teacher with ankles.

译文一：那个年轻的出纳员、威斯康星州的女教师的咯咯笑声和一双漂亮的脚弄得马丁有点心慌意乱。（柯平 译）

译文二：望着眼前的这位年轻出纳，来自威斯康星州的女教师，马丁被她的咯咯笑声和轮廓清晰的漂亮脚踝弄得有点心旌荡漾。（曾利沙 译）

译文三：眼前的这位出纳曾是威斯康星州的中学教师，她年轻，总是发出咯咯的笑声，拥有一对漂亮的脚踝，见到她，马丁不免有点心情激荡。（李明 译）

四、翻 译 练 习

句子翻译

1. The whole station was astir when news came that there was an explosion in the train.

2. Later in the day, when the sun had leached the last of my enthusiasm, my father took the bow for his final turn.

3. Rogge says his surgical career has taught him about having a sense of responsibility, and remaining humble, calm and cool.

4. For students of composition, an awareness that rhetorical patterns differ from one culture to another can help them become more quickly proficient in a writing pattern that is not native to them.

5. The machine would have to be able to move about in a house designed for human beings and would therefore have to go through a normal door, open such a door and close it, and walk up and down stairs over irregularities on the floor.

6. If North America and Europe renew their moral life, build on their culture commonality, and develop closer forms of economic and political integration to supplement their security collaboration in NATO, they could generate a third Euro-American phase of western affluence and political influence.

7. They were, in fact, very fine ladies; not deficient in good humor when they were pleased, nor in the power of being agreeable when they chose it; but proud and conceited.

8. At 6:10 p.m., December 6, 1973, Gerald Rudolph Ford, raised his right hand in the US House of Representatives, where he had spent twenty-five years working toward but never getting the top office of Speaker, and became Vice President of the United States.

9. The mantle of your high office has been placed on your shoulder at a time when the world at large and this Organization are going through an exceptionally critical phase.

10. The new leaders may be better educated, more technologically inclined, and more cosmopolitan.

篇章翻译

篇章翻译 1

Life is never just being. It is becoming, a relentless flowing on. Our parents live on through us, and we will live on through our children. The institutions we build endure, and we will endure through them. The beauty we fashion cannot be dimmed by death. Our flesh may perish, our hands will wither, but that which they create in beauty and goodness and truth lives on for all time to come.

Don't spend and waste your lives accumulating objects that will only turn to dust and ashes. Pursue not so much the material as the ideal, for ideals alone invest life with meaning and are of enduring worth.

Add love to a house and you have a home. Add righteousness to a city and you have a community. Add truth to a pile of red brick and you have a school. Add religion to the humblest of edifices and you have a sanctuary. Add justice to the far-flung round of human endeavor and you have civilization. Put them all together, exalt them above their present imperfections, add to them the vision of human kind redeemed, forever free of need and strife and you have a future lighted with the radiant colors of hope.

篇章翻译 2

1) Lexicography provides at its best a joyful sense of busyness with language. 2) One is immersed in the details of language as in no other field. 3) Sometimes the details are so overwhelming and endless they sap the spirit and depress the mind. 4) Often at the end of a hard day's work one realizes with dismay that the meager stack of finished work one has accomplished has an immeasurably slight impact on the work as a whole. 5) As I hope the readers of this work will come to understand, dictionaries do not sprint into being. 6) People must plan them, collect information, and write them. 7) Writing takes time, and it is often frustrating and even infuriating. 8) No other form of writing is at once so quixotic and so intensely practical. 9) Dictionary making does not require brilliance or originality of mind. 10) It does require high intelligence, mastery of the craft, and dedication to hard work. 11) If one has produced a dictionary, one has the satisfaction of having produced a work of enduring value.

第二章 翻译的过程

> 要做好翻译工作，必得对于原文有彻底的了解，同时对于运用本国语文有充分的把握。
>
> ——吕叔湘

一、理论探讨

翻译的过程就是理解和表达的过程。换句话说，翻译的过程是由理解和表达两个阶段组成的。有人认为，翻译还有一个校核阶段。但我们认为，校核实际上是对原文的再理解和对译文的再表达。

翻译是把一种语言（即原语）的信息用另一种语言（即译语）表达出来，使译文读者能理解原作者所表达的思想，得到与原文读者大致相同的感受。那么，翻译的关键首先在于充分理解原文所表达的信息，充分领略原文给译者带来的感受，接下来才是表达。充分理解了原文作者所表达的信息而不进行表达，就称不上翻译。只有将理解同翻译联系起来才可以称得上翻译。在翻译过程的理解阶段中，如果译者曲解了原文作者所要表达的思想，就违背了"信"的翻译原则。但如果译者充分理解了原文作者的思想，而在表达阶段，由于译入语的语言基本功问题以及翻译能力等问题而不能充分地传达出原文作者的思想，则违背了"达"的翻译原则。由此可见，"理解"和"表达"相辅相成。只有充分理解了的信息才有可能被充分表达，不理解的东西不可能被充分表达出来；反过来，被充分表达出来的信息一定是被充分理解了的信息。

在对源语进行理解的阶段中，译者首先要对源语作表层结构（语音形式部分＋逻辑形式部分）的分析和理解，接着便是对其中介层结构（即语用修辞部分）的分析和理解，最后是对其深层结构（即语义内容部分）的分析和理解。在目的语的表达阶段，译者首先要从源语的深层结构中走出来，考虑使用怎样的目的语的深层结构传达源语语义内容，接着考虑如何使用目的语的中介结构，即采用怎样的语用修辞，再到目的语的表层结构，即采用怎样的语音形式加上逻辑形式来传达源语信息（张泽乾，1994：239-240）。理解和表达既是一个连续体，同时又相辅相成、相互促进，不断反复。

总之，要做到对源语理解正确与充分，译者必须能够从各种角度（如句法分析法、语义分析法、语体分析法、语用分析法、语篇分析法、文化分析法等等）对原作进行深入细致的分析。对于理解了的信息要在译入语中正确、充分地表达出来，译者必须对目的语语言有很好的把握，并能够运用灵活的翻译技巧，传达原文神韵，运用地道的目的语句子结构和搭配再现源语信息。

翻译的全过程由具体的翻译步骤来实现。根据刘宓庆（1999：141-161）的研究，将源语的一个句子翻译成目的语的典型过程可分为以下六个步骤：在理解阶段有紧缩主干、辨析词义、分析句型、捋清脉络等四个步骤，在表达阶段有调整搭配、润饰词语两个步骤。下面就刘宓庆对这六个步骤的阐述摘录如下：

紧缩主干是指找出句子的主谓（宾）。句子的主谓（宾）是一个纲，纲举目张。抓住主干，举纲而后张目，以确定句子的基本格局。尤其是在将英语的长句翻译成汉语时，抓住英语句子的主干成分尤为重要。

辨析词义是翻译中最基础、工作量最大的工作。在英汉互译中辨析词义的主要途径有以下八个方面：一是捋清形态语义关系（meaning in lexical and semantic context）；二是弄清语法层次关系（meaning in grammatical context）；三是确定词语的联立关系（meaning in textual context）；四是考察语言文化关系（meaning in cultural context）；五是领会情态色彩关系（meaning in emotive context）；六是分析指涉呼应关系（meaning in referential context）；七是把握思维逻辑关系（meaning in logical context）；八是观照专业领域关系（meaning in professional context）。

分析句型是指对句子结构成分的分析，它对翻译至关重要。英语注重形态，主语和谓语之间有一致关系，词语均有词性标志，主语、谓语比较容易定位。英语句法分析比较障目的地方有以下几点：一是后置成分很多，这与汉语的表达法刚好相反；二是插入成分很多，使以汉语为母语的人难免产生思维阻断；三是一词多义、多词一义现象比较突出。因此，在分析句型时，重点把握好这几个方面是成功进行英汉翻译的关键所在。

捋清脉络是指捋清思维的表达层次，即句子与句子或主句与分句的组合关系。比如英语句子的基本扩张式有递进并列、环扣（主与从、被修饰与修饰成分）等方式，且这些方式常常综合运用，句子可以很长。在翻译中，只有区分出了句子的主从、修饰与被修饰等关系之后，才有可能根据句子的思维脉络与组合关系进行有条不紊的表达。

调整搭配是指调整目的语整个句子的主谓（宾）以及其他句子成分的搭配形式（搭配在此是指广义的搭配，而狭义的搭配只是指词与词之间的搭配），使整个句子符合目的语的约定俗成性和习惯表达方式。在上面四个步骤进行完毕时已经可以形成"句坯"了，对该"句坯"应该进行搭配方面的调整，这种调整要参照以下原则来进行：

一是"句坯"是否表达了源语的全部语义内容，是否与源语句子的语义内容完全一致；

二是"句坯"是否再现了源语所表现的文体色彩（语域、章句组织形式、言外意义、效果等），是否同源语句子的文体色彩一致；

三是"句坯"是否符合目的语的语法规范和修辞规范；

四是"句坯"是否符合目的语的习惯用法，是否为当代读者所接受，它在上下文中是否适得其所。

按照这四个原则对"句坯"进行搭配调整之后就可以使所得的句子成为定型的句子。

翻译的最后一个步骤是润饰词语。润饰词语需遵循以下原则：一是统观全局，包括词、词组、句、语段以及语篇，拙词、拗句是在对译文的全局性的审读中才能发现。通读全句、全段乃至全篇，拙词拗句往往能在衬托、比映中相形见绌，引起语感障碍而得以改正。二是遵循准确、精炼、隽美的标准对词语进行润饰。"精确"功在达意，"精炼"功在行文，"隽秀"功在风韵。未经润饰的词语章句有一些通病，如词不切意，文不顺理；用词粗糙芜杂，造句生硬梗塞。这时就需要我们给以润饰，将"句坯""抛光"，在琢磨推敲中使译文达到准确、精炼、隽美的要求。在英译汉中尤其要特别注意汉语虚词的用法，去掉误用、拙用或赘用的虚词。

以上六个步骤是一种典型化的操作程序。在实际翻译活动中，六个步骤往往需要反复地、交错地加以运用。翻译不是一个一次性流程，往往要在语义、语法、结构及情态风格几个平面上同时地、相辅相成地进行扫描优化成型操作；因为，归根结底，翻译思维是一个十分复杂的逻辑意念发展和审美体验过程。人类的智能潜力的发挥是逐步的，但它能达到的水平则是任何处理信息的计算机所望尘莫及的。

二、译例举隅及翻译点评

【例1】

原　文：The heavily laden infantry, though enjoying a superiority of six-to-one, simply could not keep to schedule and lost 60,000 men in one day.

译文一：这支负载很重的步兵，尽管享有六比一的优势，完全不能遵守时间表，并且在一天内损失六万人。

译文二：这支步兵尽管（在数量上）享有六比一的优势，由于个人负重量很大，根本无法按时行动，因而在一天内损失六万人。

译文三：这支步兵尽管在数量上享有六比一的优势，但是由于个人负重量很大，根本无法按时行动，因而在一天内就损失了六万人。

【点评】着手翻译一个句子时，首先要进入理解阶段，具体步骤是：紧缩主干、辨析词义、分析句型、捋清脉络，在进行这些步骤之后便可进入表达阶段，从而给出初步译文，如译文一。接下来就是润饰阶段，在这一阶段，译者要根据原文句子所表达的意义及其逻辑关系，参照译文的惯用表达方式及逻辑思维模式对译文一进行调整。这一阶段对于能否给出高质量译文非常关键。具体说来，本阶段可以采取以下步骤：

第一，"负载很重"实际上是步兵完全不能够遵守时间表的原因所在，因此将该短语置于"完全不能遵守时间表"之前比较恰当，同时，在"负载很重"之前增加"由于"一词表示原因，就比较顺畅了。

第二，在"享有六比一的优势"这一表达法中，"六比一"是指数量上的优势，因此在"六比一"之前加上"在数量上"就比较符合逻辑，文字上也更加通畅。这在翻译中叫做"增词翻译法"（amplification），增词翻译法只增加词语，不增加意义。

第三，步兵由于负载很重，就"完全不能遵守时间表"这样表述有一定的问题。负载很重所导致的结果应该是"不能够按照时间表的要求行动"才更合乎逻辑，或者简而言之，"根本无法行动"。

第四，译文一中的"并且"所表示的是并列关系。但从整句话来看，原文中的and并不表示并列关系，而是表示因果关系。因此，将其翻译成"因而"才恰当。

这样我们就得出了译文二。

但润饰阶段到此并没有结束，我们需要再回过头来从整个句子或者篇章的角度对译文作进一步润饰。这也就是我们上文中所说的将"句坯""抛光"，从而使译文在琢磨推敲中达到准确、精炼、隽美的要求。这时我们发现，译文使用了"尽管"，但没有接续连词与之呼应。根据汉语习惯表达，"尽管"往往与"但是"相呼应，表示转折。下文中的"根本无法按时行动"同其前面的从句以及后面的从句构成了因果关系，但我们到底是说"由于……，因而……，因而……"呢，还是"由于……，由于……，因而……"呢，抑或是"由于……，……，因而……"呢？经过仔细揣摩，认为第三种表达既简洁又易懂。最后，在分句"因而在一天内损失六万人"中分别增加"就"和"了"这两个语气词，就将损失惨重这种语气表达了出来。这样就有了最终的译文三。

【例2】

原　文：The sea is rippled with little white ponies.

译文一：大海掀起涟漪，像奔腾的小马驹。

译文二：大海掀起波浪，活像奔腾着的小小的白马驹。（李明 译）

【点评】 凡是做英汉翻译，首先要对英语原句进行理解和剖析。对于本句原文，从逻辑形式部分看，该句使用了 … is rippled …，为被动语态结构；从语用修辞部分看，句子使用的是带 with 结构的隐喻修辞格，且使用了 ponies 一词（试比较，若使用 horses 则感情色彩大打折扣），表示小而可爱的感情色彩；从语义内容部分看，该句的深层含义为"大海可以比作被一群矮小的白马驹掀起的细小的波浪"。在表达阶段，译者反其道而行之。首先，他要透过理解原文的全部内涵，并在自己的形象思维中呈现出一幅绚丽的画面：大海微微掀起细小的波纹，细浪像一群在草原上奔腾飞驰的小白马。这样，原文的深层结构也就包含了两个核心句：The sea is caused to move in very small waves 和 The small waves of the sea is compared to the galloping little white horses。然后，译者再根据删除、替换等翻译原则对其加以简化，并根据传译风格之需要，把"细小的波纹"转换成"涟漪"，把"小白马"转换成"小白驹"。最后在汉语的表层生成以上译文。（参见张泽乾，1994：240）

【例3】

原　文：Mao Zedong was well bred, but inside he was made of steel, of hard resistance, of tough tissue—the kind of tissue the Boxers thought they had by magic, and bared their solar plexuses to foreign bullets. (Helen Snow, *My China Years*)

译文一：毛泽东有很好的教养，内部是钢，有坚强的抗力，是坚韧的材料制成的；这是义和团设想的由于神力具有的、可以把腹部袒露给外国人的子弹的那种材料。

译文二：毛泽东教养有素，精神支柱铁铸钢打，不怕高压，是由坚韧的组织构成的。这种组织，就是义和拳认为他们通过魔法得到的那种组织——袒胸露体，刀枪不入。

译文三：毛泽东看似温文尔雅，但内心深处却钢铸铁打，既坚韧，又抗压——在他的身上可以看到当年义和团自信所具有的那种神力，面对洋枪洋炮也敢袒胸露怀。

【点评】 对于 was well bred 的翻译，三种译法都没有错误，但在翻译时，所选词语要适切人物的身份。原文主语为"毛泽东",是中国历史上有身份的人物,说他"有很好的教养"或者"教养有素"均不合适,译文三用"温文尔雅"较为恰当。并列句 inside he was made of steel 是比喻式说法,要作恰当翻译不容易,译成"内部是钢"太过直译,译成"精神支柱铁铸钢打"又有些走样,译成"内心深处却钢铸铁打"能体现比喻意义。另一个棘手的词语是 tissue,将它译成"材料"或者"组织"可谓译犹不译也。译文三对该词语进行了虚化和调整,使得译文意义清晰顺畅。

【例4】

原　文: "It should be possible to make a precious stone that not only looks like the real thing, but that is the real thing," said a chemist many years ago, "The only difference should be that one crystal would be made by man, the other by nature."

译文一: "应该有可能制造出不仅看起来是真的而且就是真的宝石,"一位化学家许多年前说,"唯一的区别是一种晶体是人造的,另一种则是大自然造的。"

译文二: 许多年前,一位化学家宣称:"应当有可能制造出宝石,这种宝石不仅看起来像真的,而且本身也是真的。唯一的区别在于一种晶体是人造的,另一种则是天然形成的。"

译文三: 许多年前,一位化学家曾经宣称:"人类应该有可能制造出宝石。这种人工宝石不仅看起来逼真,而且它的的确确就是宝石。唯一的区别在于:人工宝石的晶体是人工合成的,而天然宝石的晶体则是自然形成的。"

【点评】上面的三种译文可以说都是通顺的译文,但三者之间还是有优有劣的。译文一是根据原文完全顺译的;译文二基本上是照着原文进行顺译,在文字上没有过多的修饰,只是在个别语序上做了一些调整。译文三则在文字上做了更多的修饰,在译文的句法上做了较大调整,把定语从句翻译成了独立的句子,并且还增加了一些词汇。这样,译文的可读性就非常好了。

　　在翻译过程中,译者首先应该做的就是将原文按照原文的顺序翻译成目的语文字,接着仔细揣摩译文在逻辑上、表达习惯上、可读性上等各个方面是否自然、通顺、流畅。如果需要做文字上的修饰和语序上的调整才能再现原文信息，那就要进行修饰和调整，使译文以符合译文读者表达习惯的方式充分再现原文信息。

【例5】

原　文：It applies equally to traditional historians who view history as only the external and internal criticism of sources, and to social science historians, who equate their activity with specific techniques.

译文一：它同样适用于将历史仅仅看作是对历史材料来源的内部的和外部的批评的传统历史学家，和把历史研究活动等同于具体研究方法的社会科学历史学家。

译文二：它同样适用于传统历史学家和社会科学历史学家，传统历史学家（或前者）将历史仅仅看作是对历史材料来源的内部的和外部的批评，社会科学历史学家（或后者）把历史研究活动等同于具体的研究方法。

【点评】英语重结构，汉语重语义。英语和汉语属于两种完全不同的语言。英语句子往往比较复杂，它往往是通过结构上的安排使许多层意思在一个句子中表达出来。

此例中英语原文整个句子包含30个单词，是典型的复杂句。从内容上讲，它主要提供两方面信息：一是 It applies to... historians，二是 historians 的具体情况；从结构上讲，它是一个主句带两个由 who 所引导的从句。尽管结构复杂、信息量大，这句话在英语里并不紊乱，因为句子结构环环相扣，语义清楚：who 所引导的定语从句放在名词后面修饰这个名词，这是英语中较常见的表达形式，两个从句的语义既相对独立，又和主句连成一体。如果把这个句子改成：It applies equally to traditional historians and to social science historians. Traditional historians (or the former) view history as only the external and internal criticism of sources. Social science historians (or the latter) equate their activity with specific techniques. 表达的意思完全一样，但是表达方式略显平淡、啰唆，这说明英语表达非常重视句子结构，句子结构上的适当安排往往可以达到更好的表达效果。

　　从汉语的表达习惯来看，句子一般不宜写得太长，修饰成分过多或过长会造成喧宾夺主、语义含混。译文一是按照原文的语义结构进行直译的。这样的译文的确很忠实，但在表达上却不像是中文，译者译的时候费劲，读者读的时候也费劲。但如果把译文调整一下，效果就大不相同，如译文二。

　　很显然，译文二给人更清楚、更顺畅的感觉。很巧的是，它与改写后的英语句子在结构上更加接近，这说明汉语不需要通过复杂的结构来提高表达水平，只要意思清楚、正确，表达方式上允许有更多的自由。

【例6】

原　文：As relations between China and Australia develop, the continuing importance of expanding trade will be balanced by the development of close contact over a broad range of political issues.

初　译：随着中澳两国关系的发展，继续扩大贸易的重要性将被在一系列广泛的政治问题紧密接触所平衡。

【点评】原文是一个主从复合句。既然是一个主从复合句，弄清从句的类型很重要。对于这个由 as 引导的从句，大多数中国学生对它的理解都不会有什么问题，并且能够正确地将这句话翻译成汉语：随着中澳两国关系的发展。但也有的学生把 as 理解成"因为"或者"由于"，那样的话就与下文的逻辑关系不相符合。

　　原文的主句是一个被动语态，如果按照英语的句式和语态进行翻译，就不符合汉语的表达习惯，中国读者就会不知所云。这样就需要我们对它的汉语译文进行加工调整。原文中的主语是 the continuing importance of expanding trade，中国学生很容易将它翻译成"继续扩大贸易的重要性"。这样翻译一方面意思模糊不清，另一方面会导致整个译文佶屈聱牙。在英语的句子中，有很多短语在深层结构上实际上相当于一个句子。原文中的这个主语实际上相当于 Expanding trade between China and Australia has been important. And it will be continuingly important to expand trade between China and Australia. 因此我们可以将 the continuing importance of expanding trade 翻译成"扩大贸易仍然是很重要的"。

对于谓语动词部分 will be balanced by the development of close contact over a broad range of political issues 的处理，初译为"将被在一系列广泛的政治问题紧密接触所平衡"很不通顺，不符合汉语的表达习惯。对于这一部分，我们可以这样理解：will be balanced by（将被……平衡），也就是以前只是在一方面有所发展，另一方面没有或欠缺，而现在需要两方面同时并重，只有这样才能平衡。因此可以把 will be balanced 翻译成副词"与此同时""相应地""一方面，另一方面"等。而 the development of 短语既可以译成主谓关系"……发展"，也可以译成动宾关系"发展……，开展……"。在 close contact over a broad range of political issues 中，close contact 为"密切接触"，over 在这里表示范围"在……"，broad range of political issues 为"广泛的、一系列的"，而汉语的习惯是"一系列广泛的"，political issues 为"政治问题"之意。基于以上考虑，我们可以将上面的英文句子翻译成：

"随着中澳两国关系的发展，扩大贸易仍然是重要的，相应地还要在一系列广泛的政治问题上展开密切的联系。"

【例 7】

原　文：This is the boy that chased the dog that bit the cat that caught the rat that stole the egg that the boy hatched.

译文一：追那条狗的就是这个男孩。他孵了个鸡蛋，被老鼠偷了。猫去抓老鼠，那狗反来咬猫。

译文二：这就是追赶那条狗、那条狗咬了那只猫、那只猫逮住了那只老鼠、那只老鼠偷吃了男孩子所孵鸡蛋的那个男孩子。（李明 译）

【点评】在翻译过程的理解阶段，关键是要充分理解原文所表达的信息。要做到对原文理解充分，译者首先要对原文的表层结构（语音形式部分＋逻辑形式部分）进行分析和理解，接着便是对其中介层结构（即语用修辞部分）进行分析和理解，最后是对其深层结构（即语义内容部分）进行分析和理解。在翻译过程的表达阶段，译者首先要从源语的深层结构中走出来，考虑使用怎样的目的语的深层结构传达源语语义内容，接着考虑如何使用目的语的中介结构，即采用怎样的语用修辞，再到目的语的表层结构，即采用怎样的语音形式加上逻辑形式来传达源语信息（张泽乾，1994：239-240）。

本例的英语原文由五个由关系代词 that 引导的定语从句构成，是一个主从复合句，每个关系代词均有各自的先行词，但它们最终修饰的是第一个关系代词之前的先行词 the boy。由于该句中的定语从句太多，而汉语当中充当定语的成分又只能放在被定语所修饰的中心名词之前，因此，要将这样的句子翻译成通顺地道的汉语实在不易。正是这个原因，译文一采用了拆分和逆序的翻译方法。但经过拆分并进行逆序行文之后，原文的结构、语态、叙事方式都发生了根本性的变化，其完整的信息也被拆得七零八落。我们以为，这样的翻译方式不值得提倡，并建议仍然按照原文的行文方式进行翻译。译文二便是基于这样的翻译理念进行翻译的。尽管如此翻译让读者一下子难以明白原文之意，但经过仔细斟酌和玩味，原文的旨趣在译文当中还是能够找到影子的。

三、翻译比较与欣赏

【例1】

原　文：It is a truth universally acknowledged that a single man in possession of a good fortune must be in want of a wife.

译文一：凡有产业的单身汉，总要娶位太太，这已经成了一条举世公认的真理。（王科一 译）

译文二：有钱的单身汉总要娶位太太，这是一条举世公认的真理。（孙致礼 译）

译文三：饶有家资的单身汉男子必定想要娶妻室，这是举世公认的真情实理。（张玲、张扬 译）

译文四：举世公认，一个拥有一大笔钱财的单身男人，必定想娶一个女人做太太。这已成为一条真理。（义海 译）

译文五：世间有这样一条公认的真理——凡财产丰厚的单身男人势必缺太太。（马红军 译）

译文六：寰宇间有一条举世公认的真理：凡是有钱的单身男人一定会娶一个太太。（李明 译）

【例2】

原　文：Therefore, shelf life dates should be included on packages whenever possible to help consumers evaluate product freshness.

译文一：因此，只要有可能，食品包装上都应标明食品可以留置在货架上的期限，以便帮助顾客判断食品的新鲜程度。（顾祖良、陈桂清 译）

译文二：食品包装应标明食品的存架期限，以助顾客随时了解食品的新鲜程度。（黄忠廉、李亚舒 译）

【例3】

原　文：Everything about him was old except his eyes and they were the same color as the sea and were cheerful and undefeated. (Ernest Hemingway, *The Old Man and the Sea*)

译文一：他这人处处显老，唯独两只眼睛跟海水一个颜色，透出挺开朗、打不垮的神气。（赵少伟 译）

译文二：他身上的每一部分都显得老迈，除了那一双眼睛，跟海水一样蓝，是愉快的，毫不沮丧的。（海观 译）

译文三：他全身都已显得苍老，唯独那双眼睛，同海水的颜色一样，碧蓝碧蓝的，充满活力，让人振奋，透着永不言败的神气。（李明 译）

【例4】

原　文：The fair breeze blew, the white foam flew,

　　　　The furrow followed free;

We were the first that ever burst

Into that silent sea. (Samuel Taylor Coleridge, "The Rime of the Ancient Mariner")

译文一：和风吹荡、水花飞溅，

船儿破浪前进，

闯入那沉寂的海洋领域，

我们是第一群人。（王佐良 译）

译文二：惠风吹拂，白浪飞溅，

船儿轻快地破浪而前；

我们是这里的第一批来客，

闯进这一片沉寂的海面。（顾子欣 译）

译文三：和风拂，银浪翻，

波练翩翩逐航船；

我们是古来第一人，

划破沉沉沧海天。（马红军 译）

四、翻 译 练 习

句子翻译

1. As a nation, the French are no more eager to learn about their wartime failings than are the Japanese.

2. Casual photographs taken in relaxed circumstances give a richer and more intimate slice of life than a formal picture.

3. There are signs that, after more than two weeks of political stalemate, progress is now being made towards the formation of a coalition government.

4. I steered the conversation so that we were deep in chat when we pulled up outside my door, making it seem the most natural thing in the world to ask her in for a drink.

5. It won't tell us exactly what's going on, but it will certainly sharpen our understanding of the general principles.

6. The nature of the department store puts them at a disadvantage compared with more specialized retailers when it comes to exerting leverage over suppliers.

7. He's the least naturally talented of the four of us but for mental toughness he's as tigerish as any of us and sometimes more so.

8. In 1980 the country was one of the world's biggest debtors and had a sick economy; without relief it cured itself, repaid the debts and can now raise foreign capital.

9. As the months have gone by and he has largely failed to deal with the country's pressing economic and social problems, his popularity has plummeted.

10. The acquisition of this technology places a great burden on the foreign currency resources of the underdeveloped countries, although as we shall see later on this may be lessened by various forms of aid.

篇章翻译

【篇章翻译 1】

Since Darwin, biologists have been firmly convinced that nature works without plan or meaning, pursuing no aim by the direct road of design. But today we see that this conviction is a fatal error. Why should evolution, exactly as Darwin knew it and described it, be planless and irrational? Do not aircraft design engineers work, at precisely that point where specific calculations and plans give out, according to the same principle of evolution, when they test the serviceability of a great number of statistically determined forms in the wind tunnel, in order to choose the one that functions best? Can we say that there is no process of natural selection when nuclear physicists, through thousands of computer operations, try to find out which materials, in which combinations and with what structural form, are best suited to the

building of an atomic reactor? They also practise no designed adaptation, but work by the principle of selection. But it would never occur to anyone to call their method planless and irrational.

篇章翻译 2

1) There is more agreement on the kinds of behavior referred to by the term "intelligence" than there is on how to interpret or classify them. 2) But it is generally agreed that a person of high intelligence is one who can grasp ideas readily, make distinctions, reason logically, and make use of verbal and mathematical symbols in solving problems. 3) An intelligence test is a rough measure of a child's capacity for learning, particularly for learning the kinds of things required in school. 4) It does not measure character, social adjustment, physical endurance, manual skills, or artistic abilities. 5) It is not supposed to—it was not designed for such purposes. 6) To criticize it for such failure is roughly comparable to criticizing a thermometer for not measuring wind velocity. 7) Now since the assessment of intelligence is a comparative matter we must be sure that the scale with which we are comparing our subjects provides a "valid" or "fair" comparison.

第三章 直译与意译

> 能够使用甲语言表达的东西一定能够使用乙语言进行表达，除非语言形式是信息的基本元素。
>
> ——无名氏

一、理论探讨

翻译按照所使用的方法划分，可以分为直译（literal translation）和意译（free/liberal translation）。在我国，直译与意译之争，自东晋时就开始了。近一个世纪以来，学者们就直译和意译的问题发表了许多不同的看法。如傅斯年在其《译书感言》一文（1919年）中说："老实说话，直译没有分毫藏掖，意译却容易随便伸缩，把难的地方混过！所以既用直译的法子，虽要不对于作者负责任而不能；既用意译的法子，虽要对于作者负责任而不能。直译便真，意译便伪。"朱光潜在《谈翻译》一文（1946年）中，则认为"所谓'意译'是指把原文的意思用中文表达出来，不必完全依据原文的字面和次第。""直译不能不是意译，而意译也不能不是直译。"林汉达在《英文翻译原则方法实例》一书（1953年）中，也反对直译意译的区分，他认为："真正主张直译所反对的，其实并不是意译，而是胡译或曲译。同样，真正主张意译的人所反对的也不是直译，而是呆译或死译。我们认为正确的翻译就是直译，也就是意译。"

近些年来，学者们经过深入的钻研，以及借鉴了前人和国外的经验，对直译和意译的探讨取得了进展，趋向把直译和意译看成是一个形式与内容的问题，如许渊冲在《翻译中的几对矛盾》一文（1978年）中说："直译是把忠实于原文内容放在第一位，把忠实于原文形式放在第二位，把通顺的译文形式放在第三位的翻译方法。意译却是把忠实于原文的内容放在第一位，把通顺的译文形式放在第二位，而不拘泥于原文形式的翻译方法。无论直译、意译，都把忠实于原文的内容放在第一位。""当译文的形式和原文的形式一致的时候，就无所谓直译、意译。……当译文的形式和原文的形式不一致的时候，就有直译或意译的问题，而且直译可以有程度不同的直译，意译也可以有程度不同的意译。"（赖余，转引自《中国翻译词典》，第852页）

其实，直译和意译相互补充，相得益彰。一个句子到底应该直译，还是应该意译往往要考虑到上下文、语域、体裁、读者等因素，没有一成不变的定理。辜正坤先生认为，直译，意译，各有千秋，译者依据功能、审美、读者层等三要素，宜直译就直译，宜意译就意译，能神游于规矩之内，亦能神游于规矩之外，能循规蹈矩，亦能叛道离经，方称得上翻译的行家里手（叶子南，2001：8）。

在翻译一篇文章抑或是一段话、一个句子时，直译和意译往往交织在一起。直译和意译没有优劣之分、高下之别。采用直译和意译两种方法的前提都是译文要通顺、地道、明白、晓畅，能让译文读者理解所译出语言的意义。如果采用直译的方法不能达到这个前提，就采用意译的方法；如果没有必要采用意译的方法就能够让译文读者理解所译出语言的意义，就直接采用直译的方法。如果为了传递源语文化信息，也可以采用直译的方法，但假如采用直译的方法不能充分传达源语信息，就可以采用直译加注的办法进行翻译。

但在讨论直译与意译时，我们要注意避免两种倾向。第一个倾向是要避免死译（rigid translation），死译是指不顾目的语的表达习惯而采用同原文的语言形式亦步亦趋的翻译方法。除了在英汉两种语言中语言结构完全相同的特例之外，一般来说，在英汉翻译中采用死译的方法翻译出来的译文往往很难符合汉语的语言习惯。除了在进行两种语言之间句子结构的对比而需要采用死译的翻译方法之外，一般是避免采用死译的翻译方法的。直译不等于死译。在直译过程中，译文中除主语和谓语之外的其他句子结构可以依据目的语的语言习惯进行局部调整，但不得改变源语形象。比如，如果将 The development of an economical artificial heart is only a few transient failures away 一句翻译成"发展一个经济的人工心脏只是几个短暂的失败。"就属于死译；如果将该句翻译成"只消再经过几次失败，就能造出价格低廉的人工心脏了。"就属于直译。从对上面例子的翻译中就可以窥见直译同死译之区别。

第二个倾向是要避免过度意译（unduly free or over-free translation）。过度意译实际上就是胡译、乱译或者曲译。胡译、乱译或者曲译在翻译中都是不可接受的。它们的具体表现是，要么附加了过多的额外信息，要么信息含量不能够等同原文的信息含量，要么改变了原文的信息，要么歪曲了原文的历史、文化等背景信息。

总之，在翻译过程中应该遵循的重中之重的翻译原则就是——以目的语的自然形式来通顺、地道地再现源语所表达的意义。

二、译例举隅及翻译点评

【例1】

原　　文：A man may usually be known by the books he reads as well as by the company he keeps, for there is a companionship of books as well as of men.

译文一：人们往往可以从一个人所交往的朋友以及所阅读的书目中看到他的为人，因为，人与人之间存在友谊，人与书之间也存在友谊。

译文二：所谓欲知其人，先观其友；观其阅读书目，亦能知其人，因人可与人为友，亦可与书为友。

【点评】译文一从总体上讲为直译，但译文也做了一些调整，比如原文中的被动语态 may be known 被译成了汉语中的主动表达式"人们……可以看到（他的为人）"；由 for 引导的原因状语从句被译成两个分句"因为，人与人之间存在友谊，人与书之间也存在友谊"。译文意思明确、浅显易懂。译文二主要为意译，且文字典雅，符合层次较高的读者的阅读趣味。这里的直译和意译，真是各有千秋，但在具体的上下文中，译者还是要依据语篇的功能、读者的审美情趣和层次等三个要素来确定所选择的翻译方法。

【例2】

原　　文：The Negro lives on a lonely island of poverty in the midst of a vast ocean of material prosperity.

译文一：黑人依然生活在物质富裕的汪洋大海中贫乏的孤岛上。

译文二：那个黑人生活在贫困的孤岛上，而孤岛四周广阔的海域却是一片繁荣景象。

【点评】译文一是比较接近原文的直译法，保留了原文的形象——"汪洋大海"，但可读性很不佳，不仅行文比较别扭，而且将"汪洋大海"这个常有负面涵义的比喻和"物质富裕"放在一起显得很不协调（叶子南，2001：6），使得译文的意义含混不清。译文二调整了语义表达的方式，采取意译的办法，使译文的可读性大大增强。

【例3】

原　文：The development of an economical artificial heart is only a few transient failures away.

译文一：要发展一个经济的人工心脏只隔几个短暂的失败。

译文二：只消再经过几次失败，就能造出价格低廉的人工心脏了。

【点评】翻译有直译与意译之分，但假如译文过于直译，即译文纯粹是以原文的语言形式为基础进行翻译，这时翻译就变成了硬译或者说死译。在学术著作中，为了探讨两种语言在结构上或者表述上的差异或者再现不同语言的语言特点等而进行不同文字间隔行对照的翻译，硬译或者说死译是必要的。但是，以传达意义为目的的翻译就不能够采用硬译法或者死译法。上面的译文一就是硬译成汉语的，因而读来文不从，字不顺。译文二就对原文的语序进行了相应调整，译文读来清楚明了、通顺地道。应该说，译文二采用的也是直译法，但由于译文二对原文内容的表述进行了适当调整，使之符合汉语的习惯表达，因此，译文在汉语中非常通顺地道地传达了原文内容。

【例4】

原　文：It seems to me what is sauce for the goose is sauce for the gander.

译文一：我觉得煮母鹅用什么酱油，煮公鹅也要用什么酱油。

译文二：我认为如何律人就应如何律己／两种情况都适合。

【点评】what is sauce for the goose is sauce for the gander 是一个习语，意思是 what is thought suitable treatment for a woman should be so for a man、behavior etc. expected from one class of person should be expected from another，即"适于此者亦适于彼""要求别人怎样自己也应怎样"（秦秀白，2000：1834）。对这个习语进行翻译，如果直译就是译文一所给出的译文。但对于习语的翻译不能像对于非习语的翻译那样，因为习语蕴涵着深厚的文化内涵，习语的意义不是习语中各个单词意义的简单相加，而是有其特殊内涵和特殊意义的。因此，在翻译习语时，多数时候是不能直译而应该是意译的。

【例 5】

原　文：His retort was delivered with a strong note of vinegar.

译文一：他的反驳是带着强烈的醋意发出的。

译文二：他用非常尖酸刻薄的口气进行了反驳。

【点评】这里原文中的 vinegar 以及译文中的"醋意"均是负载有文化信息的（culturally-loaded）词语。译文一采用直译方法，将 vinegar 翻译成"醋"，将 (a) note of vinegar 翻译成"醋意"。中国人读到此译文时乍一看觉得这就是原文所表达的意思，但实际上这只是取了 vinegar 的字面意思而进行主观臆断的译法。假如译者仔细查阅词典就不会给出这样的译文：vinegar 的字面意思的确是"醋"，但若用于比喻意义，其意思为"尖酸刻薄"，这是"醋"给予英美人的感受，因此他们将"醋"引申为"尖酸刻薄"。而汉语中的"醋意"则是指"妒忌心"，多用于描述男女关系，其英文对等语是 jealousy。因此，译文二才是正确的译文。在不同的语言中，同一种事物在用于比喻意义时，可能会有不同的文化含义，翻译时我们必须时刻小心，避免将假朋友当成真朋友。

【例 6】

原　文：I gave my youth to the sea and I came home and gave my wife my old age.

译文一：我把我的青春献给了大海，我回到家里，给了我的妻子我的老年。

译文二：我把青春献给了大海，我回到家里和我妻子共度晚年。

译文三：我把青春献给了海洋，等我回到家里时，已经是白发苍苍了。

【点评】上面的三种译文中，译文一是硬译，因而读来很不通顺。译文二和译文三均属于意译，但两相比较，译文三要胜于译文二，译文三也正是原文所传达的意义，因为译文二可以说是意译中的超额翻译（over-translation），因为，如果说"我和我妻子共度晚年"，那就意味着"我的妻子"也步入了晚年，而原文中没有提供这个信息。尽管有这种可能，但既然原文没有提供这个信息，译者就不能够主观臆断。超额翻译是初学翻译的人最容易犯的毛病，而犯了这种毛病时，译者还浑然不知。作为译者，我们必须严谨，并时时警惕犯超额翻译的错误。

【例7】

原　文：New York has the poorest millionaires, the smallest great men, the haughtiest beggars, the plainest beauties, the lowest skyscrapers, the dolefulest pleasures of any town I ever saw.

译　文：纽约有的是最为贫穷的富翁，最为渺小的伟人，最为傲慢的乞丐，最为平常的美女，最为低矮的摩天大楼和最为悲哀的欢乐，这一切比我所见到过的任何城市都有过之而无不及。

【点评】这里的原文涉及英语中的矛盾修辞法（oxymoron）。所谓矛盾修辞法是指把意义上相互矛盾或者不协调的词语/词组放在一起使用，这些词语/词组从字面上看似乎截然相反，但仔细体会则回味无穷、意味深长、妙趣横生。矛盾修辞法的作用就在于揭示人和事物之间矛盾性的同时，在矛盾中寻求一种哲理，造成一种出人意料的修辞效果。在将英语中的矛盾修辞法翻译成汉语时，可以根据其所处的语境，如果直译能让人心领神会就采用直译的办法。这里均采取了直译的方法进行翻译，译文意义明确。

三、翻译比较与欣赏

【例1】

原　　文：A: Why is the river rich?

　　　　　B: Because it has two banks.

译文一：A: 为什么说河流是富裕的?

　　　　B: 因为它有两个银行啊!（王治奎等 译）

　　　　（注：英语原文中的 bank 一词是双关语，可指河岸，也可指银行。）

译文二：A: 为什么说河水富有?

　　　　B: 因为它总是向前流呀。或者：因为它年年有鱼呀。（马红军 译）

【例2】

原　　文：A: What does that lawyer do after he dies?

　　　　　B: Lie still.

译文一：A: 那个律师死后能干什么?

　　　　B: 静静地躺着。可译为：仍然撒谎。（勒梅琳等 译）

　　　　（注：lie 兼有"躺"和"撒谎"之意；still 兼有"安静地"和"仍然"之意。）

译文二：A: 那个律师死后还能干什么?

　　　　B: 躺着说鬼话。（马红军 译）

译文三：A: 那个律师死了以后干啥?

　　　　B: 身子动弹不得，口里却依然撒谎。（傅敬民等 译）

译文四：A: 那个律师死后还能干什么?

　　　　B: 即使安静地躺下了仍然要撒谎。（李明 译）

【例3】

原　　文：As a demanding boss, he expected total loyalty and devotion to the company from all his employees.

译文一：作为一个苛刻的老板，他要求所有雇员对公司完全忠诚和奉献。（夏立新 用例）

译文二：作为一个苛刻的老板，他要求所有的雇员对他忠心耿耿，鞠躬尽瘁。（夏立新 用例）

译文三：他当老板非常苛刻，要求所有雇员对公司忠心不二，竭尽全力。（李明 译）

【例4】

原　文：If I can stop one heart from breaking,

　　　　I shall not live in vain;

　　　　If I can ease one life from aching,

　　　　Or help one fainting robin

　　　　Unto his nest again,

　　　　I shall not live in vain.

译文一：假如我

　　　　能弥合一个破碎的心灵

　　　　我就没有虚度此生；

　　　　假如我

　　　　能使一个饱受折磨的人的痛苦得到减轻，

　　　　或者帮助一只小鸟，一只垂危的知更，

　　　　重新回到它的鸟巢，去见他的双亲，

　　　　我就没有虚度此生。（杨立民、徐克容 用例）

译文二：假如我

　　　　能够不让一个人的心灵破碎，

　　　　我就没有虚度我那年年岁岁；

　　　　假如我

　　　　能够给一个忍受痛苦的生命以抚慰，

或者帮助奄奄一息的知更鸟

重新回巢，

我就没有虚度我那年年岁岁。（李明 译）

四、翻译练习

句子翻译

1. Career planning includes gathering information about ourselves and about occupations, estimating the probable outcomes of various courses of action, and finally, choosing alternatives that we find attractive and feasible.

2. John can be relied on. He eats no fish and plays the game.

3. He walked at the head of the funeral procession, and every now and then wiped his crocodile tears with a big handkerchief.

4. It was an old and ragged moon.

5. And as she considered, the light came again, and she saw two dark figures lying in the path ahead of her. She leaped forward and saw that one was Kino and the other a stranger with dark shiny fluid leaking from his throat.

6. It is possible that they never imagined that any considerable amount of public opinion would be rallied in their favor.

7. John was upsetting the other children, so I showed him the door.

8. A woman without a man is like a fish without a bicycle.

9. Smashing a mirror is no way to make an ugly person beautiful, nor is it a way to make social problems evaporate.

10. Mao Zedong was well bred, but inside he was made of steel, of hard resistance, of tough tissue—the kind of tissue the Boxers thought they had by magic, and bared their solar plexuses to foreign bullets.

篇章翻译

篇章翻译 1

A commonplace criticism of American culture is its excessive preoccupation with material goods and corresponding neglect of the human spirit. Americans, it is alleged, worship only "the almighty dollar". We scramble to "keep up with Joneses". The love affair between Americans and their automobiles has been a continuing subject of derisive commentary by both foreign and domestic critics. Americans are said to live by a quantitative ethic. Bigger is better, whether in bombs or bosoms. The classical virtues of grace, harmony, and economy of both means and ends are lost on most Americans. As a result, we are said to be swallowing up the world's supply of natural resources, which are irreplaceable. Americans constitute 6 percent of the world's population but consume over a third of the world's energy. These are now familiar complaints. Indeed, in some respects Americans may believe the "pursuit of happiness" to mean the pursuit of material things.

篇章翻译 2

1) Most ironic was the image of government that was born of these experiences. 2) As any scholarly treatise on the subject will tell you, the great advantage bureaucracy is supposed to offer a complex, modern society like ours is efficient, rational, uniform and courteous treatment for the citizens it deals with. 3) Yet not only did these qualities not come through to the people I talked with, it was their very opposites that seemed more characteristic. 4) People of all classes—the rich man dealing with the Internal Revenue Service as well as the poor woman struggling with the welfare department—felt that the treatment they had received had been bungled, not efficient; unpredictable, not rational; discriminatory, not uniform; and, all too often, insensitive, rather than courteous. 5) It was as if they had bought a big new car that not only did not run when they wanted it to, but periodically revved itself up and drove all around their yards.

第四章 词义的选择

> 色彩会褪去，庙宇会倒塌，帝国会衰亡，唯有充满智慧的言语会永恒。[3]
>
> ——爱德华·索代克

一、理 论 探 讨

谈论翻译不可能不涉及词语的选择。词语的选择与翻译之间存在着紧密关系。可以说，一篇译作成功与否在很大程度上取决于词语的选择是否精当、得体。选择了精当、得体的词语就可以为译文的通顺、流畅、地道铺平道路，也可为整个语篇和语篇的文体打下坚实基础。那么，什么是词语的选择呢？词语的选择是指在翻译过程中，基于对源语文本的精确理解在目的语中选择恰当的词语或表达法，使之符合译文语境的表达需要。

对译者来说，最头痛的问题莫过于在译文中选择恰当的词语了。严复的名言"一名之立，旬月踟蹰"可谓是对翻译过程中如何在译文中选择恰当词语的最好描述了。当然，严复先生在此主要是就如何确立一个恰当的术语而言。但作为一个译者，很多时候都需要为了寻找一个符合上下文的表达而冥思苦想、斟酌再三，"旬月踟蹰"在翻译过程中实际上是家常便饭。

要做到在翻译中能够选择精当的词语，必须把握以下两点：

一是要正确看待翻译时所使用的词典。尽管每个单词的含义在词典中都能找到，但绝对不能把词典当成选择词义的万能钥匙。如果生硬地把词典的释义照搬到译文中去，常会犯一些非常荒谬的错误。英汉两种语言的词义不仅仅是点的对应，也不仅仅

---

[3] 爱德华·索代克（Edward Thorndike）的原话是：Colors fade, temples crumble, empires fall, but wise words endure.

是在一个平面上的线性交叉对应，而是成立体交叉对应关系。因此在翻译时，译者寻求的不只是词义的静态对应，而是要在这种立体交叉的词义关系中寻求动态对应。

二是要弄清英汉两种语言的差别。我们知道，英语词汇所包含的意义往往颇具游移性（vacillant）和灵活性（flexible），这主要是因为英语词汇的意义多依据各自的前后搭配和语境而变化；英语词汇常常是集引申义（extended meaning）、内含义（intensional meaning）、扩展义（extensional meaning）、内涵义（connotative meaning）、外延义（denotative meaning）等多种意义于一体。在具体语境中一个词语到底为何意完全取决于其所在位置或该词语同其他词语的搭配或组合关系。正如刘宓庆（1986：100）所说，英语词汇"涵义范围比较宽，比较丰富多彩，词义对上下文的依赖性比较大，独立性比较小"。当英语中的词语孤立存在的时候，严格地说，我们无法说出它的具体意义，因为它的词义游移不定，因而具有它在使用中可能具有的一切词义。难怪英国哲学家维特根斯坦有"词汇的意义即是其在语言中的运用"[4]之说。这也就是英语词语往往具备一词多义的原因所在。

现代汉语[5]里的词语同英语里的词汇大不相同，现代汉语词语的涵义范围比较狭窄，词义比较精确、固定、严谨，其伸缩性和对上下文的依赖性比较小，具有较强的独立性。因此，总体说来，现代汉语里同一个词语的词义即使在不同的上下文中也基本上是一致的。可以说，现代汉语里一词多义现象远没有英语中那样普遍。对照一下英语词典和汉语词典我们就可以发现，英语里每个词条往往有数种甚至数十种词义，很多还有数条甚至数十条同其他词汇的搭配而形成的新义，由此可见英语词汇的词义对搭配和语境的依赖性；汉语词语则不同，每个词条只有非常有限的几个词义，这充分显示出汉语词汇词义的伸缩性和对上下文的依赖性相对较小。

英语词语同汉语词汇的另一显著区别是，由于当代科技日新月异以及英语在国际上不可替代的地位，各行业、各集团都尽可能使用英语常用词汇来表达各种概念，在这种背景之下，英语词义的范围很容易扩大。换言之，英语词汇容易获得新义。汉语词汇则不然。作为因形生义、因形带来联想的象形文字，汉语语言有着悠久的历史传统，有着特殊的民族文化底蕴和内涵，再加上汉语用词讲究词义精确、稳定、规范、

---

4 原文为：The meaning of a word is its use in the language.

5 之所以专门讲解现代汉语里的词语，是因为在古汉语里，一词多义现象是很普遍的。若用英语比古汉语，恐怕只能算小巫见大巫了。（参见偶西、董乐山、张今编著《英译汉理论与实例》pp. 30-31）

严谨,历来反对生造词义和没有理据的组合,因此,汉语词语的词义很不容易受到外部环境的影响,不易于变化,并在一定程度上"流于执着、凝滞,不易变通"(刘宓庆,1986:101)。

因此,在翻译过程中,我们要正确使用词典,并根据英汉两种语言的差异,对在目的语中所选择的词语进行仔细斟酌和揣摩,充分发挥我们的创造性,选择出精当、贴切的词语,努力使我们的译文蓬荜生辉。

二、译例举隅及翻译点评

【例1】

原 文:There is the world of ideas and the world of practice; the French are often for suppressing **the one** and the English **the other**; but neither is to be suppressed. (Matthew Arnold)

译 文:存在着一个思想的世界和一个行动的世界;法国人通常赞成压制**思想的世界**,而英国人则赞成压制**行动的世界**;但两者压制不住。

【点评】原文中的 the one… the other 在篇章语言学中被称为"照应"(reference),在语用学中叫做"篇章指示语"(discourse deixis),它们在篇章的前文中已经有所指代的词语或句子。它们的功能是避免重复使用其所指代的名词,使译文更为简练。常用的照应词语或篇章指示语包括 one、such、some、any、each、both、much、many、few、little、this、that、these、those、her、there、now、then 以及 similarity、counterpart、equivalent、the former、the latter、substitute、variation 等。汉语中往往没有与英语对应的这些照应词语或篇章指示语,因此,在将英语中的照应词语或篇章指示语翻译成汉语时,多采用重复照应词语所指代名词的方式进行翻译。如该译例原文中的 the one 指前文中的 the world of ideas,the other 则指前文中的 the world of practice。再如:1) His father sent John to the university and was eager to have **him** distinguish **himself**. 他的父亲送约翰上大学,巴望他能出类拔萃。2) During his visit to China this year, George Bush Jr. will

meet his **counterpart** and discuss the Sino-US relations of the future. 在今年来中国访问期间，乔治·布什将会见胡锦涛主席并就中美未来的关系进行讨论。

【例2】

原　文：While people in other countries in the world were trying to catch wild animals and birds and were still collecting seeds and nuts, farmers in China were **developing** the science of agriculture.

译　文：当世界上其他国家还在捕猎飞禽走兽、采集种子坚果的时候，中国的农民就已经在从事农业科技研究了。

【点评】英语中，develop是一个常用词语，但它的意义可谓宽泛至极，因为在不同的上下文中它所表示的是不同的意义，在汉语中这些不同的意义要用不同的词语来表达，这从反面说明了汉语词语意义的狭窄。下面这些句子均使用了动词develop，但它在不同的上下文和搭配中具有迥然不同的意义，请比较：

1) His plane **developed** engine trouble only seven miles after take-off.
   他的飞机在起飞后只飞行了七英里就**发生**了机械故障。

2) Modern aircraft are so heavy that the wings must **develop** a very large lift force in order to sustain the aircraft.
   现代的飞机质量很大，机翼必须**产生**很大的升力才能保持飞机在空中飞行。

3) Inspired by these ideas, in 1752, Franklin **developed** a practical lightning rod.
   由于受到这些思想的启发，富兰克林于1752年**发明了**很实用的避雷针。

4) A hypothesis is a specific statement **developed** by a scientist from observations.
   一个假设是由科学家经过大量观察而**得出**的具体结论。

5) Until the domain theory of magnetism was **developed**, they did not have much success.
   直到提出了磁力学理论他们才取得了巨大的成功。

6) To **develop** the capabilities of the geophysical prospecting, the renewal of the techniques and equipment is the first thing to be considered.
   为了**提高**地球物理探矿的能力，首先要考虑的事情就是更新技术和设备。

7) Most of the money came from selling the secret of a new type of potato he had **developed**.
   大部分钱是靠出售他所**培育**出的土豆新品种的秘密得来的。

8) As young Goddard grew into manhood, he **developed** tuberculosis.
   年轻的戈达德长大成人时**患**上了结核病。

9) We must **develop** all the natural substances in our country which can make us rich.
   我们必须**开发**我们国家的可以让我们过上富足生活的所有自然资源。

10) Several attempts have been made through the years to **develop** the deposit.
    多年来，为**开采**这部分矿床已经作了几次努力。

11) In **developing** a design, the engineer must apply his knowledge of engineering and material science.
    在**进行**设计时，工程师必须应用自己在工程学和材料科学方面的知识。

12) As early as his second film, Chaplin had **developed** his own manner of acting the one that was to become world famous.
    早在他演第二部电影时，卓别林就已**形成**了他自己的表演风格，这就是他后来闻名于世的那种表演风格。

13) By the first century the making of paper in some parts of the China had been well **developed** and had been common.
    到公元一世纪时，中国一些地方的造纸业已很**发达**而且很普遍。

14) It is believed that before writing was **developed**, people in China used to keep records by putting a number of stones together.

人们认为，在书写**出现**之前，中国人常把石头放在一起来记事。

15) Some married people who are not satisfied with their family may resort to the Internet to **develop** an extramarital affair.

一些对家庭不满意的已婚男女也学会借助因特网去**搞**婚外恋。

16) And thirdly, computer games help **develop** children's interest in computers.

再者，电子游戏有助于**培养**儿童对电脑的兴趣。

【例3】

原　文：You cannot **build** a ship, a bridge or a house if you don't know how to make a design or how to read it.

译　文：不会制图或看不懂图纸，就不可能**造**船、**架**桥或**盖**房子。（范仲英，1994：166）

【点评】在这一句中，build 之意是 to make (one or more things) by putting pieces together（Procter，1978：131），陆谷孙编《英汉大词典》（p. 226）对该词该项意义的解释是"建筑，建造，修建；营造"。然而，经过译者对 build 一词的理解和加工，build 一词被分别译成了"造""架"和"盖"。顷刻之间，build 一词的形象意义跃然纸上。对此，美国作家霍桑（Nathaniel Hawthorne）也发出过这样的感叹："词语，在辞典中是那么朴实无华、势单力薄，而一旦落入深谙如何对词语运用自如者之手，则即刻会显现其巨大威力。"[6] 英国散文家艾迪逊（Joseph Addison）也说过，"词语，如果选择精当，其力量巨大无比，往往足以使某种描述让我们享有更丰富的想象空间，而不是词语本身的就事论事。"[7]

英语中一个动词 build 可以很协调地同它的三个宾语 a ship、a bridge 和 a house 搭配，而汉语中却没有一个共用的动词可以很地道、很通顺地同这三个宾语进行搭配（因为我们只能很松散地说"造船、造桥、造房

---

[6] 原文为：Words... so innocent and powerless as they are, as standing in a dictionary, how potent for good and evil they become, in the hands of one who knows how to combine them!

[7] 原文为：Words, when well chosen, have so great a force in them that a description often gives us more lively ideas than the sight of things themselves.

子",但这种选词不是精当的选词)。当我们说 build a ship 时,汉译文恐怕只能是"造船"而不能说"架船"或"盖船"了。换句话说,我们只能选择"造"这一词来和"船"搭配才能算作是精当、贴切的选词。与此类推,通常我们也不能说"架房子""盖桥"。关于精当选择用词,马克•吐温曾经有过这样的评述:"正确的用词同几乎正确的用词之区别就好比闪电同萤火虫之区别"[8]。的确,选择了恰当的词语,真乃犹如闪电,让你眼前一亮,仿佛看到智慧的光芒。

【例 4】

原　文:On the wings of hope, of love, of joy, Miss Meadows sped back to the music hall, up the aisle, up the steps, over to the piano.

译　文:美多斯小姐仿佛插上了希望的翅膀、爱情的翅膀、欢乐的翅膀,一路飞奔回到音乐厅,她穿过通道,跃上台阶,三步并作两步走到钢琴前。

【点评】在英汉翻译中,由于英语中的介词很发达,而汉语中的介词不够发达,因此,在将英语中的介词翻译成汉语时,往往需要使用汉语中的动词。在将本例中的介词短语 up the steps 翻译成汉语时,对于该如何将 up 翻译成汉语确实颇费斟酌。根据 up 同 the steps 的搭配,可以将其翻译成"跳上""登上""跨上""蹦上""跑上""爬上""走上""跃上"等等。但到底选择哪一个表达最精确,最符合上下文呢?根据前后文,选择"跃上"最能够体现该句中所描述的欢快气氛,在感情色彩方面符合上下文。选择"爬上"可以说是不正确的,而选择"跳上""登上""跨上""蹦上""跑上""走上"等不能说不可以,但却欠精确、得当,非上乘的选择。作为译者,很多时候都要从类似的多种表达法中选取一个最恰当、最符合上下文感情色彩的表达法,或者斟酌再三、反复揣摩,直到找出一个精当、贴切、符合语境的表达法。

---

8 原文为:The difference between the right word and the almost right word is like the difference between lightning and the lightning bug.

【例 5】

原　文：Zhou came through to Kissinger as subtle, brilliant, and indirect, a politician of vision who refused to get bogged down in petty details.

译　文：在基辛格眼里／看来，周恩来敏锐、聪慧、含蓄，具有政治家的远见卓识而从不斤斤计较任何细节。

【点评】任何一种语言中的词语，在具体使用时，都不可能不带有一定的感情色彩，都不可避免地显露出原作者的立场和观点。作为译者，应该充分理解和体会原文所传达的意义，并在译文中选用适当的语言手段加以表达。英语中有相当大比重的词语属于中立词，它们集褒义和贬义于一身，这些词语的褒贬意义只能通过分析句子本身或者上下文所描述的事件等来确定，从而做出正确判断。上文中所使用的词语如"敏锐""聪慧""含蓄"以及"远见卓识"等都是褒义词，他们均用来描述周恩来总理。如果这里所描述的人是另外一个人，这里的用词一定会是另一个样子。比较下面的三个例句及其译文：1) This typewriter is indeed **cheap** and fine. 这部打字机真的是**价廉物美**。2) He is making himself **cheap**. 他这么做正使自己**名誉受损**。3) Her feelings come too easily, too **cheaply**. 她的感情来得太容易，也太**廉价**。

【例 6】

原　文：The home of your dreams **awaits** you behind this door. Whether your taste **be** a country **manor estate** or a penthouse in the sky, you will find the following pages filled with the world's most **elegant residences**.

译　文：打开门，恭候着您的就是梦寐以求的家。无论您企盼的是一座乡间宅第，抑或是一间摩天大楼的顶屋，翻开下面几页就可以看到世界上最高雅的住宅供您选择。

【点评】这里的英语原文是一则广告，该广告中所使用的 await、be、manor、elegant、residence 等均属正式语汇，代替了口语体的 wait、is、house、nice、place。该广告制作人选择文雅用词用意深刻：一方面能烘托出该种商品的高贵品质，另一方面又能满足这类商品消费者讲究身份、追求上乘的心理需求。在译文中，所列文雅用词分别以"恭候""企盼""宅第""高雅的住宅"译出，在语体色彩方面与原文基本对应。

在翻译时，再现原文词语的语体色彩，即注意词语的"雅"与"俗"，非常重要。所谓词语的"雅"就是指优雅而正式的书面语，"俗"则是指口语、俚语和非正式用语。如果原文中使用了优雅正式的书面语，译文当中也应该选择优雅正式的书面语与之对应，这样才能取得语体上的近似或对等。要做到这一点，译者首先必须能够充分领悟原文用词的语体色彩，其次是译者必须能够具备较好的译语文字功底，能够在译语中找到符合原文词语语体色彩的词语与之对应。

【例7】

原　文：**Moms** depend on Kool-Aid like **kids** depend on **moms**.

译　文：**妈咪依赖果乐，就像宝宝依赖妈咪一样。**

【点评】这又是一则广告，原文使用了俗语 moms 和 kids，分别代替 mothers 和 children。广告制作者这样选词的用意是让读者读来感到亲切，尽管这句话是通过大人之口说出，但非常符合儿童用语的特点，将妈咪对果乐的依赖程度表现得淋漓尽致，真乃上乘之作。译文在选词上充分再现了原文的神韵和语体色彩，也可谓是上乘之作。

翻译时，目的语读者对象是译者必须考虑的一个重要因素。这是因为，读者不同，所使用的语言自然不同，比如，我们不能使用同大人讲话的那种口气对小孩子讲话等等。要恰如其分地做到这些，必须选词得体。

【例8】

原　文：There is a Chinese maxim that says: The best plan for one year is to **cultivate** grain, that for ten years is to **cultivate** trees and that for a hundred years is to **cultivate** people. Once **cultivated**, grain may bring about a crop within the year, and trees may bring about benefits lasting scores of years. People may bring about benefits lasting for a hundred years.

译文一：中国有句格言：一年树谷，十年树木，百年树人。种下庄稼，一年就有收获，树木也可以带来几十年的收益，而人才的培养却有着百年的效益。

译文二：中国有句格言是这样说的：一年最好的规划是**种植**谷物，十年最好的规划是**种植**树木，百年最好的规划是**培养**人才。一旦种植好了，谷物可以带来一年的收成，树木可以带来持续几十年的利益。所培养的人才可以带来持续百年的利益。（李明 译）

【点评】英语原文中有四处使用了 cultivate 一词。对它的词义的选择取决于它同后面所接宾语的搭配。to cultivate grain 和 to cultivate trees 可分别翻译成"种植谷物"和"种植树木"，可是，to cultivate people 就不能翻译成"种植人才"了。根据搭配，只能将该短语翻译成"培养人才"。因此，在进行词义选择时，一定要随时注意所关涉词语的前后搭配。

三、翻译比较与欣赏

【例1】

原　文：Vast lawns that extend like sheets of vivid green, with here and there clumps of gigantic trees, heaping up with rich piles of foliage.

译文一：草地宽阔，好像地上铺了鲜艳的绿绒似的毡毯，巨大数株，聚成一簇，绿叶浓密，一眼望去，草地上东一簇，西一簇，这类的大树可不少。（王寅，1993：13）

译文二：宽阔的草坪宛如翠绿的地毯，成片的参天大树点缀其间，绿叶浓密，层层叠叠。（马红军 译）

译文三：一片片宽阔的草坪犹如翠绿的地毯铺展开来，处处可见成片成片的参天大树，树叶叠翠、茂盛浓密。（李明 译）

【例2】

原　文："You promised to tell me your history, you know," said Alice, …

第四章　词义的选择

"Mine is a long and a sad tale!" said the Mouse, turning to Alice, and sighing.
"It is a long tail, certainly," said Alice, looking down with wonder at the Mouse's tail, "but why do you call it sad?"…

译文一："我的故事说来真是又长又伤心！"耗子转身向阿丽思叹口气说。
"你的尾巴确实很长，"阿丽思惊奇地朝下看着耗子尾巴说，"可是你干吗说它伤心呢？"……（陈复庵 译）

译文二：那老鼠对着爱丽丝叹了口气道："唉，我的历史说来可真是又长又苦又委屈呀！"
爱丽丝听了，瞧着那光滑的尾巴说："你这尾巴是长呀！可是为什么又说它苦呢？"……（赵元任 译）

译文三：老鼠对着爱丽丝叹了口气道："唉，说来话长！真叫我委屈！"
"尾曲？！"爱丽丝听了，惊讶地瞧着老鼠那光滑的尾巴问："你这尾巴明明又长又直，为什么要说它曲呢？"（马红军 译，有改动）

【例3】

原　文：…and, therefore, I say that if you should still be in this country when Mr. Martin marries, I wish you may not be drawn in, by your intimacy with the sisters, to be acquainted with the wife, who will probably be some mere father's daughter, without education. (Jane Austin, *Emma*)

译文一：所以我说等马丁先生结婚的时候，你若是还待在这个地方的话，我愿你不要因为同她姐妹的亲近关系而结识他太太，她可能只是一个农民的女儿，没有受过教育。（刘重德 译）

译文二：所以，如果马丁先生结婚时你还住在这儿，可千万别碍着她两个妹妹的情面去搭理他的太太。说不定他会娶个十足的乡下人的女儿，没有一点教养。（张经浩 译）

译文三：所以我说呢，等马丁先生结婚时，要是你还住在这儿的话，我希望你不要碍于自己同他姐妹的情面去同他妻子交往。他妻子有可能只是某个父亲的女儿，没有读过半句书。（李明 译）

49

【例 4】

原　文：　　　　**The Eagle**

He clasps the crag with crooked hands,
Close to the sun in lonely lands,
Ringed with the azure world, he stands.

The wrinkled sea beneath him crawls;
He watches from his mountain walls,
And like a thunderbolt he falls. (Alfred Tennyson)

译文一：　　鹰

钢爪握崖岩，
独立太阳边；
岩高万籁寂，
四外尽蓝天。

身下海涛翻，
只见微皱面；
绝壁傲视久，
忽坠如雷电。（根据汪榕培原译文而作）

译文二：　　老　　鹰

荒原高高立，
雄爪扣崖壁，
低头做环视，
万物收眼底。

头顶近苍穹，

脚下波涛涌，

目光下峭壁，

迅疾做俯冲。（李建军 用例）

四、翻 译 练 习

短语翻译

第一组：

delicate skin

delicate porcelain

delicate upbringing

delicate living

delicate health

delicate stomach

delicate vase

delicate diplomatic question

delicate difference

delicate surgical operation

delicate ear for music

delicate sense of smell

delicate touch

delicate food

第二组：

enjoy free medical care

enjoy advantages

enjoy national protection

enjoy mass support

enjoy access to Internet

enjoy prosperity

enjoy a special place

enjoy a double-digit growth

enjoy a revival

enjoy an economical honey moon

enjoy a fine day

enjoy constant attention

句子翻译

1. This war is becoming the most important **story** of this generation.
2. It is quite another **story** now.
3. Some reporters who were not included in the sessions broke the **story**.
4. He'll be very happy if that **story** holds up.
5. The Rita Hayworth **story** is one of the saddest.
6. A young man came to Scott's office with a **story**.
7. Last December, the Post first reported that probes were being made in each of those cities, but officials refused to confirm the **story**.
8. The **story** about him became smaller and by and by faded out from the American TV.
9. Tell me the **story** of what happened to you.
10. The **story** of the opera was printed in the program.
11. He halted in the district where by night are found the **lightest** streets, hearts, vows and librettos.

第四章　词义的选择

篇章翻译

篇章翻译 1

The three sacred words "duty", "honor" and "country" reverently dictate what you should be, what you can be, and what you will be. They urge you to build courage when courage seems to fail, to regain faith when there seems to be little cause for faith, to create hope when hopes become abandoned. I am convinced that these words teach you to be proud and unbending in honest failure, but humble and gentle in success; not to substitute words for action; to seek the path of comfort, but to face the stress of difficulty and challenge; to learn to stand up in the storm, but to have compassion on those who fail; to have a heart that is clean, a goal that is high; to learn to laugh, yet never forget how to weep; to reach into the future, yet never neglect the past; to be serious, yet never take yourself too seriously; to be modest so that you will remember the simplicity of true greatness, to open mind of true wisdom, the meekness of true strength. In short, these words teach you to be both a militant fighter and a gentleman.

篇章翻译 2

Opera is expensive: that much is inevitable. But expensive things are not inevitably the province of the rich unless we abdicate society's power of choice. We can choose to make opera, and other expensive forms of culture, accessible to those who cannot individually pay for it. The question is: why should we? Nobody denies the imperatives of food, shelter, defense, health and education. But even in a prehistoric cave, mankind stretched out a hand not just to eat, drink or fight, but also to draw. The impulse towards culture, the desire to express and explore the world through imagination and representation is fundamental. In Europe, this desire has found fulfillment in the masterpieces of our music, art, literature and theatre. These masterpieces are the touchstones for all our efforts; they are the touchstones for the possibilities to which human thought and imagination may aspire; they carry the most profound messages that can be sent from one human to another. (1997 年高等院校英语专业八级考试样题）

第五章 语境对词义选择的作用

> 语境是决定语义的唯一因素，舍此别无意义可言。
>
> ——马林诺夫斯基

一、理论探讨

英国语言学家弗斯（Firth）曾经说："每个词语在用于新的语境中时则是一个新词。"[9] 19世纪诗人霍姆斯（O. W. Holmes）对于词义因语境的变化也有过下面的评论："一个词语不是一个水晶体，晶莹剔透，永无变化，而是充满生命力的思维的外壳，它可以依据其使用的情景和时间的变化而在色彩和内容上有很大变化。"[10] 这里所依据的情景和时间就是语境。

人们在言语交际过程中要想顺利地交流思想和理解话语始发者的信息，必须运用语言所依赖的各种表现为言辞的上下文或不表现为言辞的主客观环境因素。这里的表现为言辞的上下文和不表现为言辞的主客观环境因素统称为语境。语境有广义的语境与狭义的语境之分。广义的语境是指对语言交际产生制约的社会的、自然的、交际者本身的等各种因素，也称"情景语境"（situational context）或"超语言学语境"（extralinguistic context）。它涉及韩礼德等人提出的交际过程的三个方面，即"语场"（field of discourse）[11]、"语式"（mode of discourse）[12] 和"语旨"（tenor of discourse）[13]，主要体

---

[9] 原文为：Each word when used in a new context is a new word.

[10] 原文为：A word is not a crystal, transparent and unchanging; it is the skin of a living thought and may vary greatly in color and content according to the circumstances and time in which it is used.

[11] 指言语活动的主题。

[12] 指言语活动的方式。

[13] 指言语活动双方的地位关系。

现为同语言环境密切相关的"社会性因素"（social factors）。狭义的语境是指交际过程中某一话语结构表达某种特定意义时所依赖的各种表现为言辞的语境，它既包括书面语中的语境，也包括口语中的前言后语所限定的环境。换句话说，它是指词语在原文中所处的实际语言环境（verbal context），即言语活动在一定时间和空间里所处的境况。语境是制约词义的首要因素，尤其在英语中，没有语境，就无法确定词义。有人曾发出这样的感叹：几乎任何单词，只有看了语境才能了解其意义，这是我们在翻译时必须牢记的一点，就连 we、you、they 等词语也不例外。另外，社会生活的方方面面、世间的万事万物、人类自身的一切——时间、地点、场合、话题、交际者身份和地位、交际者心理背景和文化背景、交际目的、交际方式、语码、信息的始发者和接受者以及与话语结构同时出现的各种非语言符号（如姿势、表情）等——都可以成为语境。

　　语境对于语言的使用和顺利交际以及对于语言的表达和理解起着制约和补衬作用，而且这种作用是绝对的、普遍的。任何时候，语境都决定着语言活动的顺利进行，制约着语言材料的选择和加工提炼。反言之，语言交际必须以一定的语境为依据，一个人所说的话、所写的文章必须切合具体的语境。我们也可以这样说，离开具体的语境人们就无法进行语言交际，就无法实现信息传递的目的。生活中具体的语言材料之所以产生意义就是因为有了特定的语境。汉语中一个个孤立的汉字，就它们的意义而言具有游移性（oscillation）[14]，正因为如此，作为砖瓦的这些"建筑材料"就可以根据交际的需要和语言规则进行相互组合，从而构成词语、句子、段落乃至篇章，组成意义的大厦。这些单个汉字在相互组合之前，往往具有多义性（polysemy），且它们本身只有指称意义（referential meaning）[15]（即它们在词典中的意义，或曰辞面意义。比如汉语中的"狗"所指称的是一种家畜）。但当它们用作语言材料而组成大于字的单位并跟一定的语境结合时，其多义性就变成了单义性（monosemy），它们本身所具有的指称意义也就转化成言内意义（linguistic meaning）或/和语用意义（pragmatic meaning）了，并且词义固定下来。这就是为什么尽管汉语中有一词多义现象但在具体的语境中意义仍然明确、具体且不会出现歧义的原因所在。由此看来，语境在确定

---

14 借用周方珠所采用的术语，参见《中国翻译》，1995（1）第 8 页。
15 根据符号学的观点，语言的意义分为三个方面：（1）指称意义，指符号与所指称对象之间的关系所体现的意义；（2）言内意义，指符号相互之间的关系所体现的意义；（3）语用意义，指符号与符号解释者之间的关系所体现的意义。

汉语单字的意义方面起了决定性作用。著名人类学家马林诺夫斯基（B. Malinowsky）说得好："语境是决定语义的唯一因素，舍此别无意义可言"[16]。

英语是拼音文字。英语里没有完全等同于汉语里的"字"的单位，只有接近汉语里的"字"的单位，这便是"语素"（morpheme），即语言中最小的、赋有意义的单位。它可以是一个词根，也可以是一个词缀，例如 gentlemanliness 就是由词根 gentle 和 man 以及词缀 -li 和 -ness 四个语素组成的词。英语是有形态的语言，每个词类都有一个固定形态。故英语词语的特征之一就是有形态变化。比如 investigate、criticize、develop、analyze 等词，一看便知道它们是动词；investigation、criticism、development、analysis 等词，一看便知道它们是名词；suggestive、beautiful、resistible 等词，一看便知道它们都是形容词，因为它们的词性都是通过形态体现出来的。

英语词语的另一个特征是一词多义性。翻开任何一本中型英语词典，一个词条下只有一个意义的词语只占词典的少数，一般情况是一个词条下至少有两至三个义项，多者则达十几个或几十个。比如陆谷孙主编的《英汉大词典》对 get 一词用作及物动词时列举了三十个义项，用作不及物动词时列举了七个义项，用作名词时列举了五个义项，这些还不包括 get 与其他词语搭配而形成的新的意义。同汉语词语一样，英语词语的一词多义性大大提高了词语的使用率，简化了语言的表达手段。英语辞格中的轭式搭配法（zeugma）、一笔双叙法（syllepsis）、借代（metonymy）、双关（pun）等正是运用了英语词语的一词多义性。

英语词语的第三个特征是一词具有多词性的特点。英语的名词动用和动词的名词化等均得益于英语词语可以具有一词多词性的特点。英语词语的一词多词性也大大地丰富和简化了语言的表达手段，使得英语语言生动活泼、异彩纷呈。比如 Don't trouble trouble until trouble troubles you 和 Father has succeeded in bedding the naughty child 等句便是利用一词多词性的特点来充分而又生动地传达原文意义的极佳例子。

正是由于英语词语具有这些特征，在英汉翻译过程中首先要解决的问题便是确定原文各词语的词义，再在译文中选择恰当的词语表达出来。如前所述，英语词语的特征决定了在英汉翻译过程中对词义的确定必须依赖语境。同一词语在不同语境中会产生出不同意义，在译文中需要用不同词语再现出来。翻译主要涉及语言语境。语言语

---

[16] 原文为：Context is the sole determiner of meaning without which meaning does not exist.

境有大小语境之分，小语境可以是句子、短语乃至词组等，大语境可以是句段、段落乃至篇章等。

二、译例举隅及翻译点评

【例1】

原　文：I **got** on horseback within ten minutes after I **got** your letter. When I **got** to Canterbury, I **got** a chaise for town, but I **got** wet through, and have **got** such a cold that I shall not **get** rid of it in a hurry. I **got** to the Treasury about noon, but first of all **got** shaved and dressed. I soon **got** into the secret of **getting** a memorial before the Board, but I could not **get** an answer then; however I **got** intelligence from a messenger that I should **get** one next morning.

译　文：**接到**来函后，不到十分钟，我就骑马**动身**了。**到达**坎特布里时，我**换乘**四轮马车进城，但我浑身淋得透湿，**患了**重感冒，一时**痊愈**不了。大约中午时分，我**到达**财物委员会，但做的第一件事就是**刮脸换衣**。不久，我打听到在委员会前竖碑的内情。可当时我没能**接到**通知。不过，我从送信者口里**获悉**翌日上午会**有**通知的。

【点评】　在这段不到100词的英文句子中，一共含有14个get这个词。尽管是同一个词语，但在各自主要以句子为单位的语境中，它们含有不同的意义。这些意义的不同在汉语中必须使用不同的词语才能再现。英语中这样的例子还有很多，尤其是源自盎格鲁－撒克逊民族的英语本土词语，如make、do、take等，它们的词义非常丰富，搭配能力非常强，我们在翻译中必须非常注意这些词语。

【例2】

原　文：This is the first **round**. (*n*.)

译　文：这是第一轮。

原　　文：There is a **round** table in the room. (*adj*.)

译　　文：屋里有一张圆桌。

原　　文：**Round** the corner slowly. (*v*.)

译　　文：慢慢绕过这个角。

原　　文：He walked **round** the house. (*prep*.)

译　　文：他绕过那座房子而行。

原　　文：Come **round** tomorrow. (*adv*.)

译　　文：明天来吧。

【点评】英语中有许多词语具有一词多词性的特点。比如，在英语中，很多名词可以直接用作动词，很多动词可以直接用作名词等。在本例中，round 一词分别用作名词、形容词、动词、介词和副词。该词拥有那么多词性，实在令人叹为观止！对于英语中的词语，我们一定要结合语境来确立其词性，确定词性后再确定其意义。

【例3】

原　　文：——"Since she left, I have done the cooking and baked the cakes, but mine are never as good as hers."

——"**Nonsense**, my dear; I don't think Lissie's cakes were any better than yours," said Mr. Priestly loyally.

译　　文：——"自她走后，煮饭、烤饼的事就由我来做了，可我做的怎么也没有她做的好吃。"

——"哪儿的话，我亲爱的，我觉得你做的饼和莉茜做的饼一样好吃。"普里斯特利先生认认真真地说。

【点评】由上下文决定的词义有时候要从词典的多条释义中挑选出来，但有时候一般词典所提供的释义会无一适用。此时，上下文所提供的社会场合或情景即语境便起着决定性作用，当然，要准确把握词义，译者必须有足够的语言水平和社会文化修养以及认真负责的态度和一丝不苟的精神。

本例句中的 nonsense 是口语中常用的词语，按照英汉词典的释义，大多数词典都将其释义为"胡说""废话"或"愚蠢的举动"，但在此处显然不能够照搬照抄。由此可见语境对于词义的选择起了多么重大的作用。再如：There was no **lady** about him. He was what the woman would call a manly man. That was why they liked him.（他这个人可没有一点女人气，他正是女人们称之为男子汉的那种人，这正是她们喜欢他的原因所在。）

【例4】

原　文：We are now in a **wet** season.

译　文：我们现在进入了**多雨的**季节。

原　文：He is **wet** through.

译　文：他浑身**湿透**了。

原　文：If you think I am for him, you are **all wet**.

译　文：你若认为我支持他，那你就**大错特错**了。

原　文：She had **a wet nurse** for the infant Elliot.

译　文：她雇了一名**奶妈**，为襁褓中的艾略特喂奶。

原　文：But Smith showed unexpected strength, especially in the **wet districts**.

译　文：但是史密斯出其不意地得到很多选票，特别是在那些**非禁酒地区**。

原　文：To Big Tim that day he (Roosevelt) looked like a cocky college kid, still **wet behind the ears**.

译　文：在大个子蒂姆看来，罗斯福那天活像一个毛头大学生，仍然有些**乳臭未干**。

原　文：The teenagers won't invite Bob to their parties because he is **a wet blanket**.

译　文：青少年们不愿意邀请鲍勃参加他们的聚会是因为他是**一个令人扫兴的人**。

【点评】上面这些例子中，wet 一词由于处于不同的语境，与不同的前言后语搭配，因而产生不同的搭配意义（collocative meaning）。搭配意义是指一个词语通过与其他词语搭配而形成一种惯用短语或者常用搭配，进而产生某种联想意义，这种联想意义已经超越了该词语本身的字面意义。比如，

pretty 和 handsome 这两个词语就具有搭配意义，因为前者通常与表示女性的词语搭配使用，后者则通常与表示男性的词语搭配使用。再如，如果我们将"北京路关闭了"这句话翻译成 Beijing Road is shut 就没有考虑到搭配意义，因为 shut 这个词语表示"关闭"时通常与"门""窗"搭配使用，这也就是 shut 一词的搭配意义；如果说道路关闭的话，往往要使用 closed，这也是 closed 的搭配意义。

【例 5】

原　文：This typewriter is indeed **cheap** and fine.

译　文：这部打字机真的是**价廉**物美。

原　文：He is making himself **cheap**.

译　文：他这么做正使自己名誉**受损**。

原　文：Her feelings come too easily, too **cheaply**.

译　文：她的感情来得太容易，也太廉价。

【点评】 在上面三句话的翻译中，第一个 cheap 被翻译成"价廉（物美）"，"价廉"是褒义词；第二个 cheap 被翻译成"受损"，"受损"是贬义词；第三句话中的 cheaply 由 cheap 派生而来，被翻译成"廉价"，"廉价"是贬义词。任何一种语言里的词语，在具体使用时，都带有一定感情色彩，都不可避免地反映出原文作者或说话人的立场和观点。作为译者或者听话人，必须对原文有正确的理解。在翻译时必须选用恰当的语言手段表达出来。另外，有些词语属于中性词，它们集褒义和贬义于一身，这类词语在英语中占有相当比重。它们的褒贬意义只能通过语境来确定，这就需要我们增强语境意识，做出正确判断。例如：1) He was a man of integrity, but unfortunately he had a certain **reputation**. 他为人正直，但不幸有某种**坏名声**。2) She has made a **reputation** for herself through hard work. 她勤奋工作，为自己赢得了声誉。

第五章　语境对词义选择的作用

【例6】

原　　文：When the country calls for your **help**, you cannot but go.

译　　文：当祖国需要你的**奉献**时，你应义无反顾，奋勇当先。

【点评】　此处如果把 help 翻译成"帮助"，就会显得分量太轻，而且就整个句意而言，也很不妥当。不管是英语还是汉语，在用词时均有一个轻与重的问题，所谓词义的轻重，就是指词语的意义在具体语境中所承载的分量。英语中有些词语，本身可轻可重，甚至轻重悬殊，不可同日而语，但到底选用分量重的还是分量轻的取决于语境。例如：teacher 教师，导师；leader 领导，领袖；activist 积极分子，活动家；originator 发起人，创始人；writer 作者，作家，等等。再如：My military career had been **inglorious**. 我的部队生涯**不足称道**（不能译成"不光荣的"）。

【例7】

原　　文：The autumn leaves blew over the moonlit pavement in such a way as to make the girl who was moving there seem fixed to a sliding walk, letting the motion of the wind and the leaves carry her forward. Her head was half bent to watch her shoes stir the circling leaves. (Ray Bradbury, Fahrenheit 451)

译文一：秋叶卷过洒满月光的小径，走在上面的女孩看起来就像是站在自动人行道上，由风和叶推动着前行。她稍稍低着头，看自己的鞋尖拨动打旋的落叶。（某学生译文，转引自郑军荣，2013：51）

译文二：秋风吹落叶，卷过月光流照的人行道，袅袅婷婷的一位姑娘仿佛并未移步而是乘风履叶，若飞若扬。她低着头，望着脚下随风转的乱叶。（于而彦译，转引自郑军荣，2013：51）

译文三：秋天的落叶随风飘落到月光流照的人行道上，让那位在上面行走的姑娘好像止住脚步滑行了起来，任凭那秋风的肆虐和落叶的运动把她往前推去。她的头微微低下，望着自己的鞋子在搅动着那些不断旋转的落叶。（李明译）

【点评】　马林诺夫斯基说，"语境是决定语义的唯一因素，舍此别无意义可言。"

这可谓是翻译过程中如何确定词语意义所发表的真知灼见。任何词语，若没有语境或上下文，其意义都是游移的。一旦有了语境，其意义基本上就具有单一性了，读者也就能够弄清其在具体语境中的含义了。作为译者，在理解阶段和表达阶段，都需要依赖语境。本例英语原文中，尽管有语境，但对于诸如 blew、was moving there、fixed、a sliding walk、letting、the motion、carry her forward、stir、circling 等到底如何翻译，译者都会非常纠结。译文一是某学生的译文，其中的不足显而易见。对于译文二，郑军荣（2013：51）做了如此评论："译文2彻底摆脱了原文细节的束缚，对整体的意义的把握堪称完美。译者把 moonlit 译成'月光流照'，可谓神来之笔；把下一句 letting the motion of the wind and the leaves carry her forward 译成'乘风履叶，若飞若扬'，真令人击节三叹。这该是钱钟书所谓的'化境'。"

对此评论，我们不敢苟同。诚然，将 moonlit 翻译成"月光流照"的确是不错的选择，可在其他方面，译文可谓是问题多多。首先，原文开头的主语是 The autumn leaves，不是 The autumn wind，因此，用"秋风"充当译文的主语，没有理据地出现了"秋风吹落叶"这样一个事件，这是原文当中没有表述的内容。另外，从逻辑上讲，"秋风吹落叶，卷过月光流照的人行道"，后半句中，动词"卷过"的主语只可能理解为"（秋风）卷过月光流照的人行道"，而不是"（落叶）卷过月光流照的人行道"，而前者是不符合逻辑的。其次，在"袅袅婷婷的一位姑娘"这一表达中，"袅袅婷婷的"从何而来？很多时候，有些译者就是使用这样一些形象化的语言或者"甜言蜜语"把读者给蒙骗了。第三，译文二将 to make the girl who was moving there seem fixed 翻译成"仿佛并未移步"太过简化，没有传达出原文中的细节描写。难道摆脱原文细节的束缚是随意简化原文中的细腻描述吗？第四，原文所描述的是"秋风和落叶把女孩子往前推去"，可是，译文二却表述为"（一位姑娘）乘风履叶，若飞若扬"。这不是改变了原文所表述的视角吗？第五，译文二将原文中的 the circling leaves 翻译成"随风转的乱叶"，这"乱叶"中的"乱"字从何而来？添加一个"乱"字，将整个段落的意境糟蹋得一塌糊涂。

对于这样的文字的翻译，作为译者，一定要移情，也就是说，要将自己置于原文作者所描写的情景当中去体验、去感受当时的情景。只有这样，我们的译文才有可能符合原文作者所描述的情景。正是在移情的基础上，我们才给出了译文三。

三、翻译比较与欣赏

【例1】

原　　文：Able was I ere I saw Elba.

　　　　（注：原文据说为1814年各国联军攻陷巴黎后，拿破仑皇帝被放逐到地中海的厄尔巴岛（Elba）时所写，其妙处就在于它是一个回文句。）

译文一：我在看到厄尔巴之前曾是强有力的。（钱歌川 译）

译文二：不见棺材不掉泪。（许渊冲 译）

译文三：不到俄岛我不倒。（许渊冲 译）

译文四：落败孤岛孤败落。（马红军 译）

译文五：若非孤岛孤非弱。（马红军 译）

【例2】

原　　文：Better late than the late.（注：原文为美国高速公路上矗立的安全警示牌）

译文一：迟到总比丧命好。

译文二：晚了总比完了好。（马红军 译）

译文三：迟了总比死了好。（马红军 译）

译文四：宁迟一时，不迟一世。（马红军 译）

译文五：慢行回家，快行回老家。（马红军 译）

【例3】

原　　文：By experimentation, imagination, and reasoning, mathematics are discovering new facts and ideas that science and engineering are using to change our civilization.

译文一：通过实验，想象和推理，数学一直在不断地发现各种新（事实）现象和新概念，以便科学和工程不断地利用它们来改造我们的文明。（易明华 用例）

译文二：数学家们通过实验、想象和推理，一直在不断的发现各种新（事实）现象和新概念，以便科学家和工程师可不断的用它们来改造我们的文明世界。（易明华 用例）

译文三：通过实验、想象和推理，在数学领域内一直在不断地挖掘出新的事实，创造出新的概念，科学家和工程师们正是运用这些事实和概念在改变着我们文明的进程。（李明 译）

【例4】

原　文：　　　**A Nation's Strength**

Not gold, but only men can make

A people great and strong;

Men who, for truth and honor's sake,

Stand fast and suffer long.

Brave men who work while others sleep.

Who dare while others fly—

They build a nation's pillars deep

And lift them to the sky. (Ralph Waldo Emerson)

译文一：　　　国　力

什么才能使一个民族伟大强盛？

不是金子，

而只有人;
只有那些英雄,
他们为了真理,为了民族的光荣,
坚定不移,不惜牺牲。

在懒汉们酣睡的时候,
勇敢的人们都在忘我地劳动。
当懦夫们望风而逃,
我们的英雄却在奋勇冲锋。
是他们建造了支撑祖国大厦的柱石,
使它们拔地而起,高耸入云。

译文二: 　　　国　　力

民族的伟大昌盛靠什么?
不靠金子而只靠人。
靠那些为了真理和祖国荣誉的人们
坚定不移,吃苦受饥。

靠那些勇敢的人们
在他人酣睡时的冲锋不息,
在他人逃逸时的奋勇出击……
他们牢固地搭起民族的柱石
撑起一片辽阔的天地。(李明 译)

四、翻译练习

句子翻译

第一组：

1. He is always the first to bear hardships and the **last** to enjoy comforts.

2. Miniskirts are the **last** things she'd like to wear.

3. This is the **last** thing in labor-saving devices.

4. I wouldn't marry you if you were the **last** man on earth.

5. This is a question of the **last** importance.

6. The Japanese militarists committed the **last** crime.

7. I've said my **last** word on this question.

8. "Women always have the **last** word!"

9. I want to comment on your **last** issue of September, 1995, No. 5.

10. You are late for the **last** time.

11. He is the **last** person to be blamed.

第二组：

1. Health is above wealth, for **this** cannot give so much happiness as **that**.

2. I hate blue shirt; white shirt suits me, but gray shirt is the **most preferable**.

3. Although the country's long-term strategy of **developing** the vast western region is still at an early stage, both the government officials and economic experts are keen to discuss the ways to narrow the economic gap between the west and the east.

4. He is bright and **ambitious**.

5. He is **ambitious** for fame and power.

6. I feel greatly **flattered** by your invitation.

7. Don't be deceived by her **flatteries**.

8. If there are those who don't want to vote for me because I am a deeply **committed** Christian, I believe they should vote for someone else.

9. He said, "I feel that my existence in the world is completely mine, more than when I was a committed Nazi."

10. He loved particularly to tell us how he had made Mr. Churchill unhappy by teasing him about his "bad boy", General de Gaulle.

11. There was much traffic at night and many mules on the road with boxes of ammunition on each side of their pack-saddles and gray motor trucks that carried men, and other trucks with loads covered with canvas that moved slower in the traffic. (A Farewell to Arms)

篇章翻译

篇章翻译 1

A major source of anxiety about the future of the family is rooted not so much in reality as in the tension between the idealized expectation in the culture and the reality itself. Nostalgia for a lost family tradition, which, in fact, never existed, has prejudiced our understanding of the conditions of families in contemporary society. Thus, the current anxiety over the fate of the family reflects not only problems in the family but also a variety of fears about other social problems that are eventually projected onto the family.

The real problem facing American families today are not symptoms of breakdown as is often suggested; rather, they reflect the difficulties of adaptation to recent social changes, particularly to the loss of diversity in household membership, to the reduction of the variety of family functions and, to some extent, to the weakening of the family adaptability. The idealization of the family as a refuge from the world and the myth that the work of mothers is harmful has added considerable strain. The continuous emphasis on the family as a universal private retreat and as an emotional haven is misguided in light of historical experience.

篇章翻译 2

1) There are 39 universities and colleges offering degree courses in Geography, but I have never seen any good jobs for Geography graduates advertised. 2) Or am I alone in suspecting that they will return to teach Geography to another set of students, who in turn will teach more Geography undergraduates? 3) Only ten universities currently offer degree courses in Aeronautical Engineering, which perhaps is just as well, in view of the speed with which the aircraft industry has been dispensing with excess personnel. 4) On the other hand, hospital casualty departments throughout the country are having to close down because of the lack of doctors. 5) The reason? University medical schools can only find places for half of those who apply. 6) It seems to me that time is ripe for the Department of Employment and the Department of Education to get together with the universities and produce a revised educational system that will make a more economic use of the wealth of talent, application and industry currently being wasted on diplomas and degrees that no one wants to know about.

第六章　省词翻译法

> 翻译中的可译性只能是相对的，绝对的可译性是不存在的。
> ——刘宓庆
>
> 没有加减就没有算术，对翻译来说，也是如此。
> ——贝亚德·泰勒

一、理论探讨

从事英汉翻译，并非任何时候都要把英语原文中的每个词语翻译到译文中来。为使行文简洁易懂并符合译文的语言表达习惯和修辞特点，很多时候往往需要省略某些词语不译。这种翻译方法称作"省略法"或"省词翻译法"。由于翻译所涉及的两种不同语言之间存在差异，在一种语言里惯常使用的词语或表达，在另一种语言里按照其语言规则和习惯则有可能显得累赘或多余。在翻译过程中，对于在译文中显得累赘或多余的词语和表达就应略去不译，这样才能保证译文的简洁和精练。

同英语相比，汉语中没有冠词，而代词、连词、介词使用的频率也远远没有英语中使用的频率那么高。这样，在英汉翻译时，若碰到句子中使用了这些词语，就要考虑在译文中省略它们，以使译文简洁通畅。另外，英语中的系动词和先行词在汉译中也经常可以省略不译。这类由于英汉两种语言在句子结构上的差异而引起的省词翻译法叫做结构性省词翻译法。结构性省词翻译并非一点也不涉及信息，也并非只是句中个别字词的省略。由于英文句子有追求结构完整的倾向，汉语则有突出重点部分而不计其余部分的倾向，故有些在英语句子中不得缺少的部分，若在汉语句中可有可无或译出后反而显得重复累赘，则可省去不译（王宏印，2002：32）。

另一种省词翻译法叫做精炼压缩法。这种翻译方法在用于科技翻译中时，是指将英语中较为复杂的结构包括从句压缩成精炼的汉语词组。如将 We are all familiar with the fact that a body expands when heated 译成"众所周知，物体热胀冷缩"，将 Scientific exploration, the search of knowledge, has given man the practical results of being able to shield himself from the calamities of nature and the calamities imposed by other men 译成"科学探索,即对知识的追求,使得人类真正能够不受天灾人祸的袭击"等均属精炼压缩法。文学作品更加讲究语言的精炼优美,避免逐字逐句地死译使译文冗长生硬,而又在精炼中更多体现汉语的特点。如将 There is no month in the whole year, in which nature wears a more beautiful appearance than in the month of August 译成"四季之美,八月为最"(周方珠 译),将 So fine was the morning except for a streak of wind here and there that the sea and sky looked all one fabric, as if sails were stuck high up in the sky, or the clouds had dropped down into the sea 译成"清晨晴朗,清风徐徐,水天一色,征帆如插高天,浮云似坠海底"等均属精炼压缩翻译法。精炼压缩翻译法将在第九章作进一步讨论。

有人(王宏印,2002:32)将结构性省词翻译看作是消极的省译手段,而将精炼压缩法看作是积极的省译手段,因为前者明显,后者隐晦。省词翻译是针对原文而言的。在英汉翻译中,在汉语译文中可省略的英语词语有代词(尤其是物主代词)、系动词、介词、连词、冠词、先行词、引导词等。对这些词语省译并非因为它们在原文中不重要,而是它们在译文中不必要。

省词翻译同增词翻译(见第七章)相辅相成,是一个问题的两个方面,但词语的增补是针对译文而言的。作为译者,对省词翻译法和增词翻译法的运用都要慎重,所遵循的原则就是:增词不能蛇足,减词不能损意(王宏印,2002:174)。

二、译例举隅及翻译点评

【例1】

原　文：They had ground him beneath their heel, they had taken the best of him, **they** had murdered his father, **they** had broken and wrecked his wife, **they** had crushed his whole family.

译　文：他们把他踩在脚下,压得粉碎,他们榨干了他的精髓,害死了他的父亲,摧残了他的妻子，毁灭了他的全家。

【点评】对比原文和译文，不难发现原文中一共使用了五个代词they，但译文中仅使用了两次"他们"，其余三个代词they都被省略未译。汉语中如果连续几个句子共用同一个主语，这时通常只在第一句话中提及主语，其余句子里通常可以省略主语。汉语中省略主语可以作为句子与句子之间的衔接手段（cohesive devices）之一，但在英语中却没有这种衔接手段，因为英语是主语显著（subject prominent）的语言。

英汉翻译中，在汉语译文中省略英文原文中的代词属于结构性省略，即省略英语原文中因为结构而需要但在汉语译文中因为汉语的结构而不需要的词语。在英汉翻译中，除了作主语的代词可以省略之外，作宾语的代词以及作定语的所有格代词很多情况下也可以省略。如：1) That dishonest boy is not at all ill. He is alive and kicking in the swimming pool. We all saw **him**. 那个不诚实的男孩子根本没病，他在游泳池里还活蹦乱跳的，我们都看见了。2) John got up vary early in the morning. He put on **his** jacket, (**his**) trousers and (**his**) shoes, sat down at (**his**) desk and began to do **his** homework. 清晨约翰起得很早。他穿上夹克、裤子和鞋子，就在书桌那里坐下来开始做家庭作业。（试比较：清晨约翰起得很早。他穿上他的夹克、裤子和鞋子，就在书桌那里坐下来开始做他的家庭作业。）

【例2】

原　文：Winter is the best time to study **the** growth of trees. Although **the** leaves are gone and the branches are bare, **the** trees themselves are beautiful.

译　文：冬天是研究树木生长的最好季节。虽则树叶落了，树枝光了，但树木本身却是美丽的。

【点评】本例句中，定冠词the表示泛指，故汉语译文中没有将其翻译出来。在汉语译文中省略英文原文中的冠词不译也属于结构性省略。英语中的冠词分为两种：定冠词（the）和不定冠词（a和an），汉语中却没有冠词。那么在英汉翻译中，如何在汉语译文中处理英语中的冠词呢？对于英语

中的冠词，有两种处理方式：如果不定冠词表示"一（个）""每一"之意，那么在汉语译文中必须译出；如果不定冠词用来表示泛指，则在汉语译文中需要省略。同理，英语中的定冠词如果表示"那个""这个"等特指意义，就需要在汉语中译出；如果定冠词表示泛指，则在汉语译文中需要省略。再如，下面句子中不定冠词 a 表示泛指，故汉语译文需要省略不译该词：

Any substance is made of atoms whether it is **a** solid, **a** liquid, or **a** gas.（任何物质，不论固体、液体或气体，都由原子组成。）

【例3】

原　文：No man can be brave who considers pain as the greatest evil of life; **or** temperate, who regards pleasure as the highest goal.

译　文：把痛苦视为生活中最大不幸的人不可能勇敢；把快乐当作生活中最高目标的人不可能自我节制。

【点评】本例中，汉语译文省略了英语原文中的连词 or 未译，属结构性省略。连词在英语中的使用频率很高，但在汉语中的使用频率就要低得多了。这是因为，英语是一种以形合（hypotactic）为主要特点的语言。在形式上，英语多使用从属连接词（如 because、although、since 等）、关系代词或关系副词（如 who、which、where 等）以及动词不定式结构等。由于英语中连词已经清楚地表明主从句之间的关系，因而其从属分句既可置于主句之前、之后，有时也可以镶嵌在主句之中。换言之，形合法是指，在组织语言时，通过连接手段将一个分句置于另一个分句的从属位置上，使得主句和从句之间以及其他各个句子成分之间的关系非常分明。

与英语相对应，汉语是一种以意合（paratactic）为主要特点的语言。汉语最重要的特点就是通常不使用明显的连接词来将句子连接在一起，这样，对于句子与句子之间以及分句与分句之间的关系需要靠读者从上下文的相关性中找到解释。具有意合特点的语言在行文时有两种方式，其一是将片语、分句、句子放在一起，通常不使用连接词，即使使用连接词时也只使用诸如 and、but、or 这样的连接词，或者最小限度地使用或者干脆不使用表示从属关系的连接词连接句子。其二是在两个或两个以上意义完整的句子之间用逗号或分号隔开，把这些句子看成是一个句子，比如英文中的例子：1) The rain fell; the river flooded; the house was washed away. 2) I came, I saw, I conquered.

由于英语主要以形合为特点，汉语主要以意合为特点，在英汉翻译时，英语中的连词在汉语译文中通常予以省略。如：1) **Because** everyone uses language to talk, everyone thinks he can talk about language. (Johann Wolfgang von Goethe) 人人都用语言交谈，人人也就自认为能够谈论语言。（歌德语）2) He liked his sister, **who was** warm **and** pleasant, **but he** did not like his brother, **who was** aloof **and** arrogant. 他喜欢他那热情、可爱的妹妹，不喜欢他那冷漠、高傲的哥哥。（张培基等，1980：133）

【例4】

原　文：Scientific exploration, the search for knowledge, has given man the practical **results** of being able to shield himself from the calamities of nature and the calamities **imposed by other men**.

译　文：科学探索，即对知识的探求，使得人类真正能够不受/免遭天灾人祸的袭击。（李明 译）

【点评】对照英语原文和汉语译文就不难发现，英语原文中的 results 一词和过去分词短语 imposed by other men 在汉语中被省略而没有翻译出来，但它们各自的意义实际上已经隐含在译文当中。这种省略是因表达需要而进行的省略。因表达需要而进行的省略在英汉翻译中非常常见。很多时候，在表达同一种意思时，英语中需要使用的词语在汉语中可以省略，但英语中使用词语所含的意义在汉语译文中已经隐含。再如：1) We think we have freed our slaves, but we have not. We just call them by a different name. Every time people reach a certain status **in life** they seem to take pride **in the fact that** they now have a secretary. 我们总以为已经解放了奴隶，但事实上并没有。我们只不过使用了另一个名称来称呼他们罢了。每当人们上升到某个位置，他们似乎就以拥有一名秘书而自豪。（李明 译）2) There was no snow, the leaves were gone **from the trees**, the grass was dead. 天未下雪，但叶落草枯。

【例5】

原　文：At the birth of her second child she went into a long coma and emerged with a clear case of schizophrenia or "**split personality**".

译　文：生第二个孩子时，她陷入了长时间的昏迷，等醒来后，又出现典型的精神分裂症症状。（张经浩 译）

【点评】在英语中，schizophrenia 是一个专业术语，而 split personality 则是一个常用短语。在汉语中，不管是专业术语还是常用词语，通常只有一种表达，即"精神分裂症"，这是因为语言表达差异而采取的省略翻译法。再如：1) Bacteria capable of causing disease are known as pathogenic, **or disease-producing**. 能引起疾病的细菌称为致病菌。2) Remember: you are not any old **Tom, Dick or Harry** giving his opinion. You're a man who was sent as a representative of the British Government. 你要记住，你不是一个普普通通的老百姓，可以随便发表意见。你是英国政府派出的代表。3) **The late** Mrs. Achson had passed to her Maker somewhere about 1930. 亚奇逊太太升天大约是在1930年。（张经浩 译）

【例6】

原　文：Instead of one old woman knocking me about and starving me, everybody of all ages **knocked me about and starved me**.

译　文：那时打我并且使我挨饿的不只是一个老太婆，而是老老少少各式各样的人。（张培基 译）

【点评】这里的汉语译文将英语原文中的 knocked me about and starved me 承前省略不译。这种省略属于因修辞需要而进行的省略。如果将本例中汉语译文的后半句翻译成"而是老老少少各式各样的人打我并且使我挨饿"就会使译文非常啰唆。再如：1) University applicants who had worked at a job would receive preference **over those who had not**. 报考大学的人，有工作经验者优先录取。(张培基 译) 2) **China is also a country of people** with a passionate love of flowers and trees and intense dedication to the welfare of children and to the work ethic. 中国人还热爱鲜花和树木，专心致力于儿童的福利事业，并且严格恪守工作道德。

【例 7】

原　文：People will be alert and receptive if they are faced with information that gets them to think about things they are interested in.

译文一：如果人们遇到的信息能使他们想起感兴趣的事情，他们就会很留心而且愿意接受。

译文二：假如人们碰到那些引发他们对自己所感兴趣的东西进行思考的信息，他们就会非常关注并愿意接受的。(李明 译)

【点评】省词翻译并不意味着随译者自己的意愿将原文信息进行整合，从而改变原文的句子结构或信息结构。译文一的误译就在于：将原文关于 people 及其所衍生出的 they 的信息或话题改成了"人们碰到的信息"(即将所谈论话题的"人们"变成了"信息")，这就从根本上改变了原文句子的信息出发点，因而是不忠实的翻译。这样的翻译应该极力避免。译文二同原文所表达的信息保持了一致。尽管译文二在语言的使用上也许显得比译文一更长一些，但它充分传达了原文信息且没有冗余信息的字眼，因而该译文可视为好的、简洁的译文。

三、翻译比较与欣赏

【例 1】

原　文：A: What flower does everybody have?

　　　　B: Tulips. (Tulips = two lips)

译文一：A: 人人都有的花是什么花？

　　　　　B: 郁金香。(郁金香的英文与双唇的英文发音相似)（勒梅琳等 译）

译文二：A: 人人都有的花儿是什么花儿？

　　　　　B: 泪花儿。（马红军 译，有改动）

【例 2】

原　　文：It isn't strange for a woman to want her old husband back, for respectability, though for a man to want his wife back—well, perhaps it is funny, rather!

译文一：（一个）女人为了体面（的关系）而要（她的从）前（的那个）丈夫回来，这并不（是）奇怪（的事），虽然（一个）男人要（他从）前（的那个）妻（子）回来，也许是很有趣的事。（括号中的成分可以省略，见王宏印，2002: 30）

译文二：女人为了体面而要前夫回来，这并不是什么奇怪的事情，而男人要前妻回来，那或许可就是非常有趣的事情了！（李明 译）

【例 3】

原　　文：Up Broadway he turned, and halted at a glittering café, where are gathered together nightly the choicest products of the grapes, the silkworm and protoplasm.

译文一：他拐到百老汇街上，在一家灯火辉煌的饭店前停了下来。那里每晚汇集着葡萄、蚕和原生质最优异的产品。（易明华 用例）

译文二：他拐到百老汇街上，在一家灯火辉煌的饭店前停了下来。那里每晚汇集着上等的美酒、华丽的衣服和有地位的人物。（易明华 用例）

译文三：他拐上百老汇大街，在一家灯火辉煌的咖啡店门前停了下来。这里每天晚上都汇集了各种上等的葡萄美酒，展现了各色华丽的服装，聚集了各种显赫的人物。（李明 译）

【例 4】

原　　文：I love my love with an E, because she's enticing; I hate her with an E, because she's engaged; I took her to the sign of the exquisite, and treated her with an elopement; her name's Emily, and she lives in the east. (Charles Dickens, *David Copperfield*)

译文一：我爱我的爱人为了一个 E，因为她是 Enticing（迷人的）；我恨我的爱人为了一个 E，因为她是 Engaged（订了婚了）。我用我的爱人象征 Exquisite（美妙），我劝我的爱人从事 Elopement（私奔），她的名字是 Emily（爱弥丽），她的住处在 East（东方）。（董秋斯 译）

译文二：我爱我的所爱，因为她长得实在招人爱。我恨我的所爱，因为她不回报我的爱。我带着她到挂着一幅美妙之处招牌的一家，和她谈情说爱。我请她跟我一起潜逃私奔，为的是我和她能长久你亲我爱。她的名字叫爱弥丽，她家住在爱仁里。（张谷若 译）

译文三：我爱我的心上人，因为她那样地叫人入迷（enticing）；我恨我的心上人，因为她已订婚将作他人妻（engaged）；她花容月貌无可比拟（exquisite），我劝她私奔跟我在一起（elopement）；她的名字叫埃米莉（Emily），她的家就在东城里（east），我爱我的心上人呀，一切都是因为这个 E！（陆乃胜 译）

译文四：我爱我的爱人，因为她很迷人；我恨我的爱人，因已许配他人；她在我心中是美人，我带她私奔，以避开外人；她名叫虞美人，是东方丽人。（姜秋霞、张柏然，1996：18）

译文五：吾爱吾爱，因伊可爱；吾恨吾爱，因伊另有所爱。吾视吾爱，神圣之爱，吾携吾爱，私逃为爱；吾爱名爱米丽，吾东方之爱。（姜秋霞、张柏然，1996：18）

译文六：我爱我的那个"丽"，可爱迷人有魅力；我恨我的那个"丽"，要和他人结伉俪；她文雅大方又美丽，和我出逃去游历；她芳名就叫爱米丽，家住东方人俏丽。（马红军 译）

四、翻 译 练 习

句子翻译

1. When the students finished all the books **they** had brought, **they** opened the lunch and ate it.

2. Knowledge is a comfortable and necessary retreat and shelter for **us** in an advanced age; and if **we** do not plant it while young, it will give **us** no shade when **we** grow old.

3. For two weeks, he had been studying the house, looking at **its** rooms, **its** electric wiring, **its** path and **its** garden.

4. **Her** dark hair waved untidy across **her** broad forehead, **her** face was short, **her** upper lips short, showing a glint of teeth, **her** brows were straight and dark, **her** lashes long and dark, **her** nose straight.

5. You cannot build **a** ship, **a** bridge or **a** house if you don't know how to make **a** design or how to read.

6. **The** intensity of sound is inversely proportioned to the square of the distance measured from the source of the sound.

7. It had been a fine, golden autumn, a lovely farewell to those **who** would lose their youth, **and** some of them their lives, **before** the leaves turned again in a peace time fall.

8. **During** the whole of a dull, dark, and soundless day in the autumn of the year, **when** the clouds hung oppressively low in the heavens, I had been passing alone, on horseback, through a singularly dreary tract (地方) of country.

9. The crowd was pushing harder. Those in the middle were squeezed **against each other so tightly** they could not move **in any direction**.

10. **There are those who think** that most people are not particularly interested in analyses of climatic conditions, so there must be other reasons for strangers to start conversations by talking about the weather.

11. Patients with influenza must be separated from the well lest the disease should spread

from person to person.

12. When mineral oil is refined into petrol, it is used to drive internal combustion engine. To it we owe the existence of the motor-car, which has replaced the private **carriage drawn by the horse**.

13. He continued to order the stale bread—**never** a cake, **never** a pie, **never** one of the other delicious pastries in the showcase.

14. Mr. Jarndyce was turning to speak to us, when his attention was attracted by the abrupt entrance into the room of Mr. Gridley **who had been mentioned**, and whom we had seen on our way up.

15. He hopes that he may once again repeat, upon a greater scale than ever before, that process of destroying his enemies one by one by which he has so long **thrived** and **prospered**.

16. To our knowledge, advertisement and **commercials** do many important things for society: they convey business information, facilitate communication and help keep the business world moving.

篇章翻译

篇章翻译 1

Japan's once enviable jobless rate will soar to double-digit levels if—and the warning is a big one—firms opt for drastic Western-style layoffs to boost profits. While Japan's life-time employment system is visibly unraveling, many economists still doubt whether a scenario of soaring joblessness will occur, given that economic incentives to slash payrolls clash with social and political pressures to save jobs. A kinder, gentler approach to restructuring would soften the social instability many fear would result from doubling the jobless rate, already at a record high.

Critics believe it would also cap gains in profit margins and stifle economic vitality, especially in the absence of bold steps to open the door to new growth industries. Some economists believe different methods of counting mean Japan's jobless rate is already close to 7 percent by United States standards, not that far from the 7.8 percent peak hit in the US in 1992 when it began to emerge from a two-year slump.

篇章翻译 2

1) Under the law of competition, the employer of thousands is forced into the strictest economies, among which the rates paid to labor figure prominently. 2) The price which society pays for the law, like the price it pays for cheap comforts and luxuries, is great, but the advantages of this law are also greater than its cost—for it is to this law that we owe our wonderful material development, which brings improved conditions in its train (后果). 3) But, whether the law be benign (良性的) or not, we cannot evade it; of the effect of any new substitutes for it proposed we can not be sure; and while the law may be sometimes hard for the individual, it is best for the race, because it insures the survival of the fittest in every department. 4) We accept and welcome, therefore, as conditions to which we must accommodate ourselves, great inequality of environment; the concentration of business, industrial and commercial, in the hands of a few; and the law of competition between these, as being not only beneficial, but essential to the future progress of the race.

第七章 增词翻译法

增词不能蛇足，减词不能损意。

——王宏印

一、理论探讨

增词翻译法是指在准确理解原文的基础上在译文中添加必要词语的翻译方法。此时所增加的词语必须是译文中在句法上、语义上、修辞上或习惯搭配上不可或缺的词语，或者说，只有增加了相关的词语才能够把原文的意思在译文中说得清楚明白。增词并不是给译文增加额外的信息或意义，也不意味着译文没有忠于原文。恰恰相反，所增加的词语往往是原文中没有直接说出但却隐含其中的信息，只是由于翻译所涉及的两种语言之间的差异，原文可以隐含该信息，但译文必须明示出来。但采用增词翻译法要注意的问题是，所增加的词语必须既要同原文保持高度的一致，又要在句法结构上或者修辞上同译文保持搭配的和谐。换言之，增词翻译法是为了忠实再现原文信息和在译文中进行通顺表达之所需而使用的翻译方法。

就英汉翻译而言，在采用增词翻译法时，可以增加的词语既可以是实词，也可以是虚词。英译汉时常可以增加的词语有动词、名词、副词、结构词、数量词、概括词、范畴词、语气词等。

二、译例举隅及翻译点评

【例1】

原　文：Mao Zedong **is** an activist, a prime mover, an originator and master of strategy achieved by alternating surprise, tension and easement.

译　文：毛泽东**是**活动家，**是**原动力，**是**创始者，**是**交替运用出其不意、紧张松弛而取得成功的战略家。

【点评】　重复动词是增词翻译法中很重要的一种方法。汉语里动词使用的频率远远高于英语中动词使用的频率。本例中原文只使用了一个系动词 is，后面的 a prime mover、an originator 和 master of strategy 三个名词短语都是系动词 is 的并列表语，这在英语中是允许的，但在将该句翻译成汉语时，如果依照原文只使用一个"是"，汉语译文就会不通顺。在三个名词短语之前重复系动词 is 的汉语对应语"是"才能使译文符合汉语的习惯表达，读来也对称。

【例 2】

原　文：The daily newspaper guides, educates and encourages **the masses**.

译　文：这份报纸可指导**群众**、教育**群众**、鼓舞**群众**。（郭富强 用例）

【点评】　英语中多个动词带一个宾语的现象非常常见，在将这样的英语句子翻译成汉语时，由于必须重复这些动词，而这些被重复的动词之后又必须接宾语，因此，英语句子中的一个宾语在译文中必须重复。再如：We must analyze and solve problems.（我们必须分析问题、解决问题。）

【例 3】

原　文：For the international community the most striking consequence of these **changes** is that China has grown to be the world's eleventh largest economy, and is set to grow further.

译　文：对于国际社会来说，这些变化**所带来的**最为引人注目的结果是，中国已跃居世界第十一经济大国，而且今后定会更强。

【点评】　本例的译文中所增加的"所带来的"几个字是因为行文的需要而增加的词语。同时，由于增加了这几个词，译文的意义也非常清楚地表达出来了。

再如：1) In the evening, after the **banquets**, the **concerts** and the **table tennis exhibitions**, he would work on the drafting of the final communiqué. 晚上在**参加**宴会、**出席**音乐会、**观看**乒乓球表演以后，他还得起草最后公报。
2) My **work**, my **family**, my **friends** were more than enough to fill my time. 我要干工作，要做家务，还要招待朋友，这些足够占去我全部时间。
3) The first requisite of **a good citizen** in this Republic of ours is that he shall be able and willing to pull his weight. 要在我们这个共和国里当一个好公民，第一必备条件就是他要能够而且愿意尽自己的本分。

【例 4】

原　文：Not to educate him (the Child) is to condemn him to repetitious **ignorance**.

译　文：如果我们不对儿童进行教育的话，那就会使他们沦入世世代代的**愚昧状态**。

【点评】英语中很多抽象名词在汉语中需要增加范畴词才能使其意义明晰化，如本例中的 ignorance 在译文中被翻译成"愚昧状态"，这里的"状态"就是被增加的范畴词。再如：The **arrogance** of the aristocracy helped to lead to the French Revolution.（贵族的**傲慢态度**促发了法国革命。）在英汉翻译过程中需要增加范畴词的词语还有以下一些：

abstraction（抽象化）　　　　　jealousy（嫉妒心理）
backwardness（落后状态）　　lightheartedness（轻松愉快的心情）
commercialization（商业化）　loftiness（崇高气质）
complexity（复杂局面）　　　　madness（疯狂行为）
correctness（正确性）　　　　　oxidation（氧化作用）
dejection（沮丧情绪）　　　　　precaution（预防措施）
dependence（依赖性）　　　　　preparation（准备工作）
development（开发工程）　　　processing（加工方法）
favoritism（徇私作风）　　　　　readability（可读性）
hostility（敌对情绪）　　　　　　remedy（补救方法）

indifference（冷漠态度）　　　　tension（紧张局势）
infiltration（渗透作用）　　　　togetherness（集体感）
irregularities（越轨行为）　　　transition（演变过程）

【例 5】

原　文：In the 1960s, the Soviets posed a serious challenge to America's hegemonic position **militarily**, **politically** and **economically**.

译　文：20 世纪 60 年代，在**军事**、**政治**、**经济**等各方面，苏联人对美国的霸权地位提出了严重的挑战。

【点评】在英语中，如果要列举一系列事物往往在最后被列举的两项事物之间使用 and，而在汉语中，则往往将所需列举的事物呈现出来，最后使用"等"来加以概括。这是英美民族同汉语民族在表达方式上所体现的区别。因此，在英译汉时，我们必须既了解英语的表达，同时在译文中又要以汉语惯用的方式进行意义的传达。再如：The thesis summed up the new developments made in electronic computers, artificial satellites and rockets.（论文总结了电子计算机、人造卫星和火箭等三个领域中的新成就。）

【例 6】

原　文：Time drops in decay, like a candle **burnt out**.

译　文：时间一点一滴地逝去，犹如蜡烛慢慢燃尽。

【点评】本例中原文 burnt out 在译文中被译成"慢慢燃尽"，表面上看，原文中根本没有"慢慢"（slowly）这个词，但其意义已经隐含在 burnt out 之中。"慢慢"在这里可以看作是表示方式的副词。英语中很多动词本身已经隐含了其动作的方式，汉语中动词往往是比较单纯的动作，如果要表示方式，就需要另外增加副词。这方面的例子很多，我们以"笑"为例。请注意英语中含有"笑"的单词在汉语中的对应语：

smile 微笑

laugh 捧腹大笑

simper 傻笑，假笑

smirk 傻笑，假笑（与 simper 同义）

grin 露齿而笑，咧嘴而笑

giggle 咯咯地笑，痴痴地笑

titter（含羞地）窃笑

snigger 窃笑，暗笑

twitter 一连串又短又轻地笑

chuckle（男人）压低声音、抿着嘴而独自轻声地笑

chortle 闭嘴低声咯咯轻笑

因此，英汉翻译时，我们一定要注意英汉两种语言在这方面的差别。

再如：He **poured** out his tale of misfortunes.（他滔滔不绝地诉说了自己的遭遇。）

【例 7】

原　文：You can almost put it down as a general rule in this town that **presidents** often invite "honest criticism" from their aides.

译　文：你几乎可以把这一点看成首都的一种倾向：**历届总统经常请他们的助手们提出"直率的批评"**。（蔡基刚，2003：64）

【点评】英语中的可数名词都有其单数和复数形式，其复数形式是在名词之后加上后缀 -s 构成。汉语中的名词复数可以通过许多途径构成，如本例中在"总统"之前增加"历届"二字便成复数，也可以使用"每一届""历任"等置于"总统"之前表示复数。汉语中名词复数的表现形式可以说是汉语语言的一道奇观。我们再看下面的例子：1) They can separate **facts** from **opinions** and don't pretend to have all the answers. 他们能够把无数的事实从纷繁的意见中剥离出来，而又不会假装知晓一切。2) Cargo insurance is to protect the trader from **losses** that many dangers may cause. 货物保险会使贸易商免受许多风险所可能造成的**种种损失**。3) The judge let him off with **warnings** not to cause trouble again. 法官对他**再三**提出警告,不得重新作案,然后就将他放了。4) The simple perception of natural **forms** is a delight. The influence of the **forms** and **actions** in nature is so needful to man, that, in its lowest functions, it seems to lie on the confines of commodity and beauty. 只要一想到自然**万物**的形体,我便心花怒放。自然界里**各种形体**和**各种活动**的影响,对于人类都是非常必需的,这种影响,就其最粗浅的作用来说,似乎只局限于适用性和审美价值。(爱默生《论自然》)(夏济安 译,有改动)

【例8】

原　文:**I had imagined** it to be merely a gesture of affection, but it **seems** it is to smell the lamb and make sure that it is her own.

译　文:我**原**以为这不过是表示亲昵,但**现在**看来,这是为了闻一闻羊羔的味道,来断定羊羔是不是自己生的。

【点评】英语句子中的任何时态都是依靠动词来体现,汉语句子中的动词本身不体现任何时态,而是依靠增加表示时态概念的副词来体现。因此,在将英语句子中体现各种时态的动词翻译成汉语时,必须首先充分理解英语动词所体现时态的意义,然后在汉语译文中选取能够表示英语动词时态的副词。译文第一个分句中的"原"是"原来"的意思,表示过去完成时这一概念,第二个分句中的"现在"是翻译原文中 seems 所体现的现在时态。由此可见,在涉及英语句子动词时态的汉译时,往往需要运用增词翻译法。再如:1) We can learn what we **did** not know. 我们能够学会我们**原来**不懂的东西。2) The English language **is** in very good shape. It **is changing** in its own undiscoverable way, but it **is not going rotten** like a plum dropping off a tree. 英语**目前**的情况很好,它正按照它那不易为人发现的方式**在**起着变化,而不是像一只树上掉下来的李子那样**在**逐渐腐烂。(古今明 用例)3) I particularly want to pay tribute, not only to those who

prepared the magnificent dinner, but also to those who **have provided** the splendid music. Never **have I heard** American music played better in a foreign land. 我特别要赞扬的不仅是那些准备了这次盛大宴会的人，而且还有那些演奏了这样美好的音乐的人。我在国外从来没有听到过把美国音乐演奏得这样好的。（古今明 用例）

【例 9】

原　文：She possessed an innocence unsullied by contact with the world.

译　文：她拥有一种纯真，**这种纯真**并没有因为同外界的接触而玷污。（李明 译）

【点评】本例译文第二个分句中的"这种纯真"是增加的词语，这种增词翻译法也可以看作是重复翻译法，它是因为汉语行文和表达需要而通过增加词语来使汉语句子的意思表达得通顺流畅。如果不增加"这种纯真"这几个字，译文就无法通顺地表达。再如：As a result, a few token meetings were being set up through Foggy Bottom, the more-than-ever appropriate nickname for the Department of State. It describes Secretary Roger's influence … foggy and at the bottom.（结果在"雾谷"召开了几次象征性的会议。**用"雾谷"这个绰号来称呼**（美国）国务院是再贴切不过的词语了。它描述了国务卿罗杰斯的影响——**虚无缥缈如雾，地位低下如谷**。）这里分别有三处进行了增词处理，它们也可以被看作是解释性翻译。所增加的词语在对原文意义的顺利传达方面起了至关重要的作用。

【例 10】

原　文：A government of and by and for **the exploiting class** cannot possibly survive.

译　文：一个为剥削阶级所占有，由剥削阶级所组成并为剥削阶级服务的政府是不可能存在下去的。

【点评】本例原文中的 a government of and by and for the exploiting class 实际上是 a government of the exploiting class and by the exploiting class and for the

exploiting class 的压缩表达式,英语的这种表达可以使语言非常简洁,但汉语中就没有这种压缩式表达法,如果汉语中按照英语的形式进行简洁式表达就会意义不明确。因此,就需要将原文中被压缩的部分补充出来,这种补充既可以看作是重复翻译法,也可以看作是增词翻译法。再如:1) Matter can be changed into energy, and energy into matter. 物质可以转化为能,能也可以转化为物质。2) Courage in excess becomes foolhardiness, affection weakness, thrift avarice. 勇敢过度即成蛮勇,感情过度即成溺爱,节俭过度即成贪婪。

【例 11】

原 文:You are only young once. At the time it seems endless, and is gone in a flash; and then for a very long time you are old. (By Sylvia Townsend Warner)

译 文:人的一生只能年轻一次,年轻时总觉得时间无限,而逝去就在瞬间;然后呢,就要在漫长的岁月中度过晚年。

【点评】英语中,句子的语气要么是通过动词谓语部分所使用的情态动词来体现,要么是通过某些副词来体现,而汉语句子的语气则往往要靠语气词本身来表示。本例汉语译文中的"呢"就是一个语气词。英译汉时,必要时必须增加表示语气的词语,以体现原文句子所表示的语气。再如:1) Don't take it seriously. It's only a joke. 不要认真嘛!这不过是开个玩笑而已。(试比较:不要认真。这只是一个玩笑。) 2) Their host carved, poured, served, cut bread, talked, laughed, proposed health. 他们的主人,(又是)割啊,(又是)倒啊,(又是)布菜啊,(又是)切面包啊,(又是)谈啊,(又是)笑啊,(又是)敬酒啊,忙个不停。(试比较:他们的主人割,倒,布菜,切面包,谈,笑,敬酒。)以上两个例子更进一步说明,在英汉翻译中,语气词具有很大的效用。

【例 12】

原 文:Your invention is fantastic; you should send it to **Munich**.

译　文：你的发明真奇妙，你应该把它送到慕尼黑的德国专利局。（司显柱 译）

【点评】这里的译文如果照原文直译就是：你的发明真奇妙，你应该把它送到慕尼黑去。那样的话，由于译文读者对源语中 Munich 所传递的文化信息不了解，于是对源语所表达的意义就无法了解。在将这种负载有文化信息的英文词语翻译成汉语时，必须采取增词翻译法，将源语所传达的文化信息表达出来。再如：1) *Le Monde*, the B.B.C., *The New York Times*, the entire Arab press, all quote Heikal at length. 法国的《世界报》、英国广播公司、美国《纽约时报》以及整个阿拉伯报界，都经常大量引用海卡尔的话。2) This great scientist was born in **New England**. 这位伟大的科学家出生在**美国东北部的新英格兰**。3) The blond boy quickly **crossed** himself. 那个金发小男孩立刻在胸前划十字，**祈求上帝保佑**。4) The British people are still profoundly divided on the issue of **joining Europe**. 在英国人民中间到目前为止一直在**英国是否加入欧洲"共同市场"**的问题上存在严重分歧。

【例 13】

原　文：To attract foreign investment, the United States must offer higher interest rate, adding to domestic borrowing and financing costs, which boost inflation.

译　文：为了吸引外资，美国必须提供较高的利率，**而**这样就会加重内债和金融开支，**最终**导致通货膨胀。

【点评】这里的增词属于因句子逻辑需要而增加的词，以体现句子各成分之间的关系。如果不增加这些词语，就会使句子的意义含混不清。再如：1) I am in charge of the depot, people will hold me responsible but not you. 只有我一个人负责管理这个仓库，**出了事情**别人找我，找不到你。2) The strongest man cannot alter the law of nature. **即使是**最强有力的人也不能改变自然法则。3) The molecules of hydrogen get closer and closer with the pressure. **随着**压力的增加，氢分子越来越密集。4) Noontime came and went; Nixon, who rarely had lunch, and Kissinger, who rarely missed it, skipped the meal and went right on talking for almost four hours. 正午到了，又谈到偏午，尼

克松很少吃午饭，而基辛格则很少不吃午饭，但这回，俩人都不曾想到这顿饭，接连谈了差不多四个钟头。

【例 14】

原　　文：Gunpowder strengthened central government at the expense of feudal nobility.

译文一：火药消灭了封建贵族而巩固了中央集权政治。（何兆武、李约瑟 译）

译文二：火药用于征战，中央政府因之以强，拥据领地之公侯因之而弱。（许国璋 译）

【点评】对比两种汉语译文不难发现，译文一依照原文进行了直译，而译文二的译者许国璋先生则在译文当中对原文采取了"意义上的显化转换"（柯飞，2005：306）。如果译者在译文中增添有助于译文读者理解的显化表达，或者说将原文隐含的信息显化于译文当中，即是所谓的"意义上的显化转换"。在译文当中进行"意义上的显化转换"实际上就是增词翻译法，它可以使译文所表达的意思更为明确，逻辑更为清楚。当然，本例选自罗素的《西方哲学史》。对于哲学著作的翻译，许国璋先生（1991：248，262）认为应采取"通译""切译"或"阐译"的方法。他力主译文必须通脱、醒豁，译出词的文化史涵义。他特地翻译罗素《西方哲学史》以为其"阐译"示范。他解释说：feudal 不译"封建"，译"拥据领地（之公侯）"；anarchy 不译"无政府"（当时无中央政府），而译"诸侯纷争"；adventure 不译"冒险"，而应要么译为"猎奇于远方"，要么译为"探无涯之知"，视上下文而定。再如 antiquity 不译"古代"，而译"希腊罗马"；fame and beauty 应根据文艺复兴时期的特殊涵义而译为"享盛誉于邦国，创文艺之美"；prudential arguments 译为"保身家保名誉之考虑"等。试比较下面一段文字的两种汉语译文：

When Constantinople, the last survival of antiquity, was captured by the Turks, Greek refugees in Italy were welcomed by humanists. Vasco da Gama and Columbus enlarged the world, and Copernicus enlarged the heavens.

译文一：当君士坦丁堡，这个古代最后的残余，被土耳其人攻陷后，逃往意大利的希腊难民曾受到人文学者的欢迎。瓦斯寇·达·伽马和哥伦布扩大了世界，而哥白尼扩大了天界。（何兆武、李约瑟 译）

译文二：[15世纪中叶] 君士坦丁堡为土耳其所占。自希腊罗马之衰，古文化残存于世，仅君士坦丁堡一地。既陷，寓居于君士坦丁堡之希腊学人，相率流亡意大利，意大利倾慕希腊人文之学者，迎为上宾。达迦玛绕好望角抵印度，哥伦布西行发现新地，而世界为之扩大。哥白尼立日中心之说，而宇宙为之扩大。（许国璋 译）

对比两种译文，哪个译文意义更为清晰，读者自有判断。由此可见增词翻译法在翻译中的重要性。

三、翻译比较与欣赏

【例1】

原　文：Even the pine logs which burned all day in the fireplace couldn't keep my little house warm and dry.

译文一：火炉里成天烧着松柴，还不能使我的小屋子温暖和干燥。（周煦良 译）

译文二：火炉里成天烧着松柴，还不能使我的小屋子温暖和干爽。（马红军，2000：103）

译文三：炉子里成天烧着松柴，可我的小屋子还是又冷又潮。（马红军，2000：103）

译文四：即使壁炉里整天烧着松柴，我的小屋子也暖和干爽不起来。（李明 译）

【例2】

原　文：From the shore-line out to a distance which may be anywhere from a few miles to a few hundred miles runs the gentle slope of the continental shelf, geologically part of the continents.

译文一：从海岸线向外延伸着从几英里到几百英里的大陆架缓坡，即大陆的地质

要素。

译文二：大陆架徐缓的斜坡从海岸线向外延伸至海内数英里乃至数百英里。从地质上说，它是大陆的一部分。（赵振才 译）

译文三：大陆架的斜坡较缓，从海岸向海里延伸数英里乃至数百英里。地质学认为它是大陆的一部分。（黄忠廉、李亚舒 译）

译文四：从海岸线向远处延伸的是大陆架平缓的斜坡，其距离从几英里到几百英里不等，从地质学的角度说，它是大陆的一部分。（李明 译）

【例3】

原　文：Every man who rises above the common level has received two educations: the first from his teachers; the second, more personal and important, from himself.

译文一：每个人尖儿都接受两种教育：一个是拜师学艺；另外一个是自学成才。后一个更加个人化，也更加重要。（傅敬民等 用例）

译文二：每一个能够从众人中脱颖而出的人，他所受的教育方式不外乎两种：一种是从师；另外一种是自学。后者尤为重要，也更显个性。（傅敬民等 用例）

译文三：芸芸众生中凡脱颖而出的人往往接受过两种教育：一种来自老师，另一种来自个人。而来自个人的，更直接，也更重要。（李明 译）

【例4】

原　文：　　**Bed in Summer**

In winter I get up at night

And dress by yellow candle-light

In summer, quite the other way,

I have to go to bed by day.

I have to go to bed and see

The birds still hopping on the tree,

Or hear the grown-up people's feet

Still going past me in the street.

And does it seem hard to you,

When all the sky is clear and blue,

And I should like so much to play,

To have to go to bed by day?

译文一： 夏 之 眠

冬日里我夜里起床，

借这昏黄的烛光穿衣裳。

夏日里可不一样，

我不得不白日里就睡觉上床。

小鸟儿仍在树上蹦蹦跳跳，

大人们的脚步声

还在大街上回响，

我却得早早睡觉上床。

天空还那么蔚蓝、明亮，

我多么想嬉戏、玩耍，

你是否觉得

这时候就睡觉难入梦乡？！ （肖洪森 译）

译文二： 夏 之 眠

冬天起床天还未亮，

穿衣需借黄色烛光。

夏天的情形完全两样，

上床睡觉还有日光。

上床睡觉,既能看见
鸟儿在树上欢跳。
也能听见
大人的脚步迈过屋前的街道。

此时的天空蔚蓝明亮,
我多想去玩耍、嬉闹。
此时要你躺到床上,
是否能够进入梦乡?(李明 译)

四、翻译练习

句子翻译

1. He hated failure; he had conquered **it** all his life, risen above **it**, despised **it** in others.

2. He no longer **dreamed of** storms, nor **of** great occurrences, nor **of** great fish, nor **of** fights, nor **of** contests of strength.

3. Grammar **deals with** the structure of language, English grammar **with** the structure of English, French grammar **with** the structure of French, etc.

4. The government is waging a campaign against waste and extravagance, with **the banquet**, a mainstay of all public function in China, a prime target.

5. It is still a hard struggle. There is still **prejudice** and even some hatred, but in most walks of American life there are now more blacks than ever before.

6. **She** was so modest, so expressive, **she** had looked so soft in her thin white gown that he felt he had acted stupidly.

7. At the time of Kennedy's assassination, Kissinger felt that **a second term** would have led either to greatness or to disaster.

8. They drove in a black limousine, past **groves** of birch trees and endless **rows** of identical new buildings.

9. Smoking is harmful to the health of people. World **governments** should conduct serious campaigns against it.

10. I **have not been** satisfied with my efforts to date and I **have been constantly searching** for some sort of organized and systematic contribution which I could make to bridging the gaps between the Eastern and Western worlds.

11. Conditions **are changing** all the time, and to adapt one's thinking to the new conditions, one must study.

12. Both Britain and Americans **are experimenting** with new ideas, and pop is developing and changing, and merging with modern folk music.

13. We see folks who **have hit** bottom. They **are losing** everything, jobs, families, homes. In therapy they **experience** mood swings, nausea, muscular aches.

14. With hair a little thin on his head, and legs that could not possibly do more than three and a half miles an hour on the road, there he was, with three families behind him.

15. It was the best of times, it was the worst of times; it was the age of wisdom, it was the age of foolishness; it was the epoch of belief, it was the epoch of incredulity; it was the season of Light, it was the season of Darkness; it was the spring of hope, it was the winter of despair; we had everything before us, we had nothing before us; we were all going direct to Heaven, we were all going direct the other way. (Charles Dickens, *A Tale of Two Cities*)

16. On the wings of hope, of love, of joy, Miss Meadows sped back to the music hall, up the aisle, up the steps, over to the piano.

17. As I snooze she talks—of anything, everything, all the things that women talk of: books, music, dress, men, other women.

18. We think we have freed our slaves, but we have not. We just call them by a different name. Every time people reach a certain status in life they seem to take pride in the fact that they now have a secretary.

19. One cannot learn to produce a sound from an explanation only, or get a correct idea of a flavor from a description: a sound must be heard, a color seen, a flavor tasted, an odor inhaled.

20. The fan, with its modern, elegant, bright, and harmoniously colored design, is an excellent electrical household appliance for cooling purposes on hot summer days.

篇章翻译

篇章翻译 1

His official academic focus shifted, thanks to a promise made to his dying father that he would study law rather than science (he also took up literature and Spanish). On his return to America, he took a position as a high school Spanish teacher. Though he was popular with students—especially, according to Hubble biographer Gale Christianson, with the girls, who were evidently charmed by his affected British diction and "Oxford mannerisms"—Hubble longed to return to science.

After a year, he signed on as a graduate student at Yerkes Observatory in Wisconsin and embarked on to work that would one day make him famous: studying faint, hazy blobs of light called nebulae (from the Latin word for cloud) that are visible through even a modest telescope.

Hubble's skills as an astronomer were impressive enough to earn him an offer from the prestigious Mount Wilson Observatory. World War I kept him from accepting right away, but in 1919 the newly discharged Major Hubble—as he invariably introduced himself—arrived at observatory headquarters, still in uniform but ready to start observing with the just completed 100-inch. Hooker Telescope, the most powerful on earth.

篇章翻译 2

1) Within a very short time of coming back into power the present government had taken steps to stabilize the position. 2) First of all, we applied ourselves to identifying the root causes of our national ailments, examining contemporary evidence and refusing to be slaves to outmoded doctrinaire beliefs. 3) Secondly we embarked on a reasoned policy to ensure steady economic growth, the modernization of industry, and a proper balance between public and private expenditure. 4) Thirdly by refusing to take refuge—as the previous Government had continually done in the preceding years—in panic-stricken stop-gap measures, we stimulated the return of international confidence. 5) As a result of those immediate measures, and aided by the tremendous effort which they evoked from our people who responded as so often before to a firm hand at the helm, we weathered the storm and moved on into calmer waters and a period of economic expansion and social reorganization.

第八章　翻译中重复的运用

英语行文多"替代"，汉语行文多"重复"。

——吴群

一、理 论 探 讨

　　不管是在英语中还是在汉语中，句子中重复使用词或词组都是存在的现象。但英语中往往是在修辞时才使用重复，或曰反复，一般情况下（即不是为了修辞需要时）则往往避免重复。同英语相比，汉语则不仅在修辞时使用重复，而且在一般情况下也大量使用重复。这是汉语同英语的重要差别之一。

　　利用重复这一表达手段可达到四种目的：一可表达强调语气，二可表达生动活泼，三可使得表达更为明确，四可取得语言的反复美。

　　下面来谈谈在一般情况下英语是如何避免重复的。在英语口语和书面语中，人们都不习惯重复。他们避免重复的成分小至单词，大至句子。其原则就是：凡是意义相同或只是部分相同的词语，在再次提起时都省略不出现，以避免重复。回避重复对于英国人来说，是十分常见的语言习惯，所以一般语法修辞书都很少提及，但对中国学生来说却是值得重视的问题。

　　汉语同英语则有相当大的差别。由于汉语的固有特点和表达习惯，在很多地方非重复不可，或者说，重复了反倒意思更为清晰明了一些（当然，啰唆式的重复在汉语中也是避免的）。换言之，如果使用得当，汉语里的重复并不会给人单调乏味或者啰唆之感。相反，重复反而可以起到强调的作用，有时还可以增强文章的思想性和战斗性。因此，与英语相反，重复是汉语的一个明显特点。

第八章　翻译中重复的运用

下面是英语中常见的避免使用重复的手段，与之相对应的汉语译文则很多时候需要使用重复。

一是使用代词（人称代词、物主代词、指示代词、关系代词等）来避免重复。这是英语中最普通、最常见，也是最有效的避免重复的方法之一。如：1) I met John on the street yesterday. **He** was walking beside his sister. **They** were going to see a film. 昨天我在街上碰到约翰，他和他妹妹走在一起，他们一起去看电影。2) Mary is standing at the door, with **her** hand in **her** pocket. 玛丽正站在门口，一只手放在口袋里。

二是使用上义词、同义词或准同义词等来替换上文中已经出现的某个词语，以避免重复。这些上义词是一些具有概括意义、表示人和事物范畴的词汇。如：man、woman、people、person、child、thing、object、flower、machine、medicine、matter、idea、feeling、animal 等。如：The **monkey's** most extraordinary feat was learning to operate a **tractor**. By the age of nine, this remarkable **animal** had learned to drive the **vehicle** single-handed.（那只猴子最拿手的本领就是学会了开拖拉机。九岁时，这只了不起的动物就已经学会了用一只手驾驶这种工具。）

这一类的换词是书面英语，尤其是现代新闻英语的主要特色之一。如果换词得当，就可以避免单调乏味，使文字新颖别致，焕然生色。如电视机，可说 the television set、the TV、telly、the tube、the goggle-box、the idiot box 等。

三是使用替代法，即使用替代词语或替代句型来回避重复。英语中为避免重复常使用的替代词语有 one、ones、that、those、it、the same (thing)、so、such、there、then、likewise、identical、different、like that、in like manner、(in) this way 等。如：What kind of textbooks do you want? The **ones** with illustrations or the **ones** without?（你需要什么样的课本？是要有插图的呢还是要没有插图的？）

最常见的替代莫过于使用"主语 + do"和"主语 + 动词（如：appear、hope、think、believe、suppose 等）+ so"这类结构了。如：—He will come tomorrow. —I hope so.（——他明天来。——我希望如此。）

其他类型的替代如：1) He might be wrong. If **not**, why was he in such low spirits? 他可能错了。如果没有错，他为什么那么消沉呢？2) We have to hand in a book report

99

every month, and **that** always promptly and in English. 我们每个月得交一篇读书报告，而且要用英语写，并且总是及时交。

英语中，用省略法来回避重复是常见的手段。用省略法回避重复有以下四种情况。一是省略中心名词来避免重复，如：—I like strong tea. —I suppose weak (   ) is better for you.（——我喜欢浓茶。——我认为清茶对你更好。）二是省略核心动词来避免重复，如：They are not known to retreat. They never have (   ) and never will (   ).（退却不是他们的做法。他们从未退却过，也永远不会退却。）三是省略动词不定式以避免重复，如：—Would you like to go with me? —Yes, I'd like to (   ).（——你愿意同我一起去吗？——愿意，我愿意同你一起去。）四是省略句子以避免重复，如：This orange is ripe. I know (   ) from its color.（这个橘子成熟了。从它的颜色可以看得出来。）

在英语中，对于某些由动词、名词或形容词等加介词构成的搭配，可以通过保留介词而省略其前面的动词、名词或形容词的方式来避免重复。如：1) We talked **of** ourselves, **of** our prospects, **of** the journey, **of** the weather, **of** each other—**of** everything but our host and hostess. 我们谈到了我们自己，谈到了我们的前程，谈到了那次旅行，谈到了当时的天气，谈到了我们彼此——谈到了一切，但就是没有谈到我们的男女主人。2) Discipline is indispensable **to** victory in war, **to** success in our work, and indeed, **to** the realization of our lofty goal. 纪律对于战争取得胜利必不可少，对于工作取得成功必不可少，对于实现我们的崇高目标必不可少。3) They continue to observe the principle of depending on their own efforts as well as **of** being thrifty in everything. 他们依然遵循一切勤俭节约、一切依靠自己的原则。

在英语中为避免词语重复还可采用紧缩法。所谓紧缩法就是将语句中两个或几个相关联的成分合并在一起，以避免某些词语的重复，使文字变得简洁紧凑。这种方法一般多见于书面形式。如：1) He was particularly interested in the articles **on** and **by** Lu Xun. 他对关于鲁迅的文章以及鲁迅所写的文章尤其感兴趣。2) You should practise speaking English both **in** and **out of** class. 你既要在课内，又要在课外练习讲英语。3) She was accepted not because **of** but **in spite of** her birth. 她被接受，并非因为她的出身，而是不考虑她的出身。

通过以上对英语避免重复手段的介绍以及所列举例子的汉语译文可以看出，英语在通常情况下是尽量避免重复,而汉语则多重复。在运用重复或曰反复的修辞格时,英语同汉语是相似的。换言之,在英汉翻译时,重复的运用是很普遍的现象。

二、译例举隅及翻译点评

【例1】

原　文：We **accept and welcome**, therefore, as conditions to which we must accommodate ourselves, great inequality of environment; the concentration of business, industrial and commercial, in the hands of a few; and the law of competition between these, as being not only beneficial, but essential to the future progress of the race.

译文一：我们**接受并欢迎**环境上的不平等,**接受并欢迎**让工商业经营集中在少数人的手里,**接受和欢迎**他们之间存在竞争的法则,我们把所有这一切**看成**是我们必须适应的条件,**看成**对人类未来的进步不仅有益,而且是很有必要的。

译文二：因此,我们**接受并欢迎**在我们生活的周围存在巨大的不平等现象(我们必须把这个看作是我们必须适应的条件),**接受并欢迎**工商业的经营集中在少数几个人手中,**接受并欢迎**他们之间存在竞争的机制,这对于整个人类未来的进步不仅是有益的,而且是必需的。(李明 译)

【点评】原文中谓语动词 accept and welcome 之后分别接有三个名词短语作宾语,它们是：great inequality of environment、the concentration of business, industrial and commercial、the law of competition between these。但在汉语中,必须重复动词并在后面接上宾语句子,行文才通顺。译文一和译文二在运用重复翻译法这一点上都是成功的。但译文一在第三次重复时却使用了连词"和",这使译文的排比逊色不少。另外,原文中 as conditions to which we must accommodate ourselves 是针对 great inequality of environment 而言的,as being not only beneficial, but essential to the future progress of the race 是针对 the law of competition between these 而言的。在翻译过程中必

101

须充分理解这一点，在此基础上再努力在译文中充分再现原文信息。译文一将两个 as 短语理解成修饰所有的三个名词短语，因而将这两个 as 短语的汉语译文全部放在句末，这样处理当然是错误的。译文二充分理解了原文句子各个成分之间的关系，并且充分再现了原文句子的意义。再者，译文二将 inequality 翻译成"不平等现象"是增词翻译法；将 the law of competition 翻译成"竞争的机制"比将其翻译成"竞争的法则"似更加通顺流畅。

【例 2】

原　文：We find ourselves rich in goods, but ragged in spirit; reaching with magnificent precision for the moon, but falling into raucous discord on earth.

We are caught in war, **wanting** peace. **We**'re torn by division, **wanting** unity. **We** see around us empty lives, **wanting** fulfillment. **We** see tasks that need doing, **wanting** for hands to do them. (R. Nixon, "Inaugural Address")

译　文：我们物质丰富，但精神贫乏；我们以巨大的精确程度登上月球，但却让地球陷入极度纷争。

我们被卷入战争，我们渴望和平。我们被四分五裂，我们渴望团结。我们看到周围的人们生活空虚，我们渴望生活的充实。我们看到等待人们去做的各项任务，我们需要人手来完成它们。（李明 译）

【点评】 一般情况下，英语的句子是避免重复的，但为了修辞需要，英语中也常常使用重复，这种重复在修辞上往往叫做重复，它可以取得排比、递进、强化等修辞效果。在汉语中，重复的使用既是一般表达时的常见现象，也是为了修辞需要的常见现象，这是由汉语这种语言的特点决定的。因此，汉语中使用重复的情况比英语中使用重复的情况要多。那么，在将英语中的重复翻译成汉语时，一定要采用汉语中的重复来表达。对于上面尼克松总统就职演说的部分内容，由于原文通过使用重复来进行排比，汉语译文也要以同样的方式再现原文信息。再如：**They** vanished from **a world** where **they** were of no consequence; where **they** achieved nothing; where **they** were a mistake and a failure and a foolishness; where **they** have left no sign that they have existed—**a world** which will lament a day and forget them forever.(**他们**无足轻重，一无所成；**他们**来到这个世界就是错误，就是失败，就是荒谬；**他们**未曾留下过任何生活的痕迹，**他们**就这样**离开了这个世界，离开了这个**只有片刻会为他们悲哀、却永远会忘却他们的**世界**。)（李明 译）

【例3】

原　文：Although credit cards are becoming a more acceptable part of the financial scene, **they** are still regarded with suspicion by many as being a major part of the "live now, pay later" syndrome. Along with hire-purchase, rental and leasing schemes, **they** provide encouragement to spend more money.

译　文：尽管**信用卡**正在成为金融业更能接受的付款方式，但许多人仍然心存疑虑，**把信用卡**看成是"今日享受，明日付款／寅吃卯粮"的一种主要表现。同分期付款、租赁方式一样，**信用卡**鼓励人们消费。

【点评】英语行文多替代，汉语行文多重复，对此本例体现得非常充分。英语原文中只使用一次 credit cards，后面两次使用的都是代词 they，以替代上文已出现的 credit cards。汉语译文在需要用到 credit cards 的汉语对应语时，都进行了重复，而没有像英语那样使用替代。由此可见英汉两种语言在这一点上的差别。再如：1) He needs assistants in his research work, but he hasn't yet got a competent **one**. 他做研究工作需要几个助手，可至今他还没有找到一个能够胜任的助手。2) Jesse opened his eyes. **They** were filled with tears. 杰西睁开双眼，眼里充满了泪水。

【例4】

原　文：We recognize—and share—**China's resolve** to resist the attempts of any nation which seeks to establish global or regional **hegemony**.

译　文：我们认识到中国有**决心**——同时我们自己也有同样的**决心**来反对任何国家谋求建立全球**霸权**或地区**霸权**的企图。

【点评】本例中，recognize 和 share 共用一个宾语，即 China's resolve。在将这种搭配翻译成汉语时，对 recognize 和 share 两个动词毫无疑问要分别译出，紧跟其后的宾语 China's resolve 也要相应地被翻译出来。但由于汉语不能像英语那样采用两个动词共享一个宾语的办法，这样，原文中 China's resolve 就只有在汉语中被重复翻译了。再如：People use natural science to understand and change **nature**.（人们利用自然科学，去了解**自然**，改造**自然**。）还有在英语中一个动词带两个宾语的情况。在将这样的英语句子翻译成汉语时，由于这个动词同两个宾语进行了搭配，因此就需要将该动词进行重复。如：John quickly learned the **Chinese language** and the **Chinese customs**.（约翰很快就**学会**了汉语这门语言，还**掌握**了中国的习俗。）

另外，原文中的 …which seeks to establish global or regional **hegemony** 被翻译成了"……谋求建立全球霸权或地区霸权……"。这里的 global 和 regional 用以修饰一个中心名词 hegemony，但在汉语译文中却对 hegemony 一词重复了两次，这是汉语多重复的又一例证。再如：The chief effects of electric currents are the magnetic, heating and chemical **effects**.（电流的主要效应是磁**效应**，热**效应**和化学**效应**。）

【例5】

原　文：On the wings of hope, (　　) of love, (　　) of joy, Miss Meadows sped back to the music hall, up the aisle, up the steps, over to the piano.

译　文：美多斯小姐仿佛插上了希望的翅膀，爱情的**翅膀**，欢乐的**翅膀**，一路飞奔回到音乐厅，她穿过通道，跑上台阶，三步并作两步走到钢琴前。

【点评】英语中的某些动词、名词或形容词等可加介词构成搭配，若这种搭配需要重复或形成一个系列，则往往只保留介词而省略其前面的动词、名词或形容词。这里的英语句子中，括号里省略的是 on the wings。所以，On the wings of hope, of love, of joy 实际上就等于 On the wings of hope, (on the wings) of love, (on the wings of) of joy。在将这样的系列搭配翻译成汉语时，往往需要将介词之前被省略的成分重新补充出来。本例句就是一个典型的例子。再如：1) He no longer dreamed **of** storms, nor **of** great occurrences, nor **of** contests of strength. 他不再**梦见**风暴，不再**梦见**惊人的遭遇，也不再**梦见**搏斗和角力。2) Locomotives **are built** of steel, and airplanes of aluminium. 火车头**由**钢**制成**，而飞机**由**铝**制成**。

【例6】

原　文：We have advocated the principle of peaceful coexistence, **which** is now growing more and more popular among the nations of Asia and Africa.

译　文：我们提倡和平共处的原则，**这个原则**目前在亚非各国越来越得人心了。

【点评】英语定语从句中的关系代词所指代的是其前面的先行词（antecedent）。在将英语中的定语从句翻译成汉语时，由于汉语中没有关系代词这种语法成分，汉语中如果要指代前面所提到的名词，最常见的办法是运用重复。本例译文中的"这个原则"就是对前面所提到的"和平共处的原则"的重复。汉语中的代词"它"尽管也可以对其前面所提到的内容进行指代，但若在翻译该句时使用"它"来替换"这个原则"，则会导致指代不明，因为那样的话，"它"既可以指"我们提倡和平共处的原则"这件事，也可以指"和平共处的原则"，这样就产生了歧义。重复"这个原则"以明确其所指就不会导致歧义。再如：And their conclusions are not just pie in the sky—they're based on an astonishing experiment **in which** a dog was frozen for 15 minutes, but then revived in perfect health!（他们的结论可不是天上掉馅饼，异想天开得来的，那是有实验做依据的。**在那次令人惊讶的实验中**，一只狗被冷冻了15分钟然后复活，而且十分健康。）

【例7】

原　文：Come to my office and have a talk with me **whenever** you are free.

译　文：你**什么时候**有空，就**什么时候**到我办公室来谈一谈。

【点评】英语中有一种使用诸如 whatever、whoever、whichever、wherever 等加后缀 -ever 的强调结构，在将这类强调结构翻译成汉语时，往往要运用重复

的办法才能清晰地传达原文的意思。本例中的汉语译文就重复使用了"什么时候",通过重复,原文中强调的语气就得以强调。再如:**Whoever** violates the discipline should be punished.(**谁**违反了纪律,**谁**就应该受到批评。)

【例8】

原　文:It is miserable, we think, to be deprived of the light of the sun; to be shut out from life and conversation; to be laid in the cold grave, a prey to corruption and the reptiles of the earth; to be no more thought of in this world, but to be obliterated, in a little time, from the affections, and almost from the memory, of their dearest friends and relations.

译文一:被剥夺阳光;被摒除于人们的生活及谈资;被埋葬在冰冷的坟墓中,继而腐烂变质成为蛆虫果腹的猎物;在人世间不再为人所思念,旋即从至爱亲朋的慈爱,乃至记忆中被驱离。凡此种种,都被我们视之为至悲至惨,蔑以加矣。(宋德利,2014:124)

译文二:在我们看来,被剥夺了阳光是痛苦的;不被允许正常地生活、正常地谈话是痛苦的;被葬于冰冷的坟墓中而成为腐烂之物和爬虫果腹的猎物,是痛苦的;不再被世人所想起,而且很快就被自己的至亲和好友淡漠了记忆、忘却了关心,是痛苦的。(李明 译)

【点评】排比句属于重复的一种形式。英语原文以 It is miserable 开头,接着分别有四个动词不定式短语尾随其后,构成排比句式。由于英语是一种形式化的语言,当 It is miserable 之后带有多个充当真正主语的动词不定式时,只需要像这里的英语原文那样,重复动词不定式短语,且动词不定式短语与动词不定式短语之间使用分号,句子结构就清晰可辨。但在将该句翻译成汉语时,需要在翻译完每个动词不定式短语之后重复翻译一遍 It is miserable 所表达的意义,这便形成了汉语的排比句。汉语非常喜欢使用排比句式,汉语的排比句读来层次清晰,强劲有力。译文一的翻译方式笔者在此不敢苟同,该译文读来云里雾里、不知所云。翻译的目的就是要深入浅出,将原文中或许比较难懂或者比较晦涩的句子,在目的语当中使用浅显易懂的文字进行表达，让读者一看便明白原文作者所要表达的意思，这个至关重要。

三、翻译比较与欣赏

【例1】

原　　文：The ballot is stronger than the bullet.（林肯名言）
译文一：选举权比子弹更具威力。（陆谷孙，1993：124）
译文二：选票比大炮更具威力。（马红军 译）
译文三：选票胜于枪炮。（马红军 译）

【例2】

原　　文：The only way I know of dealing with this general human conceit is to remind ourselves that man is a brief episode in the life of a small planet in a little corner of the universe, and that for aught we know, other parts of the cosmos may contain beings as superior to ourselves as we are to jelly-fish.

译文一：据我所知，排除人类这种夜郎自大的心理状态的唯一办法是提醒自己：地球只是宇宙天体中一颗不足为奇的小星星。而人生在地球的沧桑变换过程中只是一首短暂的插曲；况且，如同人之优于海蜇一样，宇宙中别的地方也还可能存在着比人类更高级的动物，只是我们尚未知晓而已。

译文二：我所知道的对付人类这种自负通病的唯一办法即提醒自己：人类只是茫茫宇宙一隅的一颗小行星上的短暂插曲；宇宙深处也许存在着更高等的动物，他们优于人类，如同人类之优于海蜇。（吕秀一 译）

译文三：我所知道的对付人类这种自负通病的唯一办法即提醒自己：人类只是茫茫宇宙一隅的一颗小行星生命中的一支短暂插曲；宇宙深处也许存在着更高等的动物，她们优于人类，如同人类之优于海蜇。（黄忠廉、李亚舒 译）

【例 3】

原　文：The hope of early discovery of lung cancer followed by surgical cure, which currently seems to be the most effective form of therapy, is often thwarted by diverse biologic behavior in the rate and direction of growth of the cancer.

译文一：肺癌的早期发现继之于目前最有效的外科治疗的希望常因生长速度和方向等特征的不同程度而毁灭。（傅敬民等 用例）

译文二：人们希望早期发现肺癌，然后实施外科治疗，这可能是目前最有效的治疗方式。但是，肺癌生长速度和生长方向等生物学特征各不相同，这种愿望往往落空。（傅敬民等 用例）

译文三：人们希望在肺癌发病的早期就能诊断出来，然后实施就目前来说似乎是最有效的治疗方式——外科治疗，但是，癌变的速度和方向等生物行为具有多变性，这往往使这种希望化为泡影。（李明 译）

【例 4】

原　文：April is the cruelest month, breeding
　　　　Lilacs out of the dead land, mixing
　　　　Memory and desire, stirring
　　　　Dull roots with spring rain. (T. S. Eliot, *The Waste Land*)

译文一：四月是最残忍的一月，荒地上
　　　　长着丁香，把回忆和欲望
　　　　掺和在一起，又让春雨
　　　　催促那些迟钝的根芽……（李建军 用例）

译文二：四月，一年中教你最酷，
　　　　此时的荒原，只有丁香醒目，
　　　　把记忆和憧憬交互，
　　　　春雨正撼醒孤寂的根符……（李建军 用例）

译文三：人间四月最猖狂，

催生荒原紫丁香，

掺和记忆与欲望，

洒下春雨根芽长。（李明 译）

四、翻 译 练 习

> 句子翻译

1. This is not time to engage in the luxury of cooling off or to take the tranquility drug of gradualism. Now is the time to make real the promises of Democracy. Now is the time to rise from the dark and desolate valley of segregation to the sunlit path of racial justice. Now is the time to life our nation from the quicksands of racial injustice to the solid rock of brotherhood. (Martin Luther King, "I Have a Dream")

2. Languishing in port, the (former Soviet Pacific) fleet is suffering **breakdowns** of equipment, readiness and morale.

3. A smile would come into Mr Pickwick's face; the **smile** extended into a **laugh**, the **laugh** into a **roar**, and the **roar** became general. (Charles Dickens, *Pickwick Paper*)

4. **Men** perish, but **man** shall endure; **lives** die but the **life** is not dead. (A. Swinburne, "Hymn Of Man")

5. He **poured** into his writings all the pain of his life, the fierce hatred of the bourgeoisie that it had produced in him, and the conviction it had brought to him that the world could be made a better place to live in if the exploited would rise up and take the management of society out of the hands of the exploiters.

6. Avoid using this computer in extreme cold, heat, dust or humidity.

7. Let us revise our safety and sanitary **regulations**.

8. He had to win his way into the heart of a laughing girl **who** had no serious thought of loving any man … least of all, Stephen Crane.

109

9. He wandered about in the chill rain, thinking and thinking, brooding and brooding.

10. **Wherever** there is plenty of sun and rain, the fields are green.

11. You may solve the problem **whichever** way you like.

篇章翻译

篇章翻译 1

Observing laws may help investors to gain the protection of the government which is the most powerful and dependable guarantee. But as no key can open every lock, codes can only deal with specific hazards. So it is necessary for personal experience and expert advice to make up for the weakness. Personal experience and expert advice include past performances, professional education and training, and communication with policy makers, facility owners and users. For years, personal experience and expert advice have been widely used in managing risk and have proved to be very useful and practicable. During the process of designing Shanghai Pudong Airport in 1995, a coastologist, after careful investigations and scientific analysis, came up with the suggestion that the airport should be built on the seabeach instead of behind the sea wall.

Later this suggestion proved to be practicable and saved 360 million yuan. With the emergence of new computer-based tools new methods of managing risk are continuously coming out universities and research laboratories into general application. To achieve better safety and more benefits at reasonable costs people should also improve their self-qualities continuously to keep up with the technique development. In addition, both the government and the public should not only adopt a risk-based approach but also be fully prepared to deal effectively with potentially severe risks.

篇章翻译 2

For me the most interesting thing about a solitary life, and mine has been that for the last twenty years, is that it becomes increasingly rewarding. When I can wake up and watch the sun rise over the ocean, as I do most days, and know that I have an entire day ahead, uninterrupted, in which to write a few pages, take a walk with my dog, read and listen to music, I am flooded with happiness.

I am lonely only when I am overtired, when I have worked too long without a break, when for the time being I feel empty and need filling up. And I am lonely sometimes when I come back home after a lecture trip, when I have seen a lot of people and talked a lot, and am full to the brim with experience that needs to be sorted out.

Then for a little while the house feels huge and empty, and I wonder where my self is hiding. It has to be recaptured slowly by watering the plants and, perhaps, by looking again at each one as though it were a person.

It takes a while, as I watch the surf blowing up in fountains, but the moment comes when the world falls away, and the self emerges again from the deep unconscious, bringing back all I have recently experienced to be explored and slowly understood. (2004 年全国高等院校英语专业八级考试英译汉试题）

第九章　翻译中文字的简练

> 言贵简约。
>
> ——莎士比亚

一、理 论 探 讨

　　成功的翻译，最见于文字的简练。文字的简练体现于对词语使用的精致，对句式运用的恰当和地道，对篇章运用的娴熟。莎士比亚也曾言：言贵简约（Brevity is the soul of wit）。本书第六章所讨论的省词翻译法均是为了文字的简练而采用的翻译技巧。在第六章中我们谈到了结构性省词翻译和精炼压缩法。本章除继续探讨精炼压缩翻译法之外，还准备讨论另外两个问题：1. 如何使因语言水平问题而造成的不简练的译文更加简练；2. 如何将英语的形合句翻译成汉语中的意合句从而达到译文简练的目的。

　　精炼压缩翻译法也有人称之为"隐译"。根据乔海清（1999：43）的定义，在翻译中将原文中的词或更大的结构成分隐含到译文中的另一成分的含义里去，或者隐含到整个结构深一层的含义里去而不必表现到字面上来的翻译方法叫做隐译。在翻译中要达到文字的简练，隐译是非常有效的手段之一[17]。比如在将 There has not been a scientist of eminence but was a man of industry 一句翻译成"优秀的科学家没有一个不勤奋的"时，就采用了隐译翻译法。根据汉语习惯，There has been 和 man 在译文中均不用翻译出来，但各自的意义均隐含在译文中。

　　那么，如何才能使因语言水平问题而造成的不简练的译文更加简练呢？这就涉及译者的语言水平问题。作为译者，语言水平非常重要。语言水平不仅体现在对原文的理解上，而且体现在译文的表达上。在汉语文化中，关于如何"炼"字的故事有很多，

---

[17] 在译文中之所以能隐译，也反映了目的语民族在认识客观事物的习惯认识方式上同源语民族之不同。

其中以"春风又绿江南岸"中对"绿"字的推敲和炼字最广为流传。在翻译中也要精心炼字。只要译者时时留心，时时严谨，炼字的功夫会随着自己翻译经验的积累而臻于完美。请比较下面一句的两种译文：

If you are an energetic man with strong views as to the right way of doing the job with which you are concerned, you find yourself invariably under the orders of some big man at the top who is elderly, weary and cynical.

译文一：如果你是个精力充沛的人，对于如何恰当地完成你的工作有着独到的见解，你发现自己总要听命于上面某个大人物，他上了年纪，精力不支，还爱吹毛求疵。（TEM8 翻译考试样题参考译文）

译文二：即使你活力十足，对如何做好自己的工作富于创见，仍然免不了要受制于某个年长资深、精力不支（济）、不纳贤言的高层大人物，难以有所作为。（曾利沙 译）

从上面的两种译文来看，译文一读起来就显得啰唆，而译文二就非常简洁明了。当然还有选词的问题使得译文二更胜译文一一筹。对此这里不赘述。

以形合为主的语言同以意合为主的语言之最大差别就是，以形合为主的语言在句子逻辑关系上表现为显性，即一切关系都通过词汇或句法手段明示出来，而以意合为主的语言则往往通过句子的深层结构来体现句中的逻辑关系。如在翻译 Sir, Mary is absent today because she is ill 时，汉语习惯说："老师，玛丽今天生病，不能来上课。"原文主句和从句之间的逻辑关系以显性的 because 明示出来，而汉语译文中则以深层结构来蕴涵主句同从句之间的逻辑关系。在英译汉时，在译文中以意合的方式来再现英语原文中以形合的方式呈现的信息是实现译文地道、通顺的关键所在。

有一点必须注意，翻译中文字的简练并不是说译文越短越好，而是说在将原文信息充分再现于译文中时词语的最经济的运用。

另外，翻译中的简练也是节奏美学的要求。节奏是声音大致相等的时间里所生的起伏。这大致相等的时间段落就是声音的单位，与人的发音器官构造相关。人的呼吸有一定长度，有起有伏。因为有一定的长度，一口气所读出的字音也就有一定的限制；因为有起伏，一句话的长短轻重也就不能一律。超过限度就失去了节奏。（夏力力，1996：19）任何翻译不仅是文字符号的转换，更重要的是正确表达原文的意蕴，在风格上尽量保持同原文的一致。对原文的理解当然包括对原文节奏美感的理解，然后在译文中取得同原文的"异质同构，共感共鸣"的效果。下面我们来看看译文的简练对于传达原文的节奏所起的作用：

An individual human existence should be like a river small at first, narrowly contained with in its banks, and rushing passionately past boulders and over waterfalls. ("How to Grow Old")

译文一：人生应当像条河，开始河身狭小，夹在两岸之间，河水奔腾咆哮，流过巨石，飞下悬岩。

译文二：人生好比一条河，开始是峡谷细流，接着是急流勇进，冲过巨石，飞下悬岩。

在原文中作者运用比拟修辞格，以河流比作人生的三部曲：涓涓细流——汹涌澎湃——坦荡入海。作者对每一个阶段都作了生动描写，有起有伏，有明显的节奏效果。译文一没有理解这一节奏美感，除了误译了 should be like 之外，还把起重要衔接作用的 and 漏译了，造成译文思路不明，使节奏分明的两大阶段混淆起来，损害了原文的节奏美。译文二用了"开始是……接着是……"，恰当地表现了原文的节奏"气势"，同时以"峡谷细流"取代译文一拖泥带水的"河身狭小,夹在两岸之间"，显得非常简练。无论在"神韵"上还是"骨力"上，译文二再现了原文的节奏美。

二、译例举隅及翻译点评

【例 1】

原　文：I have often thought it would be a blessing if each human being were stricken blind and deaf for a few days at some time during his early adult life.

译文一：我多次这样想过：如果一个人在刚成年时经历一段瞎子与聋子的生活，可能是一件好事。（郭富强 用例）

译文二：我常常这样想：倘若让每个人在刚成年时突然失明失聪几日，那也许是天赐之福。（郭富强 译）

译文三：我常想，假如让每个人在刚成年的某个时候突然失明失聪几天，那一定是天赐之福。（李明 译）

【点评】写作也好，翻译也好，文字的简练至关重要。简练并非是指少用词语。简练的意思是，该用的词语必须用，不该用的词语必须略去，哪怕是一个"的"字。上面三种译文固然由于译者选词的不同而带来了不同的译文效果，但译文的简练与否对译文效果也产生了重要影响。译文一中使用"多次"来译 often 当然不恰当，而"这样想过"中的"这样"和"过"均属多余，因为紧接着的下文就是作者的所思所想，译文中再加上"这样"两个字实属多余。而加上"过"这个字则不仅多余，而且还改变了原文的意思，因为原文中的 have often thought 不仅表示作者曾这样想过，还表示作者一直这样想。所以，have often thought 这个现在完成时短语实际上所表示的是现在完成进行时。译文二中的"这样"也是多余的。另外，译文二中所选词语如"倘若""几日"均过于正式，与译文中的其他词语搭配不当。再者，译文一和译文二分别将 would be a blessing 中的 would 翻译成"可能""也许"均是误译，应译为"一定"才合情理。

【例2】

原　文：There is no month in the whole year, in which nature wears a more beautiful appearance than in the month of August!

译　文：四时之美，八月为最。（周方珠 译）

【点评】本例如果依照原文的语言形式进行翻译，译文将是：一整年中大自然所穿的外衣没有哪个月比八月份更美的了。这样翻译，译文不仅表达不简洁，其意义也不明确。这里周方珠的译文可谓达到译文简洁之极致了。可见，在英汉翻译中，首先要把握原文的精神实质，然后再根据汉语的惯常表达习惯予以表达。如果碰到英语中的表达同汉语的惯常表达有出入，就应在译文中对原文结构进行变通和调整，使得汉语译文简洁、清晰、明了。再如：1) Whether you die at a young age or when you are older is less important than whether you have fully lived the years you have had. 人生的意义不在于你能活多久，更重要的是要看你生活得是否充实。

2) The isolation of the rural world because of distance and the lack of transport facilities is compounded by the paucity of the information media. 广大的农村因远离城镇，交通又不便利，再加上通信严重不足，因而与世隔绝的状态更加严重。（李明 译）

【例3】

原　文：With my present level (of French), I cannot read French newspaper easily.

译文一：以我现在的（法语）水平，我还不能轻松地读法文报纸。

译文二：我的法语，看报很吃力。

【点评】原文是一个英语形合句，如果按照英语原文进行翻译（如译文一），则译文读起来尽管不能算不顺，但总觉得有一些微微的欧化迹象。译文二则完全是汉语的意合句，没有一丝欧化迹象，因而读来地道通畅。比较起来，意合句比形合句要简练，因为意合句省去了形合句中所要求的形式化的东西。汉语主要是意合型的语言，各种句子主要采取意合的方式组句。而英语则重形合，句中的逻辑关系等均需借助体现逻辑关系的句子成分来体现。比如 One must make painstaking efforts before one could succeed in mastering a foreign language 这句话，译成汉语是"要掌握一门外语，非下苦功夫不可"。（靳梅琳 译）译文除了省去了泛指代词 one 之外，还省略了 before 这个体现句子前后关系及其形式的词语。由于英语重形合，汉语重意合，英汉翻译时，要达到译文的简练，必须采用地道的汉语表达方式进行表达。再比如：His preoccupation with business left little time for his family.（他一心一意专注事业，很少有时间同家人待在一起。）

【例4】

原　文：You may find it difficult to understand the thought of Hume, and if you have no philosophical training its implications will doubtless escape you.

译文一：你会发现很难理解休姆的思想，而且如果你没有受到过哲学训练，毫无

第九章 翻译中文字的简练

疑问，你将无法理解它的含义。

译文二：要理解休谟的思想，人们会觉得很难，但如果受过哲学训练，则毫无疑问就能领会其中的含义。（李明 译）

【点评】 在翻译的过程中，为了使译文更加简练，有一种办法比较奏效，那就是采用逆向翻译法。在本例中，原文 if you have no philosophical training its implications will doubtless escape you 如果直译成汉语就是"如果你没有接受哲学训练，其中的含义毫无疑问会离你而去"。这样从反面着笔的表达在汉语中既蹩脚，又不精练。如果变换一个角度从正面着笔，则不仅文字简练，而且意思清楚明了，符合汉语表达。采用逆向翻译法来达到文字简练的目的是常见方法。再如：1) At all costs time must be gained. 要不惜一切代价争取时间。2) Nature seldom provides me with the word, the turn of phrase, that is appropriate without being far-fetched or commonplace. 我自然而然想到的词语，很少有恰当的，要么有些牵强附会，要么有些陈词滥调。3) There is nothing that does not contain contradiction. 任何事物都包含矛盾。

因此，当依据原文的表达方式进行翻译难以表达原文之义，或译文不连贯、不通顺或不简洁时，逆向翻译不失为一种很好的补救手段。正可谓"山重水复疑无路，柳暗花明又一村"。

【例 5】

原　文：They were, in fact, very fine ladies; not deficient in good humor when they were pleased, nor in the power of being agreeable when they chose it; but proud and conceited.

译文一：事实上，她们都是非常好的小姐；她们并不是不会谈笑风生，问题是在要碰到她们高兴的时候；她们也不是不会待人和颜悦色，问题在于她们是否乐意这样做；可惜的是，她们一味骄傲自大。（王宏印 用例）

译文二：事实上，她们都是一些非常贤淑的女士；高兴时不乏谈笑风生；乐意时总能讨人欢喜。但就是有一点，她们有些傲慢和自负。（李明 译）

117

【点评】 这里提供了两种汉语译文。王宏印先生在其《英汉翻译综合教程》第28页中使用了这个例子。该译文使用了共84个字,而李明译文只使用了55个字。同王宏印先生的用例相比,李明译文增加了"一些",使用了由两个字组成的短语"贤淑"而没有使用"好"这一个字,但在翻译由九个英语词语组成的句子 not deficient in good humor when they were pleased 时,只用"高兴时不乏谈笑风生"共九个汉字就简明扼要地表达了原文的意思。在翻译由十一个英语单词组成的句子 nor in the power of being agreeable when they chose it 时,也只用"乐意时总能讨人欢喜"就表达了原文的意思,而且这一句同前一句非常对称,符合汉语惯常表达的对称美。原文的最后一句 but proud and conceited 只有四个英文单词,但译文对此译为"但就是有一点,她们有些傲慢和自负"。这是增词翻译法,但增词没有增加原文的意义,而且充分再现了原文信息。由此可见,要取得翻译中文字的简练,并非总是采取省词翻译法。王宏印先生(2002:174)认为我们应该遵循的原则就是:增词不能蛇足,减词不能损意。

【例6】

原　文: When your children are grown up they want to live their own lives, and if you continue to be as interested in them as you were when they were young, you are likely to become a burden to them, unless they are unusually callous.

译　文: 孩子长大后就希望独立生活,父母如果还像年幼时那样关注他们,就会成为他们的负担,除非他们对此麻木不仁。

【点评】 本例中,英语原文总共44个英文单词(不含标点符号),汉语译文总共46个汉字(不含标点符号)。因此,此处的汉语译文结合汉语意合的特点来行文,省略了英语原文在行文过程中因形合需要而使用的一些词语,因而汉语译文的文字非常简练。对照英语原文我们发现,汉语译文省译了英语原文中很多因英语这种形合语言所需要使用的连词(如:when、and)、代词(如:your、they、their、you)等。假如将这里的英语原文翻译成汉语的"当你的孩子长大时,他们就想独立地过他们的生活,而且如果你继续对他们像他们小时候那样感兴趣,你很有可能变成他们的负担，除非他们是特别的麻木不仁"，这样的译文看上去似乎很"忠实"于原文，但实际上由于译文的不简练而使得原文信息在译文中没有得到充分而又明晰的再现。因此，要取得译文文字的简练，还必须考虑翻译中所涉及的两种语言之间的差异。

【例7】

原　文：Gradually the river grows wider, the banks recede, the waters flow more quietly and at the end, without any visible break, they become merged in the sea, painlessly lose their individual being.

译文一：后来河面渐渐展宽，两岸离得越来越远，河水也流得较为平缓，最后流进大海，与海水浑然一体，看不出任何界线，从而结束其单独存在的那一段历程，但毫无痛苦之感。

译文二：后来河面渐宽，水流也愈趋平缓，最后流入大海，与海水浑然一体，自然而然地结束其单独存在的那一段历程。

【点评】行文中理想的节奏能够打动读者的心扉。朱光潜先生曾经说过："我读音调铿锵，节奏流畅的文章，周身筋肉仿佛做同样有节奏的运动；如果音调节奏上有毛病，我的周身筋肉都感觉局促不安。"这里的译文一冗长拖沓，超过筋肉张弛的限度，因而不能达到预期所应有的满足。译文二则简明扼要，读起来省力，富有节奏感。

三、翻译比较与欣赏

【例1】

原　文：The best lubricant cannot maintain oil films between the surfaces of engineering gears.

译文一：最好的润滑油，在机械的啮合处保不住油膜。

译文二：即使最好的润滑油，在机械的啮合处也保不住油膜。（徐莉娜 用例）

译文三：即使是最好的润滑油，也保不住机械啮合处的油膜。（黄忠廉、李亚舒 译）

译文四：哪怕是最好的润滑油，也保不住机械啮合处的油膜。（黄忠廉、李亚舒 译）

【例2】

原　　文：At the very hour of dinner, when my stomach clamored for food, I have been stopped by sight of a volume so long coveted, and marked at so advantageous a price, that I could not let it go: yet to buy it meant pangs of famine.

译文一：到用晚餐的时间，当我的肚子饿得咕噜咕噜直叫的时候，我已经因为看见一本我已想要多时的书籍而站住了脚步。书上标着很合算的价格，我实在是不能错过这个大好的机会，但是如果我买下了这本书籍，那便意味着我将经受挨饿的痛苦。（毛荣贵 用例）

译文二：某日正当进餐时分，我饥肠辘辘，步履却为一书所止，此书令我心仪已久，而标价竟如此诱人，实不忍失之交臂。然而，购之便意味着忍饥挨饿。（毛荣贵 译）

【例3】

原　　文：Some fishing boats were becalmed just in front of us. Their shadows slept, or almost slept, upon that water, a gentle quivering alone showing that it was not complete sleep, or if sleep, that it was sleep with dreams.

译文一：在我们面前停泊了几条渔船，它们的影子在水面上睡着了，或者说是几乎睡着了，一个轻微的颤动，说明影子没有完全睡着，假如说是睡着了，那么，也是一边在睡，一边在做梦。

译文二：渔舟三五，横泊眼前，樯影倒映水面，仿佛睡去，偶尔微颤，似又未尝深眠，恍若惊梦。（毛荣贵 译）

译文三：几条渔船就停泊在我们面前，静悄悄的。船的倒影酣然睡去或几乎睡去，那偶尔的轻轻颤抖意味着睡眠并不深沉，或者说如果是睡眠，那是充满了梦幻的睡眠。（李明 译）

【例4】

原　文：The curfew tolls the knell of the parting day,

　　　　The lowing herd wind slowly o'er the lea,

　　　　The plowman homeward plods his weary way,

　　　　And leaves the world to darkness and to me. (Thomas Gray, "Elegy Written in a Country Churchyard")

译文一：晚钟响起来一阵阵给白昼报丧,

　　　　牛群在草原上迂回,吼声起落,

　　　　耕地的人累了,回家走,脚步踉跄,

　　　　把整个世界留给了黄昏与我。（卞之琳 译）

译文二：暮钟鸣,昼已瞑,

　　　　牛羊相呼,纡回草径,

　　　　农人荷锄归,蹒跚而行,

　　　　把全盘的世界剩给我与黄昏。（郭沫若 译）

译文三：晚钟殷殷响,夕阳已西沉。

　　　　牛群呼叫归,迂回走草径。

　　　　农夫荷锄犁,倦倦回家门。

　　　　唯我立旷野,独自对黄昏。（丰华瞻 译）

译文四：晚钟响起为即将逝去的白昼报丧,

　　　　羊群缓缓蜿蜒走过草地,咩咩叫唤,

　　　　疲惫的耕地人上路回家,步履蹒跚,

　　　　他们把世界留给了我,留给了黑暗。（何功杰 译）

译文五：晚钟声声响,日已近黄昏。

　　　　牛儿唵唵叫,迂回走草径。

　　　　农夫甚疲惫,蹒跚踏归程。

　　　　唯我立旷野,夜色已降临。（李明 译）

四、翻译练习

句子翻译

1. If you take this medicine, your illness will surely be cured.

2. You needn't care about the affairs in the home.

3. It was one of the few gestures of sentiment he was ever to make.

4. Poetry feeds and waters the passions, instead of drying them up; she lets them rule instead of ruling them as they ought to be ruled.

5. The machine would have to be able to move about in a house designed for human beings and would therefore have to go through a normal door, open such a door and close it, and walk up and down stairs over irregularities on the floor.

6. The inability to satisfy those expectations will mean increased social tensions, especially where the regimes are already a byword for corruption and instability.

7. The world is still engaged in a massive armaments race designed to insure continuing equivalent strength among potential adversaries.

8. There used to be millions of Indians in America, but their number had dropped to only about 900,000 today.

9. Without adequate management, progress in fisheries technology will lead to a decline in the very industry it is designed to support.

10. My opinion of you is that no man knows better than you when to speak and when others to speak for you; when to make scenes and threaten resignation; and when to be as cool as a cucumber.

11. I should wish to die while still at work, knowing that others will carry on what I can no longer do and content in the thought that what was possible has been done.

12. In his eagerness to draw quick profit from the trees, man has cut them down in large numbers, only to find that with them he has lost the best friends he had.

第九章 翻译中文字的简练

篇章翻译

篇章翻译 1

The word "winner" and "loser" have many meanings. When we refer to a person as a winner, we do not mean one who makes someone else lose. To us, a winner is one who responds authentically by being credible, trustworthy, responsive, and genuine, both as an individual and as a member of a society.

Winners do not dedicate their lives to a concept of what they imagine they should be; rather, they are themselves and as such do not use their energy putting on a performance, maintaining pretense, and manipulating others. They are aware that there is a difference between being loving and acting loving, between being stupid and acting stupid, between being knowledgeable and acting knowledgeable. Winners do not need to hide behind a mask.

Winners are not afraid to do their own thinking and to use their own knowledge. They can separate facts from opinions and don't pretend to have all the answers. They listen to others, evaluate what they say, but come to their own conclusions. Although winners can admire and respect other people, they are not totally defined, demolished, bound, or awed by them.

Winners do not play "helpless", nor do they play the blaming game. Instead, they assume responsibility for their own lives. (2002年英语专业八级英汉翻译考试题)

篇章翻译 2

1) It is simple enough to say that since books have classes—fiction, biography, poetry—we should separate them and take from each what it is right that each should give us. 2) Yet few people ask from books what books can give us. 3) Most commonly we come to books with blurred and divided minds, asking of fiction that it shall be true, of poetry that it shall be false, of biography that it shall be flattering, of history that it shall enforce our own prejudices. 4) If we could banish all such preconceptions when we read, that would be an admirable beginning. 5) Do not dictate to your author; try to become him. 6) Be his

fellow-worker and accomplice. 7) If you hang back, and reserve and criticize at first, you are preventing yourself from getting the fullest possible value from what you read. 8) But if you open your mind as widely as possible, then signs and hints of almost imperceptible fitness, from the twist and turn of the first sentences, will bring you into the presence of a human being unlike any other. 9) Steep yourself in this, acquaint yourself with this and soon you will find that your author is giving you, or attempting to give you, something far more definite.

# 第十章 词类转换翻译法

> 我们翻译的并非语言,而是一个个具体的文本,翻译的基本层次主要体现在译文文字的细节处理上,体现在对译文词句的调整和变通上。
>
> ——曹明伦

一、理论探讨

词类转换是指在翻译过程中,将源语中一种词性的词语用目的语中另一种词性的词语进行翻译的方法。换言之,当翻译中词语的词性在所涉及的两种语言中出现不对应时,就出现了词类转换。它是翻译中常用的一种变通手段,是突破原文词法、句法格局,化阻滞为通达的重要方法(孙致礼,2003:81)。

英语和汉语分属于完全不同的两个语系,它们在词汇、语法结构和表达方式等方面存在很大差异。不管是做英汉翻译还是做汉英翻译,要想在任何时候都能够在词汇层面或结构层面上寻求一一对应是不可能的事情。多数时候,译者必须在忠实原文意义的前提下将原文中某些词语的词类或成分转换成汉语中的其他词类或成分才能使译文表达通顺、意义明晰。如英语中有些动词像 revolutionize、feature、characterize 等在汉语中就没有相应的动词可以表达,在将它们翻译成汉语时就需要转换成汉语中的名词,如 Steam and machinery **revolutionized** industrial production 就需要译为"蒸汽和机器引发了工业生产领域的**革命**"。另一方面,英语中有些名词实际上含有动作性,它们甚至是由动词变化而来的,而汉语中则又习惯于多用动词,这样,在将这些含有动词性质的名词翻译成汉语时,多将它们翻译成动词。如 We would be more than happy to welcome you as a guest **speaker** on Friday evening in our university 通常译为"我们非常高兴地欢迎您应邀于本星期五晚来我校作**报告**"比较恰当。(王宏印,2002:35)

由此可见，在英汉翻译中，词类转换的翻译方法是必不可少的，"离开必要的词性转换，势必会导致生硬拗口，甚至晦涩难懂的译文"（孙致礼，2003：81）。但词性转换所遵循的原则必须不违背原文之意，且有助于译文的畅达。孙致礼（2003：81）还认为，从理论上讲，翻译中的词性转换是没有限制的，比如说，名词可以转换成动词、形容词、副词等，动词可以转换成名词、形容词、副词等，而形容词、副词也可以转换成名词、动词等，不一而足。不过，从实践来看，英汉语的词性转换也有一定的规律，最明显的一点就是英语比较喜欢多用名词和介词，而汉语则是动词用得多一些。因此，我们在做英汉翻译时，词性的转换比较多地表现在名词、介词转换成动词方面。

二、译例举隅及翻译点评

【例1】

原　　文：The growing **awareness** by millions of Africans of their extremely poor and awkward living conditions has prompted them to take resolute measures and create new one.

译　　文：数以百万计的非洲人已逐渐**意识到**他们的生活状况异常贫穷落后，这就**促使**他们奋起采取坚决措施，去创造新的生活。

【点评】英语中经常使用由动词或者形容词派生出来的名词，但在将这些名词翻译成汉语时，很多时候需要将它们翻译成汉语里的动词。上句中的awareness就是由形容词转变成名词的，在汉语译文中被译成了动词。再如：1) Rockets have found **application** for the **exploration** of the universe. 火箭已经**用于探索**宇宙。2) A **glance** through his office window offers a panoramic view of the Washington Monument and the Lincoln Memorial. 透过他的办公室窗口就可以**瞥见**华盛顿纪念碑和林肯纪念馆。3) We also realize the growing **need and necessity** to industrialize certain sectors of the economy. 我们也认识到越来越**需要**使某些经济部门实行工业化。4) The **abuse** of basic human rights in their own country in **violation** of the agreement reached at Helsinki earned them the **condemnation** of freedom-loving people everywhere. 他们**违反**在赫尔辛基达成的协议，在国内侵犯基本人权，因此受到了各地热爱自由的人们的**谴责**。

【例 2】

原　文：The best books **are treasuries** of good words, the golden thoughts, which, remembered and cherished, become our constant companions and comforters.

译　文：好书**蕴藏着**金玉良言、真知灼见。将它们铭记于心、珍藏于心，它们就与我们朝夕相伴，时时给我们慰藉。

【点评】 原文中 treasury 是名词，为"宝库""宝藏"之意。按照句子结构翻译，原文主句部分的译文将是"最好的书是金玉般良言和闪闪发光思想的宝库"，如此译来，因"宝库"之前有一个那么长的修饰语，且所使用的为表达语气较弱的"是"字句，这使得原文语气大为削弱。为了充分再现原文信息，将 are treasuries of 翻译成动词"蕴藏着"，将弱势动词 are 在译文中淡出，将 treasury 转换成动词，突出其意义，这不仅使译文表达更为通顺，也准确传达了原文语气。这类词类转换可以将原文的弱势动词转化成译文的强势动词，使译文更富表达力。再如：1) Londoners are great **readers**. 伦敦人酷爱读书。2) We are **enemies** of all wars, but above all of dynastic wars. 我们**反对**一切战争，特别是反对王朝战争。3) A successful scientist must be a good **observer**. 凡成功的科学家一定非常善于**观察**。

【例 3】

原　文：We are not **afraid** of the future because of a bomb. We are **afraid** of bombs because we have no faith in the future.

译　文：我们不是因为有了原子弹而**害怕**将来，而是因为对将来没有信心而**害怕**原子弹。

【点评】 英汉翻译时，英语中表示情感的形容词往往可以同其前面的 be 动词一道翻译成汉语中的动词，上面的例子就是明证。这类表示情感的形容词包

括：confident、certain、careful、cautious、angry、sure、ignorant、afraid、doubtful、aware、content、concerned、glad、delighted、sorry、ashamed、thankful、anxious、grateful 等。再如：1) They are quite **content** with the data obtained from the experiment. 她们十分**满足**于试验中获得的数据。2) The noon sun clarified the air. I became **aware** of two surfers well out from the shore, patiently paddling their boards while they waited for a perfect wave. 正午时天气晴朗，我**瞥见**两个冲浪者离岸很远，耐心地踏着滑板，等候一个最理想的浪头。

【例4】

原　文："Coming!" Away she skimmed **over** the lawn, **up** the path, **up** the steps, **across** the veranda, and **into** the porch.

译　文："来啦！"她转身蹦着跳着跑了，**越过**草地，**跨上**小径，**跃上**台阶，**穿过**阳台，**进了**门廊。

【点评】英语句子同汉语句子的一个重要区别就在于，英语中的每个分句只能使用一个限定动词，若另需使用动词就要使用其非谓语形式，或者不使用动词而使用由动词转化过来的名词或介词等。汉语的句子则往往是依据事件发生的先后顺序进行铺陈的，由于汉语的词性没有形态变化，一个接一个地使用动词毫不让人觉得别扭。另外，由于英语使用名词——尤其是由动词转化过来的名词——的机会较多，而名词与名词之间需要介词连接，故英语中使用介词的现象比比皆是。在汉语里，句子中使用名词的概率很小，这样，汉语中介词的使用率就远远低于英语中介词的使用率。在将英语句子翻译成汉语时，碰到对介词短语的翻译往往要将介词翻译成汉语里的动词。如本例中的"越过""跨上""跃上""穿过"等都是动词。再如：1) Some longtime associates and friends wanted to protect him **from** the White House; some, to protect him **from** the public; and others, to protect him **from** himself. 有些老同事和老朋友想保护他，**使他免受白宫的连累**；有些想保护他，**使他不受公众的攻击**；还有一些人想保护他则是想使他本人**不要说错话**或者是**不要做错事**。2) Downstairs, then, they went, Joseph very red and blushing, Rebecca very modest, and holding her green eyes downwards. She was dressed in white, **with** bare shoulders as white as snow—the picture of youth, unprotected innocence, and humble virgin simplicity. 他们一路下楼，约瑟夫的脸涨得通红，丽贝卡则举止端庄，一双绿色的眼睛望着地上，她穿着洁白的衣服，**露出**雪白的肩膀。这是青春的偶像，这是烂漫的纯真，好一个温顺、纯洁的少女。

【例 5】

原　文：Mother had always told me that poor people were **basically** kind. I didn't think this man would want to hurt me.

译　文：妈妈总对我说，穷人的**本质**是好的，所以我想这个人不会害我。

【点评】英语里的副词种类繁多，使用频率很高，在句中的位置也灵活多变。在将英语中的副词翻译成汉语时，可以根据其意义和修饰关系，分别译成名词、动词或形容词。这里主要讲的是它可以翻译成汉语中的名词。再如：1) On a silent afternoon in October Harriet and William were talking **softly** together. 十月里一个静悄悄的下午，哈里特和威廉在一块儿说着悄悄话。2) Finally, a youngish, **mathematically** minded customer got out a apiece of paper and pencil and went into retirement. 最后，顾客中一个年纪轻一些的、有**数学**头脑的人拿出一张纸，一支笔，到一旁算着。3) He is **physically** weak but **mentally** sound. 他**身体**虽弱，但**精神**很好。4) They have not done so well **ideologically**, however, as **organizationally**. 但是，他们的**思想**工作没有他们的**组织**工作做得好。5) There's a growing realization about the convergence of the medical problems associated with obesity and chronic inflammation, which wasn't appreciated for a long time but is coming to the fore **scientifically**. 人们越来越认识到，与肥胖有关的一些医学问题和与慢性炎症有关的一些医学问题之间具有趋同性。这点在很长一段时间内不被人们所认识，但现在正越来越引起**科学界**的注意。

【例 6】

原　文：It was a **clear** and **unemotional** exposition of the President's reasons for willing to begin a Chinese-American dialogue.

译　文：这篇发言清楚明白、心平气和地说明了总统希望开始中美对话的原因。

【点评】英译汉时，当形容词所修饰的名词被转译成汉语里的动词时，该形容词往往需要翻译成汉语里的副词。如果形容词所描述的是某个行事的方式，该形容词也需要译成副词。如：1) She succeeded in rendering her position with this family **comfortable** and **secure**. 她巩固了自己在这个家庭中的地位，可以**安安稳稳、舒舒服服**过日子了。2) "I have a strange fancy," observed the **sensitive** minister, "that this brook is the boundary between two worlds." "真怪。"牧师**伤感地**说："我觉得这条小河就是阴阳界。" 3) **Quick** and **decided** in her ways, Emma lost no time in inviting, encouraging, and telling her to come very often; and as their acquaintance increased, so did their satisfaction in each other. 爱玛办事**利索果断**，马上邀请她，嘱咐她常来，两人相处越多越亲密。

【例 7】

原　文：She was **wisely** determined to give it up.

译　文：她很**聪明**，决定不干了。

【点评】英语中的副词多数时候是在形容词之后加上后缀 -ly 构成，因此，从构词角度看，英语中的形容词和副词之间有着天然的联系。在将英语中的形容词翻译成汉语时，必须考虑该副词同句子其他成分之间的修饰和被修饰的关系，正确理解其含义，再根据汉语的表达习惯进行灵活处理。多数时候往往要将副词翻译成汉语中的形容词。再如：1) This particular bit of Iceland was also **heavily** populated. 冰岛的这块小地方人口也很**稠密**。2) The bottle of castor oil was placed **prominently** by his bedside. 蓖麻油瓶搁在他床边**显眼的**地方。3) He **routinely** radioed another agent on the ground. 他跟另一个地勤人员进行了**例行的**无线电联系。4) The oceans contribute **immeasurably** to the earth's life support system as well as provide an untapped storehouse of food, minerals, energy, and archaeological treasure. 海洋对地球上的维持生命系统作出了**不可估量的**贡献，同时又是一座尚未打开的宝库，储有食物、矿物、能源和具有很大考古价值的东西。（陈文伯 译）

【例8】

原　文：When he catches a glimpse of a potential antagonist, his **instinct** is to win him over with charm and humor.

译　文：只要一发现有可能反对他的人，他就**本能地**要用他的魅力和风趣将这人争取过来。

【点评】英汉翻译时，英语中的名词有时候可根据其前后搭配和需要翻译成副词。这主要是因为两种语言之间存在着表达方式上的差异。再如：1) The new mayor earned some appreciation by the **courtesy** of coming to visit the city poor. 新市长**有礼貌地**前来访问城市贫民，获得了他们的一些好感。2) Britain's economic policy is now being pulled by the **magnet** of the next election. 下一次大选**磁铁般**牵引着英国的经济政策。3) I have the **honor** and **happiness** of introducing Mr. Smith to you. 我**很荣幸地**向您介绍史密斯先生。

三、翻译比较与欣赏

【例1】

原　文：Even the best of children harbor the hope that if they ignore taking out the trash long enough, or do it badly often enough, parents will give up and leave them to their play.

译文一：甚至最听话的孩子也会期望，假如他们忘记倒垃圾，或者总是干不好这件工作的话，父母亲就会偃旗息鼓而让他们去玩。

译文二：甚至最好的孩子也会心存这样的希望，如果他们迟迟不倒垃圾，或者老是把这件事干得很糟糕，那么，父母就会不让他们再干而让他们去玩。（柳盼春 译）

译文三：即使最乖的孩子也会心存侥幸，只要他们不乐意倒垃圾，或者总是干得很糟，父母就不再强求，索性放他们去玩耍了。（黄忠廉、李亚舒 译）

【例2】

原　文：Once Clara was accosted by an old lady, battered and ragged and bent, who said as she walked along, and in accents of refined madness, that once the people that had lived there had held their heads up high.

译文一：有一次，一个萎靡不振，衣衫褴褛，弯腰驼背的老妇同克莱克搭话。她一边走一边用一种典雅的迷恋之情的口吻说，过去住在这一带的可都是些很神气的人。

译文二：曾经有位年迈驼背、衣衫褴褛的老妇上前同克拉克搭话。以一种故作高雅的口气边走边说，过去住在这一带的人可是个个神气十足咧。

译文三：有一次，一位衣衫褴褛的老妇人上前同克拉克搭话。她因年迈而显得干瘪，也有些驼背。她边走边说，语调里还隐隐约约地显示出贵妇人的神气。她告诉克拉克,过去住在这一带的可都是些有头面的人物。（李建军 用例）

【例3】

原　文：He was a clever man; a pleasant **companion**; a careless **student**; with a great propensity for running into debt, and a partiality for the tavern.

译文一：他是一个聪明人，谈吐非常风趣（很好相处），可是学习却不肯用功；他老是东挪西借，又喜欢上酒店喝酒。

译文二：他人很聪明，容易相处，但学习粗心大意，喜欢借债，嗜好喝酒。

【例 4】

原　文：Between her agitation and her natural awkwardness in getting out of the cart, Peggotty was making a most extraordinary festoon of herself but I felt too blank and strange to tell her.

译文一：在她心中的激动和下车是生来的笨拙之间，辟果提把自己弄成一个最奇特的彩球，不过我觉得太扫兴太惊奇了，未告诉她这一点。（傅敬民等 用例）

译文二：坡沟提当时心烦意乱，再加上她本来下车就笨手笨脚的，所以她把身子弄得歪扭曲折，成了样子顶特别的彩绸了。不过，我当时心里一片茫然，满怀诧异，顾不得跟她说这个。（傅敬民等 用例）

译文三：佩戈蒂当时焦虑不安，再加上她下车时天生的笨拙劲儿，结果让自己出了顶级的大洋相，但我当时脑子里一片空白，也感到非常不自在，就没有告诉她。（李明 译）

四、翻 译 练 习

句子翻译

1. An economy based on free enterprise **is generally characterized by** private ownership and initiative, with a relative absence of government involvement.

2. Carlisle Street runs westward, **across** a great black bridge, **down** a hill and **up** again, **by** little shops and meat-markets, **past** single-storied homes, until suddenly it stops **against** a wide green lawn.

3. For students of composition, an **awareness** that rhetorical patterns differ from one culture to another culture can help them become more quickly **proficient** in a writing pattern that is not native to them.

4. The doctor's extremely quick **arrival** and uncommonly careful **examination** of the patient brought about his very speedy **recovery**.

5. The prospect of earning five thousand dollars a month had stimulated the **sporting** (冒险的，没有把握的) and **commercial** instinct of the villagers.

6. Millions of the people in the mountainous areas are finally **off** poverty.

7. Exchange of ideas is a constant and vital **necessity**.

8. Developed to meet the needs of very high output networks, this new socket **is characterized** first of all **by** its exceptional performance.

9. Because of Einstein's theory, scientists never again **regarded** the world as they had before.

10. Some people I know get jumpy even at the thought of being inside the crater of what is, after all, a live volcano; but Askja had said his piece very loudly in 1961 and would probably be quiet for a while. **Statistically** speaking, we were fairly safe.

11. There was **some** satisfaction in considering with what **self-denying**, **generous** friendship she had always wished and promoted the match; but it was a black morning's work for her.

12. The President had prepared **meticulously** for his journey.

13. I could not give any connected detail yesterday; but the **suddenness**, and, in one light, the **unreasonableness**, with which the affair burst out, needs explanation.

篇章翻译

篇章翻译 1

International joint ventures are people intensive. It is the people relationships that are the glue that holds them together. Good people relationships between partners are the rudders which steer joint ventures through troubled waters.

Ideally, these relationships require continuity of the people involved in the development of joint ventures, certainly for a significant period of time during their creation and when they are getting the ground, but ideally for some time thereafter. Joint ventures are basically partnerships and when the representatives of the partners change too frequently, matters often get off course, sometimes resulting in the forced dissolution of the joint venture. There is much "water over the dam" now in terms of joint ventures and one lesson that can be drawn from the experience is that "people" changes should be made with great care in the naming of company representatives responsible for working with foreign partners on international joint ventures. The fact of change in itself in these representatives frequently is just not a plus in the development of the joint venture relationship.

Joint ventures, in a number of cases don't work out because the "people" relationships become unglued and/or the business can't be made profitable. With this in mind, international joint ventures should be structured to anticipate the worst contingencies. If this is done even though the contingencies don't occur, you can feel that your company's interests have been protected. Here, I would add an additional observation, namely, that a joint venture that did not work out may be profitable for the partners when broken up if the right decisions were made on the purchase of real estate or the acquisition of the right equipment. These assets may well be worth more when sold than when they were purchased by the joint venture when formed. This has been particularly true in Japan. If the breakup is profitable, then you'll want to make sure that you get your share of these profits.

篇章翻译 2

A Watering Place

by Hayden

1) The Warwickshire Avon falls into the Severn here, and on the sides of both, for many miles back, there are the finest meadows that ever were seen. 2) In looking over them, and beholding the endless flocks and herds, one wonders what can become of all the meat! 3) By riding on about eight or nine miles farther however, this wonder is a little diminished; for here we come to one of the devouring WENS: namely, CHELTENHAM, which is what they call a "watering place", that is to say, a place to which East India plunderers, West

India floggers, English tax-gorgers, together with gluttons, drunkards, and debauchees of all descriptions, female as well as male, resort, at the suggestion of silently laughing quacks, in the hope of getting rid of the bodily consequences of their manifold sins and iniquities. 4) When I enter a place like this, I always feel disposed to squeeze up my nose with my fingers. 5) It is nonsense, to be sure, but I conceit that every two-legged creature, that I see coming near me, is about to cover me with the poisonous proceeds of its impurities. 6) To places like this come all that is knavish and all that is foolish and all that is base; gamesters, pick-pockets, and harlots; young wife-hunters in search of rich and ugly and old women, and young husband-hunters in search of rich and wrinkled or half-rotten men, the formerly resolutely bent, be the means what they may, to give the latter heirs to their lands and tenements. 7) These things are notorious; and, Sir William Scott, in his speech of 1802, in favour of the non-residence of the Clergy, expressly said, that they and their families ought to appear at watering places, and that this was amongst the means of making them respected by their flocks! 8) Memorandum: he was a member for Oxford when he said this!

第十一章　引申翻译法

> 昂贵的照相机本身造就不出摄影师，堆满书架的词典和参考书也造就不出翻译家。
>
> ——兰德斯

一、理 论 探 讨

在英汉翻译过程中我们经常发现，词典上的释义往往不能直接搬到译文之中。绝大多数情况下，需要对词义进行引申，以适合上下文需要，只有这样，译文才能在目的语当中通顺畅达。翻译中的这种做法属于引申翻译法。何谓引申翻译法？引申翻译法就是根据上下文的内在联系，从原词句基本意义出发，根据具体语境和目的语表达习惯，透过句中词或词组乃至整句的字面意义由表及里，对某些词语做一定的语义调整，将其改变为一种适于表达原文精神实质的新义，运用一些符合汉语习惯的表现法，选用确切的汉语词句，将原文内容实质准确地表达出来。

从词义角度看，引申可分为抽象化引申和具体化引申两种情况。将词义作抽象化引申是指对原文中某些字面意义明确具体的词，采用汉语中的含义抽象、概括的词语来表达出来。例如：I'm a **child** in these matters.（对于这种事我毫无经验。）将词义作具体化引申是指，用代表抽象概念或属性的词来表示一种具体事物时，用具体化的事物来表达，还其具体的本来面目，使读者一目了然。如：The car in front of me stalled and I missed **the green**.（我前头的那辆车停住了，我错过了**绿灯**。）

从句法层面来看，引申又可分为根据逻辑需要而进行的引申、根据语用需要而进行的引申和根据修辞需要而进行的引申。

英语词语多需引申方知其意义，因为英语里词语的意义多取决于语境。所以英语中有诸如"要知道一个词的意思就要看它周围是什么词"（You know a word by the company it keeps)、"词本无义，义随人生"（Words do not have meaning, but people have meaning for them）之类的说法。

同汉语词汇相比，英语里的词汇独立性较小，对语境的依赖性较强，比较灵活，其内涵和外延常随语境的不同而扩大或缩小。因此，在英译汉的过程中，要确定一个词的具体意义，往往需要在该词的语境中找出影响该词义引申的因素，即该词在该语境中所具意义的理据。当译者找到词义引申的理据时，该词的意义就会由原来空泛、笼统的意义变为具体、明确的意义。但必须注意的是，词义引申所依据的探询不应是主观的、盲目的，而应是客观的、有的放矢的。在特定语境中，词义引申的因素从其所处的范围上看有近有远，近的可立足于该词所在的词组或句子，远的可基于该词所在的语段、段落，或远离该词的其他段落，甚至语篇；最远的可源于与该词有关的文化背景。（徐莉娜，1996：35）

二、译例举隅及翻译点评

【例1】

原　文：The rather arresting spectacle of little **old** Japan adrift amid beige concrete skyscrapers is the very symbol of the incessant struggle between the kimono and the miniskirt. ("Hiroshima—the 'Liveliest' City in Japan")

译　文：在那米黄色混凝土摩天大楼丛中，漂浮着小巧玲珑**古色古香**的日本水上人家。这情景颇有点儿引人瞩目；恰好象征着和服和超短裙之间持续不断的斗争。

【点评】old 一词在辞典释义中有"年老的、陈旧的、久的、古老的"等十几种解释。Japan 作为借代辞格，在此代"水上的小屋"，它与 old 连用时，排除了 old 的其他释义，而将 old 的词义限制在与建筑物有关的词义选项中——陈旧的、古老的。little 作为一个体现了说话人感情色彩的词，表现出作者从欣赏角度来描述这种奇妙的带有浓厚民族色彩的建筑物。因而，little 中所含的这种特定的感情色彩便成了 old 的另一重要引申依据。

它排除了 old 作为"陈旧的"这一释义。在这个特定语境中，Japan 限定了 old 的所指意义——"古老的"；little 限定了它的表情意义——"年代虽久，但却具有古典色彩和情调的"。受毗邻词语的影响，old 已由词义游移不定变得稳定而明确。译文"小巧玲珑，古色古香"这两组同义重复的四字结构恰如其分地再现了原文的所指意义和表情意义。（徐莉娜 点评）

【例 2】

原　文：But consider your daughters. Only think what **an establishment** it would be for one of them. Sir William and Lady Lucas are determined to go, merely on that account, for in general, you know they visit no new comers. Indeed you must go, for it will be impossible for us to visit him, if you do not. (Jane Austen, *Pride and Prejudice*)

译文一：看女儿的份上吧。只请你想一想，她们不论哪一个，要是攀上了这样一个人家，**够多么好**。威廉爵士夫妇已经决定去拜望他，他们也无非是这个用意。你知道，他们通常是不会拜望新搬来的邻居的。你的确应该去一次，要是你不去，叫我们怎么去。（王科一 译）

译文二：可你要为女儿们着想呀。请你想一想，她们谁要是嫁给他，那会是**多好的一门亲事**。威廉爵士夫妇打定主意要去，还不就是为了这个缘故，因为你知道，他们通常是不去拜访新搬来的邻居的。你真应该去一次，要不然，我们母女就没法去见他了。（孙致礼 译）

译文三：可你也得看在女儿们的份上呀！你就想想，她们中哪一个嫁给他不会**享尽荣华富贵**的呀。威廉爵士夫妇决定去拜访他，就是这个意思。你也知道，他们一般是不会去拜访新近搬来的邻居的。的确你应该去，你去了，我们才能去拜访他呀。（李明 译）

【点评】这是《傲慢与偏见》第一章中班纳特太太对班纳特先生说的一段话。班纳特夫妇养了五个女儿，其所在的庄园新近搬来了一个富有的年轻人，班纳特太太敦促班纳特先生去拜访该年轻人，很希望自己的某个女儿能够被该年轻人看上并娶走。这句话反映了班纳特太太为女儿们所作的打算。原文中，establishment 的汉语意思是"建立""确立"，其引申义

为"家业""企业""当局"。但在翻译这里的 establishment 时，所有这些意义都不符合语境，因此王科一和孙致礼分别采用了引申的翻译办法。但到底如何引申才符合上下文行文需要？不同译者会根据自己的行文方式及文字趣味做出不同的选择，但这些不同的选择均会有高下优劣之分。在我们看来，王科一和孙致礼将 establishment 分别译为"够多么好"和"多好的一门亲事"均太过模糊，没有充分把握和传达出 establishment 作为"建立"或"确立"之基本意义的精髓。我们认为，将该词语翻译成"享尽荣华富贵"是对 establishment 基本义的更为合理的引申。

【例3】

原　文：It was clear to me that we were **soulmates** when it came to reducing government and expanding economic opportunity.

译　文：显而易见，涉及减少政府干预和扩大经济机会这个问题，我们俩是**心有灵犀一点通**的。

【点评】原文是美国前总统里根在获悉撒切尔夫人下野后，回忆两人之间的融洽关系时所说的一句话。原文句子中的 soulmate 本义是"性情相投的人""挚友""情侣""情人"等含义。为了表示对老朋友下野的慰藉，里根总统使用了这个词语，真是意味深长。如果在汉语译文中按照本义翻译就不符合此情景。这里的汉语译文对该词语进行了词义引申，将其翻译为"心有灵犀一点通"，恰到好处地再现了原文信息，这也正是里根总统所想传达的意思。

【例4】

原　文：Odd though it sounds, cosmic inflation is a scientifically plausible consequence of some respected ideas in elementary-particle physics, and many astrophysicists have been convinced for the better part of a decade that it is true.

译　文：宇宙膨胀虽然听似奇特，但它是基本粒子物理学中一些公认理论在科学上看来可信的推论，七八年来许多天体物理学家一直认为这一学说是正确的。

【点评】英语多抽象，汉语多具体。所谓抽象实际上是指一些让人似懂非懂的表达方法，英译汉如果都是一看就明白的句子，那便失去了考这种题型的意义，所以考生感觉到很多英译汉句子都比较抽象是很正常的，而翻译的最终目的是让人明白句子的意思，因此译文中不能出现让人似懂非懂的表达。从这个意义上讲，的确是英语中抽象的内容多，汉语中具体的内容多。

这句话有三个地方比较抽象：一是 consequence，二是 respected ideas，三是 for the better part of a decade。首先我们看一看 consequence，它的词典意思是"后果、结果"，用这个词义来说明 cosmic inflation（宇宙膨胀说）似乎没有切中要害，因为文章告诉我们它是从 Big Bang（大爆炸论）发展起来的一种观点，确切地说应该是一种"推论"；respected ideas 给人感觉好像只可意会不可言传，因为"受尊敬的理论"显然不是清楚明白的中文，"公认的理论"才会让人一目了然；至于 for the better part of a decade，首先 better 一词用得比较怪，根据 you know a word by the company it keeps 原则，我们应该从 part 和 decade 两个词推出 better 在此相当于 greater，而"十年中的大部分时间"又是什么意思呢？用 Get the meaning, forget the words 的办法我们便可以得到一个地道的中文表达："七八年"。经过这样从抽象到具体的引申才有了上面整句话的翻译。

在英汉翻译过程中，将抽象变为具体，需要译者具有较为深厚的英语和汉语功底才能做到，译者只有用心学习、反复实践、反复练习才能达到炉火纯青的地步。

【例5】

原　文：If a man empties his purse into his head, no man can take it away from him, an investment in knowledge always pays the best interest. (Benjamin Franklin)

译　文：倾己所有追求知识，没有人能夺走它；向知识投资，收益最佳。（富兰克林）

【点评】 这种引申是从具体向抽象方向引申,如 purse 引申为"金钱",head 引申为"知识"。之所以能够这样引申,是因为 purse 同"金钱"之间以及 head 同"知识"之间的密切联系。这在修辞格中也可以叫做借代(metonymy)。下面的两个句子是借代,只不过不是由具体向抽象引申,而是由具体向具体的引申。如:1) **The kettle** is boiling. 壶水开了。2) That man is always chasing after **skirts**. 那个男子总在不断地追逐女人。

【例6】

原　文:Television, the most pervasive and persuasive of modern technologies, marked by rapid change and growth, is moving into a new era, an era of extraordinary sophistication and versatility, which **promises** to reshape our lives and our world.

译　文:电视,这项以迅速变化和成长为标志的最普及和最有影响力的现代技术,正在步入一个新时代,一个极为成熟和多样化的时代,这将重塑我们的生活和世界。

【点评】 英语中有些动词如 manage、continue、promise 等,在其后接动词不定式时,这些动词本身不承载主要信息,它们往往用以说明其后动词不定式中动词的行事方式或时间,因此它们的功能相当于一个助动词。在翻译这一类动词时,往往要对它们的意义予以甄别,并进行适当引申。再如:He **managed** to carry the heavy suitcase into the house alone.(他好不容易一个人把那只很重的箱子搬进了屋。)

【例7】

原　文:For all its reputation as the city of tomorrow, a place that will marry capital and **cool** as effortlessly as New York City or London, the city of Shanghai, truth be told, is not a particularly pleasant place during the summer.(《英语世界》2006 年第 9 期,第 50 页)

译文一:尽管上海享有"未来之城"的美誉,像纽约和伦敦一样,将是一个毫不费力就能把资本与**时尚**融合起来的城市，但说实在话，夏天这里可不是个特别舒适的地方。(《英语世界》2006 年第 9 期，第 51 页)

译文二：尽管上海这个地方同纽约城和伦敦一样，不费吹灰之力就可以把资本与**时尚**融合在一起，从而享有"未来之城"的美誉，可是说实在的，这个地方在夏天可不是一个特别让人舒服的地方。(李明 译)

【点评】这里的译文一和译文二均将原文中的 cool 翻译成"时尚"，应该说，这是符合上下文的。cool 这个词在这里用作名词，但它的意思应是基于它的形容词 cool。作为形容词的 cool，其意为：有品位的（in good state）、潇洒的（smart）、出色的（excellent），它在美国青少年口语中使用频率非常高。该词义传到中国后，被音译为"酷"，并广泛流行开来。该词语不同于传统的汉语中的"酷"（表示"残酷"和"程度深"之意），而是一个极具感情色彩的形容词，相当于"很棒！""好极了！""很帅"等表示惊喜和赞美、羡慕之意的词汇。译文一和译文二将其引申为"时尚"，符合原文作者所表达的意思。

三、翻译比较与欣赏

【例 1】

原　文：It was a splendid population—for all the slow, sleepy, sluggish-brained sloths stayed at home.

译文一：这是一批卓越能干的人民——因为所有那些行动迟缓、瞌睡兮兮、呆如树懒的人都留在家乡了。(余立三 译)

译文二：这是一批卓越能干的人民——因为所有那些行动迟缓、头脑愚钝、睡眼惺忪、呆如树懒的人都待在了家乡了。(杨莉藜 译)

译文三：这是一批卓越的人——因为那些慢慢吞吞、昏昏沉沉、反应迟钝、形如树懒的人留在家乡。(章和升、王云桥 译)

译文四：(外出的) 这帮人个个出类拔萃——因为凡是呆板、呆滞、呆头呆脑的呆子都待在了家里。(马红军 译)

【例2】

原　文：No one will deny that what we have been able to do in the past five years is especially striking in view of the crisis which we inherited from the previous government.

译文一：考虑到上届政府遗留下来的危机,我们在过去五年里所能取得的成绩（是）尤其显著，这是没有人可以否认的。（毛荣贵 用例）

译文二：无人可以否认，我们在过去五年里所取得的成绩尤为显著，特别当我们考虑到上届政府给我们的一副烂摊子的时候。（毛荣贵 译）

【例3】

原　文：To the ordinary man, one kind of oil may be as important as another. But when the politician or the engineer refers to oil, he almost always mean mineral oil, the oil that **drives** tanks, aeroplanes and warships, motor-cars and diesel locomotives, the oil that is used to lubricate all kinds of machinery.

译文一：对于普通人来说，一种油同另一种油同样重要，但当政治家或工程师谈到油时，他们几乎总是指矿物油，即那些驱使坦克、飞机、战舰、汽车和柴油机的油，用于润滑各种机械设备的油。

译文二：在普通人看来，油和油之间也许没有主次之分。但是政治家或工程师提到油时，他们所指的几乎总是矿物油，即用来给坦克、飞机、军舰、汽车、**柴油机**等**提供动力**及润滑各种机械设备的油。

【例4】

原　文：The dress set off to perfection the seventeen-inch waist, the smallest in three counties, and tightly fitting basque showed breasts well matured for her sixteen years. (*Gone with the Wind*)

译文一：她的腰围不过十七英寸，穿着那窄窄的春衫，显得十分合身。里面紧紧绷着一件小马甲，使得她胸部特别隆起。她的年纪虽只十六岁，乳房却已十分成熟了。（傅东华 译）

译文二：她的腰围只有十七英寸，三个县里就数她腰身最细，那身衣服把她腰肢衬托得更见纤细。虽说年方十六，乳房却长得非常成熟，熨帖的紧身上衣把她乳房裹得格外显眼。（陈廷良 译）

译文三：她的腰围不过十七英寸，是附近三个县里最细小的了，而这身衣裳更把腰肢衬托得恰到好处，再加上里面那件绷得紧紧的小马甲，她的虽然只有十六岁但已成熟了的乳房便跃然显露了。（戴侃、李野光 译）

译文四：她的十七英寸的腰围，在附近三个县里算是最细的了，这身衣服把她的细腰束得尽善尽美，年方十六的她，乳房已经十分丰满，那紧而贴身的小马甲，更使其跃然显现。（毛荣贵 译）

译文五：她的腰围十七英寸，在几个县里都是最细小的。这身衣服把她的腰肢衬托得美妙绝伦，她那紧而贴身的上衣更使得她那对相对于十六岁的年龄来说发育得非常成熟的乳房非常显眼。（李明 译）

四、翻 译 练 习

句子翻译

1. It is very much like communicating with an **accurate** robot who has a very small vocabulary and who takes everything literally.

2. There comes a time to leave the world behind, forget life's pressures and rediscover the **freedom** of the great outdoors.

3. Ignorance is the **mother** of fear as well as of superstition.

4. Technology now is bringing about the opportunity to transform vision, **curiosity**, and **wonder** into practical knowledge.

5. Poison to a snake is merely a **luxury**; it enables it to get its food with very little effort, no more effort than one bite.

6. The **avalanche** unleashed by the film provided the best opportunity in a long time for the racial healing to begin.

7. He gazed at the mushroom fortress with astonishment as it loomed **indistinctly** but grandly through a morning.

8. Since then, our relations based on the anti-imperialist struggle have **blossomed** and have been diversified and considerably reinforced.

9. Although he still continued to be read, William James was considered by some of his contemporaries to be **a scientific embarrassment**.

10. Death ends all things and so is the comprehensive conclusion of a story, but marriage finishes it very properly too and **the sophisticated** are ill-advised to sneer at what is by convention termed a happy ending. It is a sound instinct of the common people which persuades them that with this all that needs to be said is said. When male and female, after whatever **vicissitudes** you like, are at least brought together, they have fulfilled their biological function and interest passes to the generation that is to come.

11. As I walked along the corridor in a beach dressing-gown on my way to the swimming pool, he looked up angrily at the **intrusion**.

12. Vietnam War was his **entrée** to the new Administration, his third incarnation as a foreign policy consultant.

13. But I suspected that if I tried to release the wolf, she would turn **aggressive** and try to tear me to pieces.

14. She had a heart so large that everybody's grief and joys **found welcome in it**.

15. Last night an uninvited guest turned up to make five for bridge. I had the kind of paper book at hand to **make being the fifth at bridge a joy**.

16. Words once **reserved for restroom walls** are now common stuff in films, plays, books and even on television.

17. And now for the good news: Stockholm residents enjoy sunbathing in November. Antarctic tourism is booming. Siberia has become the **world's breadbasket**.

18. It is very much like communicating with an **accurate** robot who has a very small vocabulary and who takes everything literally.

19. The high-ceilinged rooms, the little balconies（阳台，包厢，楼厅）, alcoves（凹室，壁橱）, nooks（隐蔽处）and angles all suggest sanctuary（避难所）, **escape**（逃亡）, creature comfort.

20. In older canes that have already paired off, dancing reinforces the union—it's a sort of annual renewal of "**vows**".

> **篇章翻译**

篇章翻译 1

Richard Wagner was equally unscrupulous in other ways. An endless procession of women marched through his life. His first wife spent twenty years enduring and forgiving his infidelities. His second wife had been the wife of his most devoted friend and admirer, from whom he stole her. And even while he was trying to persuade her to leave her first husband he was writing to a friend to inquire whether he could suggest some wealthy woman—any wealthy woman—whom he could marry for her money.

He was completely selfish in his other personal relationships. His liking for his friends was measured solely by the completeness of their devotion to him, or by their usefulness to him, whether financial or artistic. The minute they failed him—even by so much as refusing a dinner invitation—or began to lessen in usefulness, he cast them off without a second thought. At the end of his life he had exactly one friend left whom he had even known in middle age.

篇章翻译 2

A good book is often the best urn of a life enshrining the best that life could think out; for the world of a man's life is, for the most part, but the world of his thoughts. Thus the best books are treasuries of good words, the golden thoughts, which, remembered and cherished, become our constant companions and comforters. "We are never alone," said Sir Philip Sidney, "that are accompanied by noble thoughts."

Books possess an essence of immortality. They are by far the most lasting products of human effort. Temples and statues decay, but books survive. Time is of no account with great thoughts, which are fresh today as when they first passed through their author's minds, ages ago. What was then said and thought still speaks to us vividly as ever from the printed page. The only effect of time has been to sift out the bad products; for nothing in literature can long survive but what is really good.

篇章翻译 3

The true artist lets himself go. He is natural. He "swims easily in the stream of his own temperament". He listens to himself. He respects himself.

He comes into the light of everyday like a great leviathan (巨鲸) of the deep, breaking the smooth surface of accepted things, gay, serious, sportive. His appetite for life is enormous. He enters eagerly into the life of man, all men. He becomes all men in himself.

The function of the artist is to disturb. His duty is to arouse the sleepers, to shake the complacent pillars of the world. He reminds the world of its dark ancestry, shows the world its present, and points the way to its new birth. He is at once the product and preceptor (先驱) of his time. After his passage we are troubled and made unsure of our too-easily accepted realities. He makes uneasy the static, the set and the still. In a world terrified of change, he preaches revolution—the principle of life. He is an agitator, a disturber of the peace—quick, impatient, positive, restless and disquieting. He is the creative spirit working in the soul of man. (Norman Bethune, *The True Artist*)

第十二章 被动语态的汉译

> 英语常用被动句,采用物称表达法;汉语常用主动式,采用人称、泛称或隐称表达法。
>
> ——连淑能

一、理 论 探 讨

英语中被动语态使用范围很广,凡是在不必或不愿说出或无从说出施动者以及为了便于连贯上下文或者为了强调动作的承受者等场合,往往都要使用被动语态。英语的被动句有着十分规范的显性的形式标志,通常由"助动词 be + 动词的过去分词"构成,也可以由"get + 动词的过去分词"构成。这是英语这种语言重形合的重要标志之一,尤其在动词的使用方面,它一定要通过动词的形式变化来体现时态、语态、语气、体等。从思维方面看,西方哲学的"人为万物尺度",物我分明,主客体对立。所以西方人的思维方式,并非是单纯的主体意识,也并非是单纯的客体意识,而是该强调物时,就是客体意识,该强调人时,就是主体意识;该强调"物",即动作对象时,就用被动句(隋荣谊,2004:205)。

汉语中较少使用被动语态,尽管同英语相比,汉语中有好几个助词或表达方式可以被看作是被动句的形式标志,如"被""叫""受""让""给""由""把""遭""挨""予以""为……所""是……的"等,而且它们不是在任何情况下可以通用。汉语中使用被动语态时,往往表示受动的对象(即主语)遭受了某种不快或不幸。同英语相比,汉语中被动语态的使用频率之所以很低,是因为汉语属于主题显著的语言,多用"主题-述题"结构,很多时候习惯于将句中的宾语部分提前作为说话的主题来交代,被动语态是通过使用动词暗示出来而非明示出来的,或者是通过使用词汇手段表示被动的含义。另外,由于中国人秉承了"天人合一",即强调"悟性",重视"事在人为"

和个人感受的主体思维习惯,体现在语言的使用上多采用主动语态、人称表达法、无主句、主语省略句以及无形式标记的被动句(隋荣谊,2004:205)。

这样,在英译汉时,就不能完全局限于原文的语态结构,而要根据语言的习惯,在语态上做一些必要的变换。大致说来,英译汉时,英语的被动句多数情况下要译成汉语的主动句,只有在特别强调动作的被动性或特别突出句子的被动意义时才译成汉语的被动句。在具体上下文中,应以选择一种既符合汉语习惯、又保持上下文连贯的语态(可以是主动语态,也可以是被动语态)为翻译原则。同时,既要注意语态转换的一般规则,也要注意其例外情况,有的被动语态形式已习语化了,更是不可忽视的。

二、译例举隅及翻译点评

【例 1】

原　文：And it **is imagined** by many that the operations of the common mind can by no means **be compared with** the processes of these men of science, and that they have to **be required** by a sort of special training.

译　文：许多人认为,普通人的思维活动根本无法和科学家的思维过程相比较,这些(科学家的)思维过程必须经过某种专门训练才能掌握。

【点评】英语多使用被动句,汉语多使用主动句。面对这一矛盾,我们不能将英语中的每一个被动结构都机械地翻译成汉语中的被动句,一定要根据具体情况进行适当处理。

本例中原文有三个被动结构:…is imagined…、…be compared…、…be required…。第一个被动结构后有 by many 来表示动作的发出者,这种被动结构有时只要把动作发出者提到前面就可变成主动句,即把 it is imagined by many that… 变成 many imagine that… 即可,这样翻译起来就比较容易:"许多人认为……"。这属于被动句改译成主动句的第一种情况。第二种情况是在汉语中不需做任何改动就能将被动句译成主动句,句中第二个被动结构就属于这种情况，be compared with 可直接翻译为"与……相比较"，因为在汉语中没有"与……被比较"一说。第三种情况则需要对整个句子做很大调整才能正确处理好。句中第三个被动结构后面虽有介词 by 引出动作的发出者，但简单地像第一种情况那样交换主语和宾语的位置显然行不通，这种情况通常是由于词的使用造成的，如代词 they 到底指什么？动词 required 在句中究竟是什么意思？解决这些问题需要进一步了解英汉两种语言在用词上的差异。

英语中使用代词是常见现象，本例中就使用了代词 it 和 they。汉语虽然也使用代词，但使用频率明显不如英语高。翻译时为了弄清句子的确切含义，不知道代词的所指往往是不行的，尤其当代词作主语的时候，因为当我们不明白主语是什么时，谓语动词的意思往往也很难确定，而弄错了代词的所指更会影响译文的正确性和质量。如本例中的 it 是形式主语，they 指前面提到的 the processes of these men of science（这些科学家的思维过程）。由于代词在句中起着重要作用，在译成汉语时往往需将它们还原成名词，这个看起来是加大了翻译的难度，但实际上却是在考查我们对整个句子乃至上下文的理解，遇到这种情况时我们要善于从文章中寻找线索，把句子的确切含义表达出来。

【例2】

原　文：The mice which haunted my house were not the common ones which **are said to have been introduced** into the country, but a wild native kind not found in the village.

译　文：经常在我房子里出没的老鼠不是人们所说的从外面带到本地来的那种普通老鼠，而是一种在村里看不到的本乡本土的野鼠。

【点评】汉语是一种意合的语言，而且非常重视逻辑推理。正是由于汉语的这些特点，句子的被动意义往往可以采用至少三种方式进行表达，一是不明显地使用被动语态的形式而使用根据逻辑推理可以表示被动含义的表达方式；二是通过增加相关内容如施事者或者泛指概念的词语，用汉语中广泛运用的主动结构表示；三是使用无主句表示。本例中，原文有两个被动语态的形式，其一是 are said，被翻译成主动结构的"人们所说"；其二是 to have been introduced，被翻译成"从外面带到本地来"，这属于不明显地使用被动语态的形式而使用根据逻辑推理可以表示被动含义的表达方式。

【例3】

原　文：Yet these two lived together in peace and sympathy, only that now and then old Henry would become unduly cranky, complaining almost invariably that something **had been neglected or missed** which was of no importance at all.

译　文：然而两个老人一起过着宁静、相依为命的生活，只是有时老亨利有些过分急躁，几乎没完没了地抱怨忘记了做某事或者没有做某事，而这些事情根本是无关紧要的。

【点评】将英语中的主语翻译成汉语里的宾语也是英语被动语态汉译的主要方法之一。之所以会有这样的调整，是因为以英语为本族语的人们同以汉语为本族语的人们在认知方式上有差异，进而在语言表达方式上也呈现出差异。本例中的汉语译文"忘记了做某事"和"没有做某事"如果被译成"某事被忘记了做"和"某事没有被做"那将是多么别扭。再看下面两句的翻译：1) **Dr. Kissinger's qualifications for this post**, I think, **are well known** by all of you ladies and gentlemen. 我想，各位女士，各位先生一定**清楚基辛格博士能胜任这个职务**。2) But soon **this peace and quiet were broken** by the First World War. 但不久以后，第一次世界大战爆发，**打破了这种和平安静的生活**。

【例4】

原　文：**New sources of energy must be found**, and this will take time, but it is not likely to result in any situation that will ever restore that sense of cheap and plentiful energy we have had in the past.

译　文：**必须找到新的能源**，这需要时间；而要恢复以往我们曾感觉到的那种能源既价廉又充足的情况是不大可能了。

【点评】英语是一种主语突出（subject prominent）的语言，每个句子必须有主语，有时英语中的被动句没有标示出谁是动作的执行者，在将这类句子翻译成汉语时，有一种常见的办法就是使用无主句。本例就采用了这种翻译方法。再如：1) Your inquiries for all types of electric goods would **be appreciated**. 欢迎来函询购各种电器产品。2) The goods **are urgently needed**. Prompt shipment will **be appreciated**. 急需此货，请即装运。

【例 5】

原　文：One private school served notice when it opened that "no person **shall be considered as eligible** who shall not be moving in the circle of Gentlemen, no retail trader **being allowed in any circumstances to be so considered**."

译　文：一所私立学校在开张时发布通知说："非绅士者**不得进入本校**，小商贩**决不允许进入本校**。"

【点评】本例中的 shall be considered as eligible 和 being allowed in any circumstances to be so considered 均使用了被动语态，而汉语译文则均使用了主动语态，原文中的主语在译文中也以主语的身份出现。汉语中有些动词的主动语态也可以表示被动，尤其是汉语中的警示的语言。有时候，根据句子的逻辑不会出现误解时，也可以用主动语态表示被动，如：A platform **had been constructed** in a comfortable and conveniently placed tree.（台子早已搭在一棵既舒适又方便搭建的树上。）

【例 6】

原　文：During the postwar years in Germany honors **were heaped** upon Einstein.

译　文：战后那些年，爱因斯坦在德国获得的荣誉一个接一个。

【点评】本例中的被动语态 were heaped 同主语 honors 一道被翻译成"获得的荣誉一个接一个"。这种翻译方法是将被动语态前后的内容进行了意义重组。

在将英语的被动句翻译成汉语时，对原文意义进行重组也是其中的翻译方法之一。要对原文的意义进行重组，译者必须首先吃透原文所表达的意义，再结合汉语的地道表达将原文的意思表达出来。类似的句子还有：1) Many of their evenings and most of their Sundays **were passed** in each other's company. 许多夜晚和大多数星期天他们都形影不离。2) Once Einstein showed that the speed of light was as fast as anything material could possibly travel, **a terrible handicap was placed on the science-fiction writer**. It would take so long to reach even fairly close stars that tales on a galactic scale became hopelessly complicated. 爱因斯坦一证明出光速是物质运行的最大速度，**便难倒了科幻作家**。由于到相当近的恒星都要费不知多少时日，写星系间往来的故事就难以下笔了。

【例7】

原　文：Modern scientific discoveries lead to the conclusion that energy may be created from matter, and in turn, matter may be created from energy.

译文一：现代科学的发现得出这样的结论：物质可以产生能，能又可以产生物质。

译文二：现代的科学发现得出这样的结论：能量可以从物质中获取；反过来，物质也可以从能量中获取。（李明 译）

【点评】在将英语中含有被动语态的句子翻译成汉语时，通常情况下，需要将英语被动语态的主语转换成相应的汉语被动语态的主语，这样才能够将原文中所谈论的话题或原文句子所关注的焦点保持到译文当中。译文一将 energy may be created from matter 翻译成"物质可以产生能"便改变了原文的话题，因为原文所讲的是 energy（能量）可以从何而来。同样，译文一将 matter may be created from energy 翻译成"能又可以产生物质"，也是将原文中的话题 matter 变成了"能"（energy）。这样处理是不可取的。译文二便想方设法保留了原文被动语态中所关注的话题或信息焦点，将"能量"（energy）和"物质"（matter）分别充当两个被动语态的主语。翻译英语中的被动语态时，主语的处理常常令中国学生头疼。很多学生采用综合翻译法，结果将英语中被动语态的主语调整到译文中其他成分的位置上，这个一般应该尽量避免，除非万不得已才进行适度的变通。

三、翻译比较与欣赏

【例 1】

原　文：Treat people as you would like to be treated. Always offer more than expected.

译文一：要像你希望人们对待你那样去对待别人。给予他人的总要多于他们所期望的。

译文二：要像要求别人待己那样待人。给予他人的总要多于他们所期望的。（伍绐文 译）

译文三：要想别人怎样对待你，你就怎样待人。给予他人的，要多于他的企盼。（黄忠廉、李亚舒 译）

【例 2】

原　文：The mantle of your high office has been placed on your shoulder at a time when the world at large and this Organization are going through an exceptionally critical phase.

译文一：正当全世界和本组织处于一个异常危机的时期中，这个崇高职务的重担落到了你的肩上。（郭富强 用例）

译文二：整个世界和本组织正经历着一个异常危机的时期。在这样的一个时期中，这个崇高的职务的重担落到了你的肩上。（郭富强 用例）

译文三：正当全世界和本组织经历着特别关键阶段的时刻，担任这个崇高职务的重担落到了你肩上。（李明 译）

【例 3】

原　文：Many strange new means of transport have been developed in our century, the strangest of them being perhaps the hovercraft.

译文一：在本世纪，许多新的稀奇的交通工具已被研制出来。其中，最为稀奇的也许是气垫船。（毛荣贵 用例）

译文二：在本世纪内，发明许多新奇的交通工具，其中，最新奇的也许数气垫船。（毛荣贵 用例）

译文三：本世纪已经研制出许多新奇的交通工具，其中最奇特的恐怕要数气垫船了。（李明 译）

【例4】

原　文：No man is an island, entire of itself; every man is a piece of the continent, a part of the main. If a clod be washed away by the sea, Europe is the less, as well as if a promontory were, as well as if a manor of thy friend's or of thine own were: any man's death diminishes me, because I am involved in mankind, and therefore never sent to know for whom the bell tolls; it tolls for thee. (*For Whom the Bell Tolls*)

译文一：没有人可以说自己是一座孤岛；每个人都是欧洲大陆的一块泥，如果这块泥被海水冲刷而去，欧洲就残缺了，犹如大陆失去了一个岬角，犹如你自己或你的友人失去了一片邑地。任何人的死，都是"我"在消逝，因"我"已与人合而为一。因此，当教堂敲钟的时候，不要问我是为谁而鸣，因为那正是为你。（刘宓庆 译）

译文二：没有人可以成为一座孤岛，完全与世隔绝；每个人都是大陆上的一块土地，都是整体的一部分；如果这块土地被海水冲走，欧洲就会变小，就如同一个岬角被冲走，就如同你朋友的或者你自己的庄园被冲走。任何人的逝去都会削弱"我的躯体"，因为"我"与人类共存，因此，我来到这个世界永远不是为了想去知道丧钟为谁而鸣——它为你而鸣。（李明 译）

译文三：没有人能自全，

　　　　没有人是孤岛，

　　　　每人都是大陆的一片，

要为本土应卯。

那便是一块土地，

那便是一方海角，

那便是一座庄园，

不论是你的、还是朋友的，

一旦海水冲走，

欧洲就要变小。

任何人的死亡，

都是我的减少，

作为人类的一员，

我与生灵共老。

丧钟在为谁敲，

我本茫然不晓，

不为幽明永隔，

它正为你哀悼。（李敖 译）

四、翻 译 练 习

句子翻译

1. Once **Clara was accosted** by an old lady, battered and ragged and bent, who said as she walked along, and in accents of refined madness, that once the people that had lived there had held their heads up high.

2. Very late in the night he **was awakened** by a most terrible noise—a noise of fighting and screaming.

3. He **was expelled** from the Academy of Sciences; his house **was searched**; all his property **was seized**; and finally his German citizenship **was taken away**.

4. The sense of inferiority that he acquired in his youth **has never been totally eradicated**.

5. It was essential, of course, that **the game be played** in passionate seriousness. Each purchase **must be carefully considered** and, necessary, **supported** by arguments.

6. The above-mentioned funds shall be contributed in cash, in kind and in technology as mutually agreed by the Parties.

7. Though the owners of the house have departed, nowhere is there a perceptible sign of that ruin and desolation which war brings in its train; not the smallest flower dotting the lawn **has been destroyed** and it is indescribably charming to observe.

8. I was seized with sadness as I thought of how the ancient city had been spared during the Second World War and now **might be destroyed by an impending riot**.

9. Therefore, when we **are received** with so much honor and so much kindness in this great country I believe that the People's Republic of China is doing a very significant thing.

10. Animals have a few cries that serve as signals, but even the highest apes **have not been found** able to pronounce words, even with the most intensive professional instruction.

11. Most letters from his wife **are read** to him by the nurse in the hospital.

12. Radioactivity **was discovered** in 1896 and within a couple of years, it turned out that there was a vast store of energy within the atom that scientists had never previously known or suspected to exist.

13. Possibly this knowledge **was taken** from many years of close observation of cause and effect, and logical deductions made from these observations by men with very astute minds.

14. When **I was brought up I was taught** in American history books that Africa had no history and that neither had I.

15. Africa was suddenly on the stage of the world and Africans had to be dealt with in a way they had never been dealt with before.

篇章翻译

篇章翻译 1

As oil is found deep in the ground its presence cannot be determined by a study of the surface. Consequently, a geological survey of the underground rock structure must be carried out. If it is thought that the rocks in a certain area contain oil, a "drilling rig" is assembled. The most obvious part of a drilling rig is called "a derrick". It is used to lift sections of pipe, which are lowered into the hole made by the drill. As the hole is being drilled, a steel pipe is pushed down to prevent the sides from falling in. If oil is struck, a cover is firmly fixed to the top of the pipe and the oil is allowed to escape through a series of values.

篇章翻译 2

He was an undersized little man, with a head too big for his body—a sickly little man. His nerves were bad. He had skin trouble. It was agony for him to wear anything next to his skin coarser than silk. And he had delusions of grandeur.

He was a monster of conceit. Never for one minute did he look at the world or at people, except in relation to himself. He was not only the most important person in the world, to himself; in his own eyes he was the only person who existed. He believed himself to be one of the greatest dramatists in the world, one of the greatest thinkers, and one of the greatest composers. To hear his talk, he was Shakespeare and Beethoven, and Plato, rolled into one. And you would have had no difficulty in hearing his talk. He was one of the most exhausting conversationalists that ever lived. An evening with him was an evening spent in listening to monologue. Sometimes he was brilliant; sometimes he was maddeningly tiresome. But whether he was being brilliant or dull, he had one sole topic of conversation: himself. What he thought and what he did.

第十三章 翻译中句子结构的调整

> 要保留原文中信息所负载的内容,就必须改变语言形式。对语言形式改变的程度取决于始源语同目的语之间在语言上、文化上有多长的距离。
>
> ——无名氏

一、理 论 探 讨

翻译要尽可能忠实而准确地用译文形式把原作的思想内容、风格、神韵等再现出来,尽可能使译文读者的感受和反应与原文读者的感受和反应一致。对原作忠实并不是说译文在行文方式上同原文亦步亦趋,恰恰相反,在英汉翻译过程中,对汉语译文的句子结构进行调整是经常发生的事情,这是英汉两种语言在结构上存在着差异的现实造成的。

试看下面的英语原文和汉语译文:

原文:For example, they do not compensate for gross social inequality, and thus do not tell how able an underprivileged youngster might have been had he grown up under more favorable circumstances.

译文:例如,它们无法弥补巨大的社会不公,因而也不能说明一个物质条件差的年轻人所具有的实际才能,如果他在较好的环境中成长。

仔细阅读上面的译文我们会发现,这样的汉语表达有着浓厚的英语味道,即表示条件的"如果……"从句放在句子最后不大符合汉语的表达习惯。另外,将"如果……"从句置于整个句子末尾也使得整个句子所表达的意义模糊不清。

我们知道,英语句子多前重心,汉语句子多后重心。所谓前重心,就是指先说结果后说细节;后重心就是指先说细节后说结果。由于汉语句子多把重心放在后面,上述译文应该修改成：例如，它们无法弥补巨大的社会不公，因而也不能说明一个物质条件差的年轻人，如果在较好的环境中成长，他所具有的实际才能。

下面我们再看一例：

原文：There is no agreement whether methodology refers to the concepts peculiar to historical work in general or to the research techniques appropriate to the various branches of historical inquiry.

根据句子结构和语义分析，这个句子可分成五段：主句（There is no…）+ 从句（whether…）+ 后置定语（peculiar to…）+ 选择性并列从句（or…）+ 后置定语（appropriate to…）。从语义上讲，主句讲的是结果，从句说的是细节。根据汉语表达习惯，中文译文的表达顺序与原文正好相反。

译文：方法论到底是指一般的历史研究中特有的概念呢，还是指历史研究中各个具体领域适用的研究方法呢，对此人们意见不一。

如果按照英语的表达顺序来翻译，汉语译文不可能通顺、晓畅。因此，在从事英汉翻译过程中，我们必须充分了解英汉两种语言的差异，在透彻理解英语原文的基础上，按照汉语地道的行文方式，如有需要，进行必要的结构性调整，将英语原文信息充分传达出来。

二、译例举隅及翻译点评

【例1】

原　文：But just as all nations can benefit from the promise of this new world, no nation is immune to its perils. **We all have a stake** in building peace and prosperity, and in confronting threats that respects no borders—terrorism and drug trafficking, disease and environmental destruction.

译　文：但是，正如世界各国均会受益于这个新世界的美好前景一样，没有一个国家能够免遭其危险。缔造和平与繁荣，抵御不分/跨越国界的诸多威胁——恐怖主义、贩毒、疾病和环境破坏，**这些与我们大家都有着利害关系**。

【点评】在英语和汉语中都存在着包含总说和分述两个部分的句子，英语句子习惯于先总说，再分述，而汉语句子则多倾向于先分述，后总说。也就是说，在表达逻辑思维时，英语往往是判断或者结论等在前，事实或描写等在后，即重心在前；汉语则是由因到果、由假设到推论、由事实到结论，即重心在后。因此，在将英语中含有总说和分述的句子翻译成汉语时，多采用汉语的先分述、后总说的句式是可取的翻译方法，也更符合汉语的通顺表达以及汉民族的思维方式。本例句中 We all have a stake 是总说，后面的介词短语引出的部分属于分述。如果依照原文语序翻译，译文将是：
"我们在以下方面都有着利害关系：缔造和平与繁荣，抵御不分 / 跨越国界的诸多威胁——恐怖主义、贩毒、疾病和环境破坏。"这样行文让人感觉这句话似乎没有说完整。因此，在将类似的句子翻译成汉语时，调整结构至关重要。再如：

原文：It seems to me that time is ripe for the Department of Employment and the Department of Education to get together with the universities and produce a revised educational system that will make a more economic use of the wealth of talent, application and industry currently being wasted on diplomas and degrees that no one wants to know about.

译文：在我看来，就业部门和教育部门同各所大学携手合作，改革教育制度，使之更加有效地利用学校丰富的人才资源，更加充分地发挥学生们的应用能力和刻苦钻研精神，而不是像现在这样把一切都花费在无人想知道其意义的文凭和学位上，这一时机已经成熟。

试比较以下译文：

对我说来，时机已经成熟，就业部和教育部应当和各大学携手起来，改革我们的教育制度，使之更珍惜地使用学校的人才资源，学生的刻苦勤奋精神。而现在这些人才和努力都浪费在无人感兴趣的文凭和学位上。

第十三章　翻译中句子结构的调整

从以上例子不难看出，英语多前重心，而汉语则多后重心，英汉翻译时若不对这种前后重心进行调整，势必给表达造成困难。

【例 2】

原　文：The most sensible people to be met with in society are men of business and of the world, who argue from what they see and know, instead of spinning cobweb distinctions of what things ought to be.

译　文：商人和见过世面的人是我们在社会上能见到的最通达事理的人。他们讨论问题时从自己的所知所见出发，而不纠缠于事物的是非曲直。

【点评】本例的主句中谓语动词为 are，其功能相当于数学符号"="，因此，在 are 左右两边的成分可以互换位置。即在翻译这类句子时，既可依据原文语序进行翻译，也可将 are 右边的部分放到左边。但做出哪种选择取决于哪种行文更符合目的语的语言表达和目的语民族的逻辑思维方式；另外，上下文也是一个需要考虑的因素。上面的译文将原文右边的部分移至左边充当主语，理由有二：1）原文右边的部分比较简短，左边的部分比较冗长，用简短的成分充当主语容易让读者立刻明白句子述说的对象。2）原文中关系代词 who 的先行词是 men of business and of the world，而译文将这一部分调整到主语位置充当主语，这有利于翻译由 who 引导的定语从句。只要将 who 翻译成"他们"充当主语就可以了。本例中对译文的调整属于微调，这在翻译中是经常需要进行的。

【例 3】

原　文：Nature seldom provides me with the word, the turn of phrase, that is appropriate without being far-fetched or commonplace.

译　文：要做到用词、措词恰到好处，既不牵强附会，又不落俗套，我天生少有这种本领。

【点评】对照原文，译文不仅对原文语序进行了调整，而且对原文的主语也进

163

行了更换。译文用"我"来充当主语，这符合汉民族人们惯于用"人"充当主语的做法以及"天人合一"的思想观念。英语中较常用物称（impersonal）表达法，即不用人称（personal）来叙述，而是让事物以客观的口气呈现出来；汉语则多用人称主语来表达。因此，在翻译英语中含有物称的表达法充当主语的句子时，多将物称主语改换成人称主语，由此带来整个句子结构的调整和变化。再如：1) From the moment we stepped into the People's Republic of China, **care and kindness** surrounded us on every side. 一踏上中华人民共和国国土，我们就随时随地受到关怀与照顾。2) **Alarm** began to take entire possession of him. 他开始变得惊恐万状。

【例4】

原　文：We have a feeling in retrospect, amounting to a practical belief, that we could have left undone the things that we have done, and that we could have done the things that we ought to have done and did not do, and we accuse or else excuse ourselves accordingly.

译　文：回首往事，总觉得有些事情我们本来可以不做，但却做了；有些事情我们本来应该去做，但却没有做。为此我们常常责备自己，要么原谅自己。这种感觉现在已经成为一种符合实际的观念。（李明 译）

【点评】这里的译文对原文在以下方面做了调整：1) 对 We have a feeling in retrospect, amounting to a practical belief 采用拆分的办法进行翻译，先将 in retrospect 翻译成"回首往事"，再将 have a feeling 翻译成"总觉得"；译文最后一句"这种感觉现在已经成为一种符合实际的观念"所传达的也是这句话的内容。2) 对于 that we could have left undone the things that we have done 一句，如果直译就是"我们本来可以不做我们已经做过的事情"，但这样的译文不符合汉语的表达习惯，因此将其调整为"有些事情我们本来可以不做，但却做了"，既符合汉语表达习惯，又与下文相对应，使得译文文从句顺。对译文进行结构调整，有时似乎没有规律可行，但需要把握的最重要的一点是：译文要符合逻辑和目的语表达习惯。这就需要译者既要具备较强的源语语言能力，又要具备很强的目的语语感和表达能力。再如：

原文：The assertion that it was difficult, if not impossible, for a people to enjoy its basic rights unless it was able to determine freely its political status and to ensure freely its economic, social, and cultural development was now scarcely contested.

译文：如果一个民族不能自由地决定其政治地位，不能自由地保证其经济、社会和文化的发展，要享受其基本权利，即使不是不可能，也是不容易的。这一论断几乎是无可置辩的了。

【例5】

原　文：She was the product of the fancy, the feeling, the innate affection of the untutored but poetic mind of her mother combined with the gravity and poise which were characteristic of her father.

译文一：原来她的母亲虽然没有受过教育，却有一种诗意的心境，具有幻想、感情，和天生的仁厚，她的父亲呢，又具有一种沉着和稳重的性格。两者的结合，便造就她这样一个人。（毛荣贵 用例）

译文二：她的母亲从未受过教育，但却有着诗人般的智力：好幻想，易动情，天生富有爱心，而她父亲的特点是冷俊、沉着。她就是这样两种性情的人相结合的产物。（李明 译）

【点评】如果将上面的英语原文翻译成"她是她的母亲那虽然没有受过教育，但仍然含有诗意的心情的幻想、感情和天生的仁厚与作为她父亲的特征的沉重和稳重的性格相结合的产物"则完全不符合汉语的表达和行文方式。因此，碰到这种情况，我们必须对译文的行文方式进行调整，以便使译文结构符合译文表达。

【例6】

原　文：Einstein confessed, "To make a goal of comfort or happiness has never appealed to me."

译文一：爱因斯坦承认："把舒服或快乐作为人生目标，从未吸引过我。"

译文二：爱因斯坦承认："我素来不喜欢把舒服或快乐当作人生目标。"

【点评】英语原文的引文中，充当主语的是动词不定式 To make a goal of comfort or happiness，宾格代词 me 充当介词 to 的宾语，这是英语中常见的表达方式。这种表达方式叫做物称表达法。同英语中的这种物称表达法相反，汉语中更注重人称表达法，即注重思维的主体，因此在叙述客观事物时，多从自我出发或倾向于描述人及其行为，因此主语多以人称充当。正是因为英汉两种语言在注重物称和注重人称上的不同，导致英汉两种语言在转换过程中要进行物称和人称上的转换或者调整。译文一按照原文的物称主语直译成汉语，读来佶屈聱牙，不符合汉语表达。译文二则句子通顺流畅，因为译文将英语原文中的物称调整为汉语中的人称作主语。由此可见，语言的思维模式对于语言的流畅表达起着至关重要的作用。再如：The little chap's good-natured honest face won his way for him.（这小伙子长相老实，看上去脾气也好，到处有人缘。）（连淑能，1993：79）

【例7】

原　文：**My eyes** clouded with tears **as I gazed out the open window at our blue spruce, ever-green amid brown leafless trees** that **looked** as **barren** as our empty house felt.

译文一：我透过开着的窗户，凝视着我家的蓝云杉，泪水渐渐模糊了双眼。这棵云杉是常青的，而它周围那些掉了叶子的褐色树木却和我家的空房子一样显得了无生趣。（仇钰梁 译，《英语世界》2006 年第 9 期）

译文二：当我凝视开着的窗户外面我们种的那棵看上去跟我们家空房子顶上的毛毡一样贫瘠的光秃秃的褐色树林中四季常青的蓝叶云杉时，我的双眼噙

满了泪水，模糊一片。(李明 译)

译文三： 透过开着的窗户，我凝视着我们种的那棵蓝叶云杉，蓝叶云杉四季常青，它的周围都是光秃秃的褐色树木，这些树木看上去同我们家空房子顶上的毛毡一样贫瘠。看到这里，我的双眼噙满了泪水，眼前模糊一片。(李明 译)

【点评】英汉翻译时，在译文中尽可能顺着原文句子结构进行表述是每个译者必须遵循的原则。只有这样，才有可能避免在不经意间改变原文作者的写作意图或诗学价值。换言之，作为译者，在译文的表达阶段，一定要绞尽脑汁保留，而不要轻易改变原文的行文方式或句子结构。但假如源语的信息布局方式与目的语的信息布局方式不太一致、不太吻合或完全不吻合，就需要在译文当中对原文句子的信息布局方式进行调整。如此做的最终目的，无疑是要让译文通顺地道，符合目的语表达习惯。但在进行句子结构调整时，一定要确保译文的话题及中心思想同原文所谈论的话题和中心思想保持高度的一致。本例中的译文一对原文进行了调整，但在该译文的第二句中，话题变成了"这棵云杉"，接着对"这棵云杉"进行了详尽的描述。这样翻译就偏离了原文作者所要表达的中心思想，而更为重要的是，这样行文也会和下文接不上来，导致语篇衔接和语篇连贯的缺失。译文二是忠于原文句子结构的直译，但译文的前半句因定语太多而过于冗长，不符合汉语表达习惯。译文三则对原文句子结构进行了充分的调整，先将原文中所提供的背景信息进行了充分表述，并独立成句，放在前面充当第二句话的背景信息。在第二句中，译文增添了"看到这里"这一表述，该表述是为上下文的衔接需要而添加，没有额外添加任何意思。这样一来，译文就文从字顺，充分表达原文所表达的信息了。

三、翻译比较与欣赏

【例1】

原　文：The men and women throughout the world who think that **a living future is preferable to a dead world of rocks and deserts** will have to rise and demand, in tones so loud that they cannot be ignored, that common sense, humanity, and the dictates of that moral law which Mr. Dulles believes that he respects, should guide our troubled era into that happiness which only its own folly is preventing.

译文一：**希望有一个可以活下去的世界而不是一个到处是岩石和沙漠的死亡的世界的各国男男女女们**，必须起来用一种人们不能置之不理的洪亮声音大声疾呼，要求让理智、人道和杜勒斯先生所说他所尊重的道义原则，来引导这个多事之秋的时代进入只有时代本身的愚蠢在组织人们达到的幸福境地。（倜西、董乐山、张今，1984：186-187）

译文二：**充满生机的未来世界胜于遍布岩石和沙漠的荒野，凡持此观点的世人**，都应该行动起来，用无比洪亮的声音唤醒众人：正是我们今天的愚蠢做法在阻碍着人类走向幸福，我们必须依靠理智、仁慈以及杜勒斯先生所倡导的道义原则，来引导这个动乱的时代迈入幸福的殿堂。（马红军，2000：105）

【例2】

原　文：**It was really a mystery to the neighbors** that Mary, the ugly woman, could succeed in ordering about her husband, the strong-armed blacksmith, well known far and wide, and having him where she wanted him.

译文一：玛丽这个丑女人把她那远近闻名、胳膊粗力气大的铁匠丈夫支使得滴溜溜转，让他上东他不敢往西！这对于他们的邻居来说简直是不可思议。（孟庆升，2003：24）

译文二：玛丽这个丑陋的女人竟然能够将她那远近闻名、身强力壮的铁匠丈夫支使得团团转，能够叫丈夫往东他不敢往西，对于邻居们来说，这的确是个谜。（李明 译）

【例3】

原　文：The trunks of the trees were dusty and leaves fell early that year and we saw troops marching along the road and dust rising and leaves, stirred by the breeze, falling and soldiers marching and afterwards the road bare and white except for the leaves. (*A Farewell to Arms*)

译文一：军队从房子旁边的路上走过，卷起尘沙，洒在树叶上。树干积满了灰尘，树叶早落。军队一开过来，尘沙满天；微风一吹，树叶就坠，军队走完后，路上除落叶外，白白漫漫，空无一物。（吕俊、侯向群 用例）

译文二：树干上蒙满了灰尘，那一年树叶过早地凋落了。我们看到军队沿路走过时，扬起了尘沙，微风过处，树叶纷纷坠下。大军过后，大路上白白漫漫，空无一物，唯余落叶。（吕俊、侯向群 译）

译文三：那一年，树叶早早地凋落了，树干上积满了尘土。我们看到部队沿着大路行军，路上尘土飞扬，微风吹来，树叶纷纷落下，一个个士兵急速前进。行军过后，大路上除了落叶什么也没有，白茫茫一片。（李明 译）

【例4】

原　文：**Four Ducks**

　　　　Four ducks on a pond,
　　　　A grass-bank beyond,
　　　　A blue sky of spring,
　　　　White clouds on the wing,
　　　　What a little thing,

> To remember for years…
>
> To remember with tears! (William Arningham)

译文一： 小 鸭 戏 水

  塘中四鸭戏水,

  岸上绿草迂回。

  晴空春日碧丽,

  朵朵白云展翼。

  草木也有灵犀,

  相思多年难忘。

  忆起不禁泪淌。(李建军 用例)

译文二： 四 鸭 戏 水

  塘边草,绿油油,

  四鸭戏水乐悠悠。

  晴空碧,春意浓,

  片片白云飘空中。

  小灵通啊小灵通,【李明改译:小精灵,小精灵】

  多年伴我到如今,

  每每想起泪满襟。(李建军 用例)

译文三： 四 鸭 戏 水

  四鸭戏水在池塘,

  绿草茵茵两岸旁。

  晴空万里春意暖,

  朵朵白云在飞翔。

  小小精灵多可爱,

  令我思念永不忘,

  想起不禁泪沾裳。(李明 译)

四、翻 译 练 习

句子翻译

1. However, government intervention has been found necessary from time to time to ensure that economic opportunities are fair and accessible to the people, to prevent flagrant abuses, to dampen inflation and to stimulate growth.

2. The assertion that it was difficult, if not impossible, for a people to enjoy its basic rights unless it was able to determine freely its political status and to ensure freely its economic, social and cultural development was now scarcely contested.

3. What is perhaps strangest today is the keen widespread interest displayed toward people who are, on the one hand, not real celebrities and, on the other, not personally known to one.

4. He appears in the morning light as a robust, vital, appetizing sort of man of forty or thereabouts, dressed in a professional-looking black frock-coat with white linen collar and black silk tie.

5. Isabel was a tall girl with the oval face, straight nose, fine eyes and full mouth that appeared to be characteristic of the family.

6. He had cleared up those confusions which arose from different medicines that had the same name and from various names that had been given to the same substance.

7. There are swift rivers, slow, sluggish rivers, mighty rivers with several mouths, rivers that carry vast loads of alluvium to the sea, clear limpid rivers, rivers that at some seasons of the year have very much more water than at others, rivers that are made to generate vast quantities of electricity by their power, and rivers that carry great volumes of traffic.

8. On the other hand, other scientists of the brain, **noting that disease and physical damage can change personally and distort the mind**, believe the brain to be nothing more than a fantastically complex computer.

9. But the writer of these pages, who has pursued in former days, and in the same bright weather, the same remarkable journey, cannot think of it with a **sweet** and **tender regret**. Where is the road now, and its merry incidents of life?

10. For some, especially state universities, institutional autonomy and academic freedom should be strengthened by federal and state support in lieu of their domination, in order to ensure quality education.

11. The rocks presented a high impenetrable wall, over which the torrent came tumbling in a sheet of feathery foam, and fell into a broad, deep basin, black from the shadows of the surrounding forest.

篇章翻译

篇章翻译 1

One way an organization can find staff for job vacancies is to recruit outside the company. It may opt to put an advertisement in a newspaper or magazine which gives a short description of the job and invites introductory letters from applicants. Since the company would not desire applicants who do not have a good profile, it is important that an application form sent to a prospective applicant should request clear information about such things as the applicant's age, qualifications and work experience as well as references from other individuals who know the applicant well. This information assists the company's management in making a final decision on those applicants they can short list for an interview.

The staff conducting an interview together are called an "interview panel", who, prior to the interview, carefully review the job descriptions, personnel specifications, and applications. To help the panel in their selection, an interview assessment form is often used during the interview when each applicant is checked according to a number of criteria indicated on the form.

第十三章 翻译中句子结构的调整

篇章翻译 2

Some old people are oppressed by the fear of death. In the young there is a justification for this feeling. Young men who have reason to fear that they will be killed in battle may justifiably feel bitter in the thought that they have been cheated of the best things that life has to offer. But in an old man who has known human joys and sorrows, and has achieved whatever work it was in him to do, the fear of death is somewhat abject and ignoble. The best way to overcome it—as at least it seems to me—is to make your interests gradually wider and more impersonal, until bit by bit the walls of the ego recede, and your life becomes increasingly merged in the universal life. An individual human existence should be like a river—small at first, narrowly contained within its banks, and rushing passionately past boulders and over waterfalls. Gradually the river grows wider, the banks recede, the waters flow more quietly, and in the end, without any visible break, they become merged in the sea, and painlessly lose their individual being. The man who, in old age, can see his life in this way, will not suffer from the fear of death, since the things he cares for will continue. And if, with the decay of vitality, weariness increases, the thought of rest will be not unwelcome. I should wish to die while still at work, knowing that others will carry on what I can no longer do, and content in the thought that what was possible has been done.

第十四章 英语主语的汉译法

> 西方人重视自然客体，思维的目标往往指向外部世界，整个思维是开放型的，即注重客观思维；而中国人则受传统影响，重视人的伦理生活，思维往往指向自身，寻求人与自然的和谐，即注重主观思维。
>
> ——赵桂华

一、理 论 探 讨

英语是一种主语突出的语言，每个句子几乎都必须有主语。正因为主语突出是英语的特点，它在充当主语这个成分的选择上就有着广阔的余地。相比之下，汉语不是一种主语突出或显著的语言，而是话题突出或显著的语言。由于这种差异，英语主语的汉译就往往会成为英汉翻译的难点。英汉两种语言之间在主语使用上的差异既体现在语言文字方面，也体现在文化习俗、思维方式等方面。因此，在将英语句子翻译成汉语时，首先要充分理解和领会原文所传达的意义，在"灵活运用本国语言的所有长处，充分利用和挖掘它的韧性和潜力"（孙致礼，1996）的基础上，进行创造性翻译至关重要，尤其是处理英语主语的汉译。如果译者过分拘泥于原文的字面意义，译文依葫芦画瓢，其结果一定不堪卒读。作为译者，应根据汉语表达习惯，需要时就要打破原文句子结构，对原文信息进行重新布局和编码，只有这样才有可能使得译文文从字顺。

在句子主语的问题上，英语句子主语同汉语句子主语的主要差别在于：

1. "英语较常用物称表达法，即不用人称来叙述，而让事物以客观的口气呈现出来"（连淑能，1999：76），"汉语则较常用人称主语表达，往往注意'什么人怎么样了'"（连淑能，1999：77-78），如：**Penalties for overdue books** will in the future be strictly enforced.（比较译文：今后凡借书逾期不还者，必将严格按章处罚。）

2. 英语使用"无灵主语"（inanimate subjects，即使用表示抽象概念、心理感觉、事物名称或时间地点等的名词充当主语），同"有灵动词"（animate verbs，即表示人或社会团体的动作和行为的动词，如 see、find、bring、give、escape、surround、kill、deprive、seize、send、know、permit、invite、drive 等）搭配使用的句式非常之多，相比之下，汉语中则往往将"有灵动词"同表示人称的名词搭配，因为"根据汉人的思维，人或社会团体才有这类有意识、有意志的行为，非人类的、无生命的事物一般只能有一些无意识、无意志的状态、运动或变化"（连淑能，1996：80）。如：**My good fortune** has sent you to me, and we will never part from each other.（比较译文：我很幸运，能够得到你，我们将永不分离。）

3. 英语中使用非人称代词 it 作主语的情况非常之多。

第一是它可以用作先行词，代替真正的主语或宾语，如：It never occurred to me that she was so dishonest.（我从来也没有想到她这么不诚实。）或者用于诸如 it is said that…、it is thought that…、it is believed that…、it is felt that…、it is well known that…、it is considered that…、it is found that…、it is reported that… 等之类的被动句式中，it 所代替的是后面的 that 从句，如：It is well known that when fuels such as coal, oil and gas are burned, energy is released.（众所周知，煤、油和天然气之类的燃料燃烧时会释放出能量。）

第二是它可以用作虚义词，它所代替的主语是难以言明的现象或情形，如：It is only half an hour's walk from here to the campus.（只要走半个钟头就可以从这里到达校园。）

第三是它可以用作强调词，汉译时往往无法被译成汉语，如：It is here that we first met each other.（我们是在这里初次见面的。）

二、译例举隅及翻译点评

【例 1】

原　文：His weariness and the increasing heat determined him to sit down in the first convenient shade.

译文一：他的疲惫和不断增加的热量使得他下定决心要在第一个阴凉的地方坐

下来。

译文二：他很疲惫，也感到越来越热，于是决定一遇到有阴凉的地方就坐下来休息。

译文三：由于他很疲惫，而且天气越来越热，于是他决定，一遇到有树荫就坐下来歇息一会儿。（李明 译）

【点评】根据语用学的解释，his weariness 就等于 he has weariness 或者 he is weary；the increasing heat 就等于 there is increasing heat 或者 he feels increasingly hot。英语中使用诸如 his weariness 和 the increasing heat 这种无生命的名词或抽象名词充当主语的例子俯拾即是，但汉语则不习惯于使用这样的表达。在将英语中的这类句子翻译成汉语时，先要分析主语同句子谓语之间的关系。从本例来看，主语是导致谓语这个动作发生的原因。因此，在翻译这个句子时，将主语部分翻译成表示原因的从句才能传达原文的意思。本例中的译文一是直译，不符合汉语的表达习惯。译文二是一个意合句，尽管没有使用诸如"由于""因为"之类的词语，但它所表示的是后一句"于是决定……"的原因，因而是很好的译文。第三句运用了形合句，即用了"由于"一词来明示原文中的主语部分是引起谓语部分动作发生的原因，再如：A strong conviction that something must be done is the parent of many bad measures.（若对做某事非得上马说一不二，定会导致许多措施失误连连。）除此之外，英语句子中的主语部分还可表示假设，如：A man of less courage would not have dared to work inside enemy headquarters.（如果换一个勇气不足的人，那是绝对不敢在敌人的心脏地带工作的。）（李明 译）

【例 2】

原　文：Serious examination of the extent and quality of pre-college science teaching made recently has led to programs of reform and improvement that already have had profound impact on all aspects of elementary and secondary science education.

译文一：最近对入学前自然科学教育程度和质量的认真考察，导致了已经对基础科学教育和中等科学教育的方方面面产生过深刻影响的改革和改进教学计划的形成。

译文二：最近认真考察了大学入学前自然科学教育的程度和质量，从而去改革和改进教学计划，这又深刻地影响了初等和中等科学教育的方方面面。（郭富强 用例）

译文三：最近对大学入学前自然科学教育的程度和质量进行了认真考察，据此形成了目前已经对基础科学教育和中等科学教育产生深刻影响的教学改革计划。（李明 译）

【点评】 英语中将动词名词化是常见现象。这种现象在科技文献、学术文献、经济文献以及其他文体非常正式的语篇中出现的频率很高。被名词化的动词实际上所表示的是一个过程，如可以将本例中的主语部分 Serious examination of the extent and quality of pre-college science teaching made recently 转变成用过程来表达，即 The extent and quality of pre-college science teaching made recently has been seriously examined。从以上转换可以看出，将动词名词化可以使句子变为名词短语，这样这个名词短语就相当于一个句子的信息含量。另一方面，将用过程所表示的句子用名词来表达时，可以避免使用被动语态。动词被名词化之后多数用作抽象名词。英语中使用这类名词充当主语的现象非常常见。在将由动词名词化之后的名词充当主语的句子翻译成汉语时，往往不能直接按照英语的表达方式进行翻译，而要根据汉语表达的惯用方式进行调整。如上面的译文一就是按照原文的表达方式进行直译的，这样翻译不符合汉语表达习惯。译文二对原文的理解有出入。译文三才是正确的翻译。再如：The establishment of a solid manufacturing and mining industry has kept Victoria's unemployment rate the lowest in the country.（由于建立了实力雄厚的制造业和采矿业，使得维多利亚州的失业率一直是全国最低的。）

【例3】

原　文：Harriet Smith's intimacy at Hartfield was soon a settled thing.

译文一：哈丽埃特·史密斯在哈特菲尔德的亲密关系，很快成为一件固定不变的事了。

译文二：哈丽特·史密斯很快就跟哈特菲尔德建立了亲密的关系。（孙致礼 用例）

【点评】 英语主语的汉译往往是英汉翻译中的难点，这是因为，英语和汉语之间存在着巨大差异，这种差异既体现在语言文字方面，也体现在文化习俗、思维方式等方面。在将英语句子翻译成汉语时，首先要充分理解和领会原文所传达的意义，在"灵活运用本国语言的所有长处，充分利用和挖掘它的韧性和潜力"（孙致礼，1996）的基础上，进行创造性翻译。上面的译文一过分拘泥于原文的字面意义，依葫芦画瓢，结果不堪卒读。译文二打破了原文结构，对原文信息进行重新布局，所得译文文从字顺。再如：A difficulty of arranging their lips in this crude exposure to public scrutiny, an inability to balance their heads was apparent in them.（显然，硬要在大庭广众之中抛头露面，她们一个个不知道嘴唇应该做出怎样的形态，脑袋应该摆出怎样的姿势。）

【例4】

原　文：The ocean covers three quarters of the earth's surface, produces 90 percent of all its life-supporting oxygen, and is the driving force behind the entire weather system.

译　文：海洋占地球表面四分之三。地球上维持生命的氧气，90%产生于海洋，整个天气系统变化的动力也是海洋。（陈文伯 译）

【点评】 原文是一个并列句，只有一个主语，为 The ocean，其后带有三个并列谓语：1) covers three quarters of the earth's surface，2) produces 90 percent of all its life-supporting oxygen 和 3) is the driving force behind the entire weather system。译文对整个句子结构进行了调整，调整句子结构的理据是：目的语无法按照原文的语序进行通顺地表达。在调整句子结构时必然要涉及主语的位移。本例的汉语译文根据目的语——汉语——的表达需要，将原文中第二个并列谓语成分中的宾语 90 percent of all its life-supporting oxygen 进行拆分，翻译成"地球上维持生命的氧气"，作译文的主语，原文中的主语 The ocean 在译文中被置于介词"于"之后，作状语。原文第三个并列谓语成分中的表语 the driving force behind the entire weather system 被翻译成译文中的主语"整个天气系统变化的动力",原文中的主语被翻译成了译文中的表语"(也是)海洋"。

【例5】

原　文：It is the insistence, as a first consideration, upon the interdependence of the various elements in, and parts of, the United States—a recognition of the old and permanently important manifestation of the American spirit of the pioneer.

译　文：我们首先应考虑的是,坚持美国国内各种因素之间、各个部分之间的相互依赖关系——即承认体现传统的和永远重要的美国开拓精神。

【点评】　这句话选自美国前总统罗斯福在1933年的就职演说。翻译这句话时,首先要注意的一点就是要了解英语和汉语在所使用词性方面的差别,英语中名词使用较多,而汉语中动词使用较多。第二点就是,英语常用物称表达法,即不用人称来叙述,而让事物以客观的口气呈现出来(连淑能,1999:76)。而汉语则重人称,比较注重主体思维,惯于从自我出发来叙述客观事物,或倾向于描写人及其行为或状态(连淑能,1999:77)。因此,翻译本例时可把名词转译为动词。由于名词 insistence、consideration、recognition 分别源自 insist、consider、recognize 三个动词,而这三个动词的主语往往要求有灵(animate)主语,因此,将上句翻译成汉语时,主语采用人称表达法就非常符合汉语的表达了。由于英汉两种语言之间的差异,原文中的 it 在译文中就无法翻译出来。

【例6】

原　文：It seems to me that the time is ripe for the Department of Employment and the Department of Education to get together with the universities and produce a revised educational system which will make a more economic use of the wealth of talent, application and industry currently being wasted on certificates, diplomas and degrees that no one wants to know about.

译　文：在我看来，就业部门和教育部门应该同大学携起手来，修正我们的教育制度，使之更为合理地发挥学生的才能、更为充分地利用学生的勤奋和努力，他们的才能、勤奋和努力目前都浪费在无人了解其意义的证书、文凭和学位上。现在这样的时机已经成熟。

【点评】英汉翻译时，我们经常会碰到诸如 it occurs/occurred to me that、it dawns/dawned on me that、it seems/seemed to me that、it strikes/struck me that 等表达式，在汉语中我们没有这类表达式。因此，将它们翻译成汉语时，往往需要在汉语里以人称充当主语。如：1) The next morning it struck me that there was no shower in the flat. 第二天早上我突然想起这套公寓没有淋浴设备。2) It dawned on me that I had left the oven on. 我突然想起烘箱未曾关掉。3) It never occurred to me for a moment that you meant that. 我一刻也没想到你会是这个意思。4) An idiot hope struck me that they might think something had insulted me while I was writing the cheque and that I had changed my mind. (Stephen Leacock) 我突然痴人说梦似地希望他们会以为我在写支票时有人冒犯了我，因而我改变了主意。

【例7】

原　文：The summers found the kids playing soccer, building forts in the woods and bringing fish from nearby creeks to join the ducks in our pond.

译　文：夏日里，孩子们踢足球，在树林中搭城堡，从附近的小河里抓些鱼回来放到我家池塘的鸭群中。（仇钰梁 译，《英语世界》2006年第9期，第19页）

【点评】英语中使用"无灵主语"同"有灵动词"搭配使用的典型代表可以说要算由"时间名词或地点名词 + 动词 see、find、witness 的一般过去式"的句式了。再如：1) States that raised their speed limits to 70 mph or more saw a dramatic increase in the number of people killed in traffic accidents, according to a report released Monday by an auto safety group funded by insurers. 根据保险商资助的机动车安全组星期一公布的报道，把行驶速度提高到70英里每小时以上之后，因交通事故死亡的人数急剧上升。

2) However, it is certainly the case that the past few years in Europe has seen a veritable tidal wave of massive organizational and geographical restructuring by both European and non-European firms. 然而，毫无疑问是这样的情况：欧洲在过去几年中出现了真正意义上由欧洲的各家公司同非欧洲的各家公司之间进行的大规模组织重组与地理重组的浪潮。这类使用"无灵主语＋有灵动词"的句子结构能够给篇章带来巨大的生动性，让读者读来不仅感觉到其英语味道十足，而且领略到英语重客观的表达方式趣味盎然、妙趣横生。

三、翻译比较与欣赏

【例1】

原　文：Britons will have the chance in the next few months to try out an emerging technology that could put mobile telephones within the reach of even modest domestic budgets.

译文一：英国人在未来的几个月里可能搞成一种新兴的技术，这种技术能使中等收入的家庭也能用得起移动电话。（何刚强 用例）

译文二：英国人在未来的几个月里可能搞成一种新兴的技术，这种技术一投入使用，即便是中等收入的家庭也能用得起移动电话。（何刚强 译）

译文三：英国人在未来几个月里有可能研制出一种新兴技术，运用这种技术，即使只是中等收入的家庭也能用得起移动电话。（李明 译）

【例2】

原　文：An acquaintance recently remarked that it was time to get religious about his health. He is not atypical: he fancies himself too busy to eat properly, although not too busy to eat out most nights. A normal schedule justifies insufficient time for consistent exercise, etc. Implicit assumptions bespoke trouble.

译文一：最近，有个熟人说，到了用心呵护自己健康的时候了。他是个非常典型的例子：总觉得自己太忙，不能按时吃饭，尽管还没有忙到多数晚上连到外面就餐都不可能的地步。从正常的日程里也挤不出时间来坚持锻炼，不一而足。臆断必将酿出苦果。（孙建成 译）

译文二：一个熟人最近感叹道，早就到了该重视自己身体的时候了。他这种情况很典型：总是把自己想象得太忙，连饭都吃不好，尽管还不至于忙到大多数晚上都要外出吃饭的地步。常规的日程安排让人没有足够的时间来进行持之以恒的锻炼等等。各种说不清的臆断所带来的只能是苦果。（李明 译）

【例3】

原　文：Her eagerness to be gone from Norland was preserved from diminution by the evident satisfaction of her daughter-in-law in the prospect of her removal; a satisfaction which was but feebly attempted to be concealed under cold invitation to her to defer her departure.

译文一：达什伍德太太渴望离开诺兰德的心情丝毫没有减弱，因为她的儿媳看到她将要搬走，明显地露出了满意的神情，这种满意的神情只在假惺惺地请婆婆推迟她们的行期时稍微地掩盖了一下。（傅敬民 用例）

译文二：看到达什伍德要搬走，她儿媳喜形于色。她假惺惺地邀请婆婆推迟她们的行期，以便稍稍地掩盖一下这种心情。但达什伍德太太一心渴望离开诺兰德，根本不为所动。（傅敬民 译）

译文三：达什伍德太太将要搬走，她儿媳那股高兴劲儿溢于言表。尽管她不冷不热地邀请婆婆推迟行期，但那股高兴劲儿再怎么隐藏也无法遮盖住。因此，达什伍德太太渴望离开诺兰德的心情丝毫不减。（李明 译）

【例4】

原　文：While the present century was in its teens, and on one sunshiny morning in June, there drove up to the great iron gate of Miss Pinkerton's academy for young ladies, on Chiswick Mall, a large family coach, with two fat horses in blazing harness, driven by a fat coachman in a three-cornered hat and wig, at the rate of four miles an hour. (*Vanity Fair*)

译文一：当时我们这世纪（指十九世纪）刚开始了十几年。在6月里的一天早上，天气晴朗，契息克林荫道上平克顿女子学校的大铁门前面来了一辆宽敞的私人马车。拉车的两匹肥马套着雪亮的马具，肥胖的车夫戴了假头发和三角帽子，赶车子的速度不过一小时四哩。（赵前洋 译）

译文二：当时我们这世纪刚开始了十几年。在六月里的一天早上，天气晴朗，契息克林荫道上平克顿女子学校的大铁门前面来了一辆宽敞的私人马车。拉车的两匹肥马套着雪亮的马具，肥胖的车夫戴了假头发和三角帽子，赶车子的速度不过一小时四英里。（孙致礼 用例）

译文三：当时我们这个世纪刚过了十几年。在六月的一个晴朗的早晨，一辆宽敞的私人马车驶到位于契息克林荫道平克顿女子学校的大铁门前。拉车的是两匹肥硕的大马，身上套着雪亮的马具。浑身肥胖的马车夫戴着假发和三角帽，赶着马车以每小时四英里的速度行进。（李明 译）

四、翻 译 练 习

句子翻译

1. But, by the 1920s, **the influence of logical positivism and other reductionistic movements** had significantly reduced the impact of the self on social science theory.

2. **The classification of civilizations as the Stone Age, Bronze Age, and Iron Age** depends principally on the kind of tools used.

3. **The rapid advances in computer technology** provided the impetus for a general reappraisal of machine translation and methods.

4. **The data explosion** fortifies those seeking excuses for inaction—another report to be read, another authority to be consulted.

5. **The old view that every point of light in the sky represented a possible home for life

is quite foreign to modern astronomy.

6. **Interest in historical methods** had arisen less through external challenge to the validity of history as an intellectual discipline and more from internal quarrels among historians themselves.

7. **Nature** seldom provides me with the word, the turn of phrase, that is appropriate without being far-fetched or commonplace.

8. **A rope** has been stretched across the narrow lane.

9. **China's presence** is felt, more than ever, all over the world, assuming historic dimensions in the world political situation.

10. **Spectacular economic results** ultimately won impressive workers and staff support for the reformer.

11. **Memories of that historic and happy occasion** still linger.

12. **Much that we saw in 1975** has gone, **much that is new** has taken its place.

13. **The pace of the change** distinguishes Hong Kong from most other parts of the world.

14. **The improvements of the urban areas, the dramatic change in our skyline** will be highly visible to you.

15. **The quarrel** led to our breaking off our friendly relations.

16. **Pressure of work** has delayed my answer to your last letter.

17. **Shortage of suitable land in the urban areas** has made it necessary to build most new public housing in the suburbs.

18. **Simplicity of language** demands, in the first place, that the texts should be colloquial rather than literary; that they should be written in short sentences, not in long and complicated clauses.

19. **Sunday morning** found him still unwell.

20. **The 18th century** witnessed the first true English dictionary, by Dr. Samuel Johnson.

第十四章 英语主语的汉译法

篇章翻译

篇章翻译 1

On August 6, 1997, when 55,000 people gathered in Hiroshima to commemorate the 46th anniversary of the devastating bombing that killed an estimated 140,000 people and brought World War II to a sudden halt, the city's newly elected mayor broke with tradition by adding a few uncustomary lines to the annual Peace Declaration. It should also be recalled, he declared, that "Japan inflicted great suffering and despair on the peoples of Asia and the Pacific during its reign of colonial domination and war. For this we are truly sorry." Noting that this year marks the 50th anniversary of the Japanese assault on the U.S., he added, "Remembering all too well the horror of this war, starting with the attack on Pearl Harbor and ending with the atom-bombings of Hiroshima and Nagasaki, we are determined anew to work for world peace."

Usually, in Japan, when people discuss the war at all, they speak of victimization: their own victimization by the militarists who led the country into battle and by the Americans who ignored, as is Japan's aggression in China and at Pearl Harbor. The appealing image of Japan the victim has no room for the underside of Japan the aggressor.

篇章翻译 2

1) Life itself led Jack London to reject this approach in his writing. 2) He knew what it meant to be one of the disinherited, to be chained to the deadening routine of the machine and to soul-destroying labor for an insufficient reward. 3) Consequently he swept aside not only the literature that pretended that ours is a society of sweetness and light, but also that which contended that the inculcation of the spirit of Christian fellowship would put an end to class controversy. 4) He did not oppose labor organization nor balk at the strike as a weapon of labor; rather, he took his heroes and heroines from the labor movement and wove his plots within their struggles. 5) He poured into his writings all the pain of his life, the fierce hatred of the bourgeoisie that it had produced in him, and the conviction it had brought to him that world could be made a better place to live in if the exploited would rise up and take the management of society out of the hands of the exploiters.

第十五章 正说反译、反说正译法

> 语言是思维的工具。表达法的不同反映了思维方式的不同。
>
> ——姚念庚

一、理论探讨

在英汉两种语言中，对客观世界的描述有两种方法：一是以肯定方式进行描述，一是以否定方式进行描述。在英汉翻译过程中，一般情况下，当碰到英语中的肯定表达时，我们在汉语中的第一选择是使用肯定的表达法；反之，当碰到英语中的否定表达时，我们首先考虑的就是否定表达法。换言之，在翻译过程中，我们所采用的通常是正说（affirmation）正译或者反说（negation）反译的翻译方法。

但是，由于英汉两种语言的差异，有时候英语中使用正说的方式表达，但在汉语中若也使用正说的方式进行表达，则不符合汉语的审美情趣、表达习惯或审美价值，这时从反面着笔反而正好能够传达英语中使用肯定的方式所传达的意义。这样就产生了正说反译的翻译方法。与此相反，有时候英语中使用反说的方式进行表达，但在汉语中若也使用反说的表达方式则不符合汉语语言的表达习惯和审美情趣，这时从正面着笔进行翻译反而刚好能够传达原文所传达的意义。这样就产生了反说正译的翻译方法。

正说反译、反说正译在英语中均叫做反义翻译法（antonymic translation）。反义翻译法就是使用与实际表达相反的语言形式但所表达的是同样的内容的一种翻译方法。采用这种翻译方法的目的就是要适应目的语的审美情趣、审美习惯和审美价值，使目的语的措词更为自然通畅。比如，将法语中 C'est une valeur déjá ancienne 一句翻译成英文时，可以将其直译为 It is an already old value，但也可将其翻译为 It is by no means a new value（Fawcett, 1997: 31）。多数时候，将其翻译成后者更为通顺流畅，因为这种表达在英语中更为"自然"。在许多情况下，只有采用这一翻译策略才能取得预期效果。

正说与反说之间的转换是一种陈述方式的转换。其基本作用机制是双语在概念命名、话题表述、情态表达、强调分布时的角度、侧重面（dimension）、着眼点及特征选择或描摹方式（characterization）等等方面的差异。比如英语中说 self-service bookstand 为正说式，其着眼点是主观行为过程，而汉语中却要说"无人售书处"，为反说式，其着眼点是对客观现状的描述（刘宓庆，1999：176）。从此例可以看出，在译文中采用正说或者反说均是根据目的语的语言特点，使译文更加符合目的语的表达习惯。

将肯定式与否定式进行转换可能导致情态色彩的改变。一般说来，正说是一种认可式的、无异议的陈述，语气是肯定的、平铺直叙的；反说是从反面进行陈述，有时可以获得较婉转、较灵活、较少"单刀直入"的认定效果，因而具有余味或弦外之音。（刘宓庆，1999：177）

具体说来，正说和反说就是指在英语句子中是否使用了 no、not 或者带有 de-、dis-、im-、in-、un-、-less 等含有否定意义的前后缀的词语，在汉语译文中是否使用了诸如"无""非""不""没（有）""未""否""别""休""莫""勿""毋"等表示否定意义的标记（赵桂华，2002：121-122）以及是否使用了由这些字组成的词语，如"决不""毫无""否则""并非""没有""未尝"等等。如果英语句子中使用了带有 no、not 或上述这些表示否定意义的前后缀的词语、汉语中句子使用了上面所列举的这些表示否定意义的词语，那么它们就都属于反说；如果英语句子中没有使用带有 no、not 或上述表示否定意义的前后缀的词语，汉语句子中没有使用上述这些表示否定意义的词语，那就都属于正说。

在英汉翻译过程中，将英语中含有 no、not 或带有 de-、dis-、im-、in-、un-、-less 等含有否定意义前后缀词语的句子翻译成汉语时，使用汉语中不带有表示否定意义的词语而使句子从正面着笔进行表述的翻译方法叫做反说正译；与此相反，在英汉翻译过程中，将英语中不含有 no、not 或不带有 de-、dis-、im-、in-、un-、-less 等含有否定意义前后缀词语的句子翻译成汉语时，使用汉语中带有表示否定意义的词语

因而使句子从反面着笔进行表述的翻译方法叫做正说反译。原文之所以正说或者反说以及译文之所以反说或者正说，都是由于原文或者译文的修辞、语境和语气等多种因素在起作用，它们各自如此表达都是因为那样会使语言更精炼、更富有寓意、更加生动形象，更符合各自语言民族的审美情趣和语言表达习惯。例如，英文 We are quite ignorant of what he has in mind 一句是正说，其汉语译文是"我们**一点也不**知道他心里在想什么"，译文是反说；英文 And that government of the people, by the people, and for the people, **shall not perish** from the earth 为反说，其汉语译文是"一定要让民有、民治、民享的政治制度**永世长存**"，译文为正说。

二、译例举隅及翻译点评

【例1】

原　文：He killed all the chicken infected with the bird flu **without exception**.

译文一：他把感染了禽流感的鸡一只只全杀光了。

译文二：他把感染了禽流感的鸡一只不留地全杀光了。

【点评】　在将英语翻译成汉语时，有时不管英语原文是肯定表达还是否定表达，在汉语中既可以使用正译的方式，也可以使用反译的方式进行翻译。上面的译文一就是采用正译的方式翻译的，译文二则是采用反译的方式进行翻译的。两相比较，两种译文各有其特点，均符合汉语表达。再比如：

1) Don't lose hope! You are still young.

    (1) 不要失望！你还年轻呢。

    (2) 振作点儿，你还不老嘛。

2) Breakfast is free at this hotel.

    (1) 这家酒店早餐免费。

    (2) 这家酒店早餐不收费。

3) I can't remember his name.

(1) 我记不得他的名字了。

(2) 我忘了他的名字。

4) No word is meaningless.

(1) 没有一个词是没有含义的。

(2) 每个词都有它的含义。

【例 2】

原　文：All the employees strongly **disapprove of** the company's new policy.

译文一：所有雇员都强烈地不认同公司的新政策。

译文二：所有雇员都强烈反对公司的新政策。

【点评】英文句子中含有否定意义词缀的单词绝大多数都可以从正面着笔，也就是说，使用该具有否定意义单词的反义词来进行表达，如不将 disorder 翻译成"无序状态"，而翻译成"乱七八糟"，两者意思一样，但从正面着笔更加顺畅。这就是为什么上面的译文二优于译文一的原因所在。类似的例子再如：

1) The doubt **was still unsolved** after his repeated explanation.

   虽经他一再解释，可疑问仍没有得到解决。

2) The train coming from Moscow will arrive **in no time**.

   从莫斯科开来的火车**很快**就到站了。

3) He manifested a strong **dislike** for his father's business.

   他非常**讨厌**父亲所从事的行业。

4) He was an **indecisive** sort of person and always capricious.

   他是那种**优柔寡断**的人，而且总是出尔反尔。

5) Hitler's **undisguised** effort to persecute the Jews met with worldwide condemnation.

   希特勒对犹太人进行了**赤裸裸的**大肆迫害，这种行为遭到了全世界人民的谴责。

反说正译主要体现在英语句子中某个单词含有否定词缀，但在汉语译文中，使用不带否定意义的词语或短语进行表达更为通顺、流畅。如：

1) His arrogance **displeased** everyone present at the conference.

   他那傲慢的态度使得参加会议的所有人都感到气愤。

2) We were waiting for the ending of the meeting with **impatience**.

   我们当时正焦急地等待着会议结束。

3) At least he was **indirectly** responsible for the accident.

   他对这次事故至少负有间接责任。

【例3】

原　文：Winners are **not afraid** to do their own thinking and to use their own knowledge.

译文一：成功者不怕独立思考，不怕运用自己的知识。

译文二：成功者**敢于**独立思考，**敢于**运用自己的知识。

【点评】原文是反说，因为使用了 not 一词；译文一也用了反说，因为使用了"不"这个表示否定意义的词语。译文二是正说，因为没有使用否定词语。将译文一同译文二进行比较不难看出，译文一不仅不符合汉语表达，还会引起歧义；译文二采取了正说的方式，读来通顺流畅、符合汉语表达。因此，这里原文中的反说在汉语译文中应该正说才符合汉语表达习惯。类似的例子如：

1) He thought, **not very vividly**, of his father and mother.

   反说：他并**不是**很鲜明地想到了他的爸爸和妈妈。

   正说：他隐隐约约地想起了自己的爸爸和妈妈。

2) **No one** knows where the shoe pinches like the wearer.

   反说：**没有**一个人会像穿鞋者那样知道鞋子哪里夹脚。

   正说：鞋哪里夹脚，穿鞋人自己最清楚。

3) The research group **lost no time** in carrying out their new plan.

反说：研究小组**不失时间**地执行了他们的新计划。

正说：研究小组**立即 / 抓紧时间**执行了他们的新计划。

4) In the long run, **there is no doubt** that everybody would be much better off if smoking were banned altogether, but people are not ready for such drastic action.

反说：从长远的观点来看，**毫无疑问**，如果完全禁止吸烟，那么每个人的境况将得到很大改善。但对于采取这种极端措施，人们尚无准备。

正说：从长远的观点来看，**十分清楚**，如果完全禁止吸烟，那么每个人的境况将得到很大改善。但对于采取这种极端措施，人们尚无准备。

因此，在一定的上下文中，英语中带有 no、not、never 之类的反说法在汉语译文中采用正译的翻译办法非常行之有效。

类似的还有：

1) The United Nations Organization **has not**, so far, **justified** the hopes which the people of the world set on it.

到目前为止，联合国组织已经辜负了全世界人民对它所寄予的希望。

2) **No refunds or exchanges** without complete factory packing and sales slip.

商品退换须有完整包装并出示发票。

3) If you need any further help, please **don't hesitate** to contact us.

如需帮忙，请随时与我们联系。

【例 4】

原　文：Admission by Invitation Only.

译文一：只允许受邀请的人进入。

译文二：非请莫入。

【点评】以上是因表达习惯的需要而进行的正说反译。类似的例子还有许多，如：

1) Adults only. 少儿不宜。（转换视角，从"少儿"的角度而不从"成人"的角度入手。试比较：只适合于成人。）

2) Keep Upright! 切勿倒置。（试比较：请保持向上。）

3) Agreeable Sweetness 甜而不腻（试比较：甜得可口）

4) a frost-free refrigerator 无霜冰箱

5) Keep off the lawn! 请勿践踏草地!

6) Wet paint! 油漆未干!

7) Urban clearway. 市区通道，不准停车。

8) Inflammables—keep away from fire. 易燃物品，切勿近火。

【例5】

原　文：He has not sacrificed sense to sound but to words, so he **fails** to make the reader understand the verse, let alone enjoy it and delight in it.

译　文：他没有因声害意，却因词害义了，因此，他不能使读者理解原诗，更不用说"好之"或者"乐之"了。（古今明，1997：125）

【点评】原文中的动词 fail 本身具有否定的意义。这种通过使用明显的具有否定意义的词、短语等来表达否定意义的否定法叫做显形否定。英语中能起显形否定作用的有动词、名词、形容词或形容词短语、介词或介词短语、连词、副词或副词短语等等。英语中能起显形否定作用的动词有 deny、neglect、fail、refuse、lack、exclude、ignore、miss、overwork、withhold、cease、escape、refrain from、keep... from 等，名词有 absence、vacancy、deprivation、exclusion、neglect、failure、ignorance、refusal 等，形容词或形容词短语有 absent、afraid of、different、difficult、far from、few、free from、ignorant of、impatient、last、little、safe from、short of 等，介词或介词短语有 above、against、below、beyond、but、except、off、past、under、without、apart from、at a loss、at one's wit's end、at sea、beside the point、in place of、in the dark 等，连词有 before、or、rather... than、unless 等，副词或副词短语有 barely、hardly、little、otherwise、rarely、scarcely、seldom、too... to 等。因此，在将含有这些否定意义词汇的句子翻译成汉语时，往往可以将它们翻译成汉语中的否定句式，即原文正

说，译文反说。例如：

1) I think that you **are missing** the point here. 我觉得在这一点上你们**没有抓住要点**。

2) Her husband **hates** to see her stony face. 她丈夫**不愿**看到她那张毫无表情的脸。

3) Please **keep** your little brother from playing on the road. **请不要让**你的小弟弟在马路上玩儿。

4) The government official was removed from his office because of his **neglect** of duty. 那位政府官员因**玩忽职守**而被撤销了职务。

【例 6】

原　文：Catch me making the same error again.

译　文：我决不会再犯同样的错误！

【点评】在英语中有一些词、短语，它们往往为习惯用语或具有引申义，其意义是否定的。这种在句子中没有明显的具有否定意义的词语、短语属于隐形否定。如上例。再如：

1) I dare him to jump. 我量他也不敢跳。

2) You are telling me! 这事还用你说？

3) Keep it dark! 这事不可泄漏出去！

4) She bears her age well. 她一点也不显老。

5) For all I care! 这事我才不管呢。

6) It's anyone's guess. 这事谁也不清楚。

7) Your question beats me. 你这个问题令我迷惑不解。

8) There will be hell to pay. 后果不堪设想。

【例 7】

原　文：An acquaintance recently remarked that it was time to get religious about his health. He is **not atypical**: he fancies himself too busy to eat properly, although not too busy to eat out most nights.

译文一：最近，有个熟人说，到了用心呵护自己健康的时候了。他是个非常典型的例子：总觉得自己太忙，不能按时吃饭，尽管还没有忙到多数晚上连到外面就餐都不可能的地步。（孙建成 译）

译文二：一个熟人最近感叹道，早就到了该重视自己身体的时候了。他这种情况很典型：总是把自己想象得太忙，连饭都吃不好，尽管还不至于忙到大多数晚上都要外出吃饭的地步。（李明 译）

【点评】 英语和汉语中都存在双重否定的语言现象。本例英语原文中的 not atypical 是双重否定，将其翻译成"并非不典型"或"并不是不典型"也不是不通顺的汉语表达，但采用"负负得正"的肯定表达法而翻译成"很典型"似乎更符合上下文的行文需要。当然，在这一点上，不同译者有着不同的文字趣味和行文倾向。但对于英语双重否定句子的汉译，采用"负负得正"的肯定表达法进行翻译在很多场合无疑是一种有效的处理方式。再如：1) We must **never stop** taking an optimistic view of life. 我们必须对生活永远抱乐观态度。试比较：我们必须永远也不停止对生活抱乐观的态度。2) **Don't** draw your conclusion **before** the end of the year. 到年底再下结论吧。试比较：不到年底就不要下结论吧。

三、翻译比较与欣赏

【例1】

原　文：Another person runs to avoid doing anything else, to dodge a decision about how to lead his life or a realization that his life is leading nowhere. (C. Tucker, "Fear of Death")

译文一：另一个人跑步，是为了逃避其他事情，是为了规避对怎样生活下定决心，规避对意识到自己的生活碌碌无为下定决心。（李明 译）

译文二：另一个人跑步则是为了避而不做别的事，不对如何生活作出决定，不去

感受自己生活碌碌无为。（孙致礼 译）

【例2】

原　文：When the aerial are down, and your spirit is covered with snows of cynicism and the ice of pessimism, then you are grown old, even at 20, but as long as your aerials are up, to catch waves of optimism, there is hope you may die young at 80. (Samuel Vllman,"Youth")

译文一：假若你将天线收起，使你的心灵蒙上玩世不恭的霜雪和悲观厌世的冰层，那么即使你年方20，你也老气横秋；然而只要你将天线竖起，去接受乐观主义的电波，那么你就有希望即使活到80岁死去，也仍然年轻。（隋荣谊 用例）

译文二：当天线收起，当你的心灵蒙上玩世不恭的积雪和悲观主义的冰层，那么你就失去了青春，即使你只有20岁；但只要你将天线竖起，去接受乐观主义的电波，你就有希望，即使80岁死去，你也仍然青春。（李明 译）

【例3】

原　文：More important, a host of unemployed citizens face the grim problem of existence, and an equally great number toil with little return.

译文一：更重要的是，大批失业公民正面临严峻的生存问题，还有大批公民正以艰辛的劳动换取微薄的报酬。（王建华 译）

译文二：更重要的是，大批的失业公民面临严峻的生存问题，而艰苦劳动却所得甚微的人也不在少数。（邵守义 译）

译文三：更重要的是，大批的失业公民面临严峻的生存问题，而艰苦劳动却所得甚微的人也不在少数。（郑启梅 译）

【例4】

原　文：Hold fast to dreams

　　　　For if dreams die

Life is a broken-winged bird

That cannot fly.

Hold fast to dreams

For when dreams go

Life is a barren field

Frozen with snow. (Langston Hughes)

译文一：千万不能丢掉幻想

因为假如幻想破灭

生活就像小鸟断了翅膀

再也不能展翅飞翔。

千万不能丢掉幻想

因为幻想一旦离去

生活就像冬天的田野那样荒凉

冰封大地白雪茫茫。

译文二：请将梦想抓牢，

千万不要将它放跑，

否则生活就像

折翅的小鸟，

不再有自由的翱翔。

请将梦想抓牢，

千万不要将它放跑，

否则生活就像

贫瘠的土地，

还伴之风雪的呼嚎。

四、翻 译 练 习

句子翻译

1. They kept him well informed of the condition of the crops south and east, and thus he knew which articles were likely to be in demand and which articles were likely to be **unsalable**.
2. He had not the least difficulty in **discovering** the true cause of his present behavior.
3. We believe that the younger generation will **prove worthy of** our trust.
4. Obviously if our workers **lack** scientific and cultural knowledge and **fail** to learn new production skill, they can hardly master modern industrial production processes.
5. Many mistakes in her composition **escaped** the careless teacher.
6. The Internet can help us overcome the **lack** of technical data.
7. She is the last person I want to sit next to at dinner.
8. I believe then that I would die there, and I saw with a terrible clarity the things of the valley below. They were **not the less** beautiful to me.
9. Scientists are trying to find out whether there is something about the way we teach language to children which in fact **prevents children from learning sooner**.
10. Time has no divisions to mark its passage, there is never a thunderstorm or blaze of trumpets to announce the beginning of a new month or year.
11. Western society (about 1.2 billion people) cannot bring the remaining 5.1 billion people in less developed countries up the the western consumptive "standard of living" without exhausting the earth's resources.

12. She loved him too well not to detect from the deepened line between his eyes and a score of other minute sighs that he had received an unexpected blow.

篇章翻译

篇章翻译 1

In his classic novel, "The Pioneers", James Fenimore Cooper has his hero, a land developer, take his cousin on a tour of the city he is building. He describes the broad streets, rows of houses, a teeming metropolis. But his cousin looks around bewildered. All she sees is a forest. "Where are the beauties and improvements which you were to show me?" she asks. He's astonished she can't see them. "Where! Why everywhere," he replies. For though they are not yet built on earth, he has built them in his mind, and they are as concrete to him as if they were already constructed and finished.

Cooper was illustrating a distinctly American trait, future-mindedness: the ability to see the present from the vantage point of the future; the freedom to feel unencumbered by the past and more emotionally attached to things to come. As Albert Einstein once said, "Life for the American is always becoming, never being." (2003年全国高等院校英语专业八级考试英译汉试题)

篇章翻译 2

Animals' Rights

1) The point is this: **without agreement** on the rights of people, arguing about the rights of animals is **fruitless**. 2) It leads the discussion to extremes at the outset: it invites you to think that animals should be treated either with the consideration humans extend to other humans or **with no consideration at all**. 3) This is a false choice. 4) Arguing from the view that humans are **different from** animals in every relevant respect, extremists of this kind think that animals **lie outside** the area of moral choice. 5) Any regard for the suffering of animals is seen as a mistake—a sentimental **displacement** of feeling that should properly

be directed to other humans. 6) But the most elementary form of moral reasoning is to weigh others' interests against one's own. 7) To see an animal in pain is enough, for most, to engage sympathy. 8) When that happens, **it is not a mistake**, it is mankind's instinct for moral reasoning in action, an instinct that should be encouraged **rather than** laughed at.

第十六章 定语从句的翻译法

> 定语之于句子，犹如羽毛之于孔雀。只有漂亮的羽毛才能装饰成美丽的孔雀；同样，优雅的定语才能修饰出美妙的句子。
>
> ——罗伯特·瓦伦丁

一、理论探讨

"定语之于句子，犹如羽毛之于孔雀。只有漂亮的羽毛才能装饰成美丽的孔雀；同样，优雅的定语才能修饰出美妙的句子。"这是英国语法学家罗伯特·瓦伦丁的名言，它揭示了定语在句子中所发挥的重要作用。作为在英语句子中主要扮演定语角色的定语从句，毫无疑问对于使用英语的人们表达复杂的思想、建构英语的复合句起着非常重要的作用。就其位置而言，英语中的定语从句可前置（如由 as 引导的定语从句），可后置，也可被其他成分分隔。就其种类而言，英语中的定语从句可分限定性定语从句和非限定性定语从句。就其传递的信息来说，定语从句"在句子中传送辅助信息，是对主句语义的补充、修饰、限制、发展，虽然属于语义的次要部分，但常常是不可或缺的。从交际功能来看，这种结构或提供必要的背景情况，或交代事件发展的结果，或介绍有关的知识，从而使语义在不同层次上得到立体的表现。"（金微，1991：15）换言之，某些定语从句和先行词之间存在着一定的内在逻辑关系，这种内在的逻辑关系大致可分六种：原因、结果、目的、让步、条件和时间。刘重德（1991：80）认为："在语法关系上，定语从句分为两种：限制性和非限制性。但是在翻译时，我们必须要再加上一种，也就是，状语化定语从句"。有些定语从句从语法结构上看是定语从句，但从语义或功能上来看却是状语从句。Zandvoort（1975）称这种类型的从句为"半状语从句（semi-adverbial）"。（转引自刘重德，1991：80）有些语法书则把这类从句叫做"状语化定语从句"或者是"兼有状语功能的定语从句"。

第十六章 定语从句的翻译法

涉及意义方面的问题主要和状语职能的定语从句有关。在这些句子中，定语从句和先行词之间存在着一定的逻辑关系，如原因、结果、条件、目的、让步、时间。翻译这类定语从句要不拘泥于原语的字面意义和语法结构，要能跳出原语的束缚，从整体上把握全句的意义，不能被原语牵着鼻子走，只见树木不见森林。具体来说就是，在将英语中的定语从句翻译成汉语时，应根据英语定语从句在句中的功能进行翻译，可译成定语，或表示条件、原因、结果、目的、让步、时间等的状语。就译文的形式讲，可译成汉语中"……的"字结构或并列句、独立句和复合句等。

英语中的定语从句一般为右开放型，放在被修饰的词语或句子之后，而且这个被修饰的词语或句子之后可以接无数个定语从句，定语从句的结构往往呈现以下特点：1) 蔓生式，如：The rates at which the molecules move depend upon the energy they have；2) 并列式，如：The house (that) he bought in 1968, and which he sold two years later, is again on the market；3) 连环套式，如：There was one thing (that) he told me which I don't believe at all.（隋荣谊，2004：111）汉语中需要被修饰的词语之前却不能放过多的修饰语，即汉语中不能够在被修饰语的左边无限、随意地扩展，再加上英语中的定语从句同被修饰的成分之间存在着状语关系，因此，定语从句的汉译就成为中国学生翻译英语句子的重大障碍之一。

另外，英语民族的思维反映现实的顺序主要是：主体——行为——行为客体——行为标志。这一思维习惯的语言传达模式是：主语+谓语+宾语+状语，以及较长的定语必须后置等。汉语的思维方式则是：主体——行为标志——行为——行为客体。这一思维习惯所引起的语言传达模式是：主语+状语+谓语+宾语，以及定语必须前置（王东风、章于炎，1993：37）。这种逻辑思维顺序的差异是导致英汉翻译困难的一个重要原因。在翻译过程中，中文里定语的语序抑制了英语定语从句向汉语转换的灵活性。学生常常在先行词之前堆砌很多定语从句转换过来的修饰语，但修饰语过于臃肿时就不符合汉语的表达习惯。

所以，在讲解翻译时，我们应告诉学生：

1. 在翻译定语从句时，我们不能只从语法关系去把握定语从句，还要从功能上去把握它。

2. 不能把定语从句仅仅简化为"的"字结构，还要注意英汉两种语言在语序上的差别，使他们在翻译定语从句时，能够把原文的定语从句从定语结构的形式中解放出来，用灵活多样的表达方式把它译成叙述性的主从句子，或谓语宾语结构。（殷宝书，1963：19）

二、译例举隅及翻译点评

【例1】

原　文：Most of the people **who appear most often and most gloriously in the history books** are great conquerors and generals and soldiers, whereas the people **who really helped civilization forward** are often never mentioned at all.

译　文：**历史书上出现得最经常和最为显耀的人物**大多是一些伟大的征服者、将军和士兵，而那些**真正推动文明前进的人**却往往名不见经传。（孟庆升 用例）

【点评】定语从句顾名思义是用作定语的从句，汉语语法中没有该术语，但这并不意味着汉语中没有这种语法现象存在，汉语中只有带"的"字的词组，放在被修饰的名词之前作定语。英语中的定语从句同汉语中带"的"字结构的词组具有相似的功能，因此，在将英语的定语从句翻译成汉语时，最常见的做法就是将其翻译成汉语的前置定语，放在被修饰的名词之前。这种翻译法有人称之为"前置法"。本例中的定语从句属限定性定语从句，是按照"前置法"翻译成汉语的，符合汉语表达。英语中的非限定性定语从句也可以采用前置法进行翻译，如：1) The sun, **which had hidden all day**, now came out in all its splendor. 那个整天一直躲在云层里的太阳，现在又光芒四射地露面了。2) Miggle's laugh, **which was very infectious**, broke the silence. 米格尔那富有感染力的笑声打破了静默。

【例2】

原　文：He unselfishly contributed his uncommon talents and indefatigable spirit to the struggle **which today brings them (those aims) within the reach of a majority of the human race.**

译　文：他将自己非凡的才智和不倦的精神无私献给了那次奋斗，**那次奋斗今天已使人类大多数人实现那些目标。**

【点评】将英语中的定语从句翻译成汉语的前置定语只是英语定语从句汉译的方法之一。这种方法有时又不能奏效，这时我们就要尝试别的翻译方法。本例采用了将英语的定语从句翻译成后置的并列句的办法进行翻译，译文通顺流畅，符合汉语表达。再如：They have had to live the rest of their lives under the stigma **that he had recklessly precipitated an action which wrecked the Summit Conference and conceivably could have launched a nuclear war.**（他们现在不得不背着臭名终其余生，这个臭名就是：他曾贸然采取一种行动，该行动破坏了峰会，并且证据确凿地有可能已触发一场核战争。）除了上面的限定性定语从句可以采用后置的并列句的翻译法处理之外，非限定性定语从句也可以采用同样的翻译方法。如：The food supply will not increase nearly enough to match the growing population, which means that we are heading into a crisis in the matter of producing and marketing food.（食品供应的增加将赶不上人口的增长，这意味着我们在粮食的生产和购销方面正陷入危机。）

【例3】

原　文：This will be epoch-making revolution in China's social productive forces **which will lay down the material foundation for the socialist and communist mode of production.**

译　文：这将是中国社会生产力方面的一次划时代的革命，**将会为社会主义和共产主义的生产方式打下物质基础。**（王宏印 用例）

【点评】本例中的 which will lay down... production 为定语从句，在汉语译文中被译为同主句中的谓语部分并列的另一个谓语。这是在将英语中的定语从句翻译成汉语时经常采取的翻译方法。这种翻译方法也可以叫做并列

法，只不过这时的汉语译文不是作为一个并列句同主句并列，而是将从句降了一级地翻译成了一个谓语动词短语罢了。再如：His wife, Betty, is a Shanghai-born Chinese who left China at the age of eight, and whose book, Eighth Moon, tells of her sister Sansan's life in China.（他的妻子蓓蒂是一位出生在上海的华人，八岁时离开中国，写过一本名为《八月》的书，记述了她妹妹姗姗在中国的生活。）

【例4】

原　文：This was the period when Einstein began the research which resulted in the creation of his famous Theory of Relativity.

译　文：就在这期间，爱因斯坦开始了一项研究。这项研究成就了他那著名的相对论。

【点评】原文中含有两个定语从句，其一是 when Einstein began the research，其二是 which resulted in the creation of his famous Theory of Relativity。在将原文翻译成汉语时，第一个定语从句同其前面的 This was the period 被融合在一起，译文就由原来的复合句变成了简单句：就在这期间，爱因斯坦开始了一项研究。这种翻译方法叫做融合翻译法。融合翻译法是指，把原句中的被修饰词与定语从句融合在一起，用一个独立的汉语句子进行表述的翻译方法。一些带有限制性的定语从句的英语复合句，如果英语中的主句能够压缩成汉语词组并作主语，那么定语从句就可以译成谓语结构，从而将原文中的复合句变成译文中的简单句。如果主句压缩成汉语词组后用作其他成分，那么定语从句可以译成一个句子，关系代词灵活处理。一般来说，英语原文中，定语从句的主句里如果有 there be、be 结构或动词时通常把原句中的主语和定语从句融合在一起构成一个主谓结构，形成一个简单句。再如：

1) We have a social and political system **which differs in many respects from your own**.

我们的社会、政治制度在许多方面与你们的不一样。

204

2) It was a beautiful late-June morning, with fair-weather clouds and a light wind going, the grasses long in the orchard—the kind of morning **that always carries for me overtones of summer sadness**.

那是一个美丽的六月的早晨：天气晴朗,空中有淡淡的浮云,清风徐徐,果园里的草已经长得很高了——那样的早晨对于我来说（似乎）总有些不吉祥。

【例5】

原　　文：Nowhere is the clash between development and environment more visible than in China, **where the world's largest population faces pollution, deforestation and acid rain on a large scale**.

译　　文：在中国，发展与环境之间的矛盾表现得最为突出。**这个世界上人口最多的国家正面临着环境污染、森林减少以及大范围酸雨侵袭。**

【点评】英语中有些定语从句较长，结构较为复杂，或意思上独立性较强，在逻辑意义上有追述、分层叙述、转折等作用。这时，可以将英语的定语从句从主句中分离出来，译成独立的成分。再如：A gulf had opened between them over which they looked at each other with eyes that were on either side a declaration of the deception suffered.（在他们之间产生了一条鸿沟。双方隔着鸿沟相对而视，彼此的目光都在宣告各自所遭受的对方的欺骗。）

【例6】

原　　文：I should want not merely to see the outline of her face, so that I could cherish it in my memory, but to study that face and find in it the living evidence of the sympathetic tenderness and patience **with which she accomplished the difficult task of my education**.

译　　文：我不仅渴望着看到她的脸庞，好让我把它珍藏在记忆中，而且渴望着端详那张脸，并从中找出活生生的证据来窥见她那富于同情心的温柔和耐

心，因为她正是运用这种温柔和耐心，完成了教育我的这项艰难任务。）

【点评】某一语言的特定句子结构同它所表示的事物的概念和关系并非始终具有一致性。英语定语从句也可以兼有状语的职能，一般认为包括原因、目的、结果、条件、让步、假设等类型。（王宏印，2002：211）因此，在将英语中的定语从句翻译成汉语时，要根据特定的上下文中句子所承担的交际功能，仔细分析一定的语言结构所表示的实际含义，然后给予符合上下文、符合逻辑的恰当处理。再如：My assistant, **who had carefully read through the instruction before doing his experiment**, could not obtain satisfactory results, because he followed them mechanically.（我的助手虽然在做实验之前已从头至尾仔细阅读了说明书，但由于生搬硬套，就没有能够得出满意的结果。）

【例7】

原　文：We believe that it is a serious responsibility of your government to insure that weapons **which you have provided to Cuba** are not employed to interfere with this surveillance **which is so important to us all** in obtaining reliable information **on which improvements in the situation can be based**.

译　文：我们相信，贵国政府负有重大责任来保证你们提供给古巴的武器不会用于干扰这种侦察行动，因为这种侦察行动对于我们双方获取改善局势所需要的可靠信息都是非常重要的。

【点评】这里的英语原文是一个复合句，其中包含有三个定语从句，其中最后一个定语从句包孕在第二个定语从句中，这样的定语从句叫做嵌套式定语从句，即在一个句子中，定语从句套定语从句的情况。这种结构中的定语从句其实和自由式定语从句基本相似，拆开来也是一个独立的定语从句，只不过一个定语从句包孕在另一个定语从句之中而已。因此，其翻译也与简单的定语从句相同。对于这种定语从句的翻译，只要掌握好了前面所讲到的各种类型的定语从句的翻译，翻译这样的定语从句也就不会很难了。

三、翻译比较与欣赏

【例 1】

原　文：In addition English is the language of commerce and the second language of many countries which formerly had French or German in that position.

译文一：此外，英语还是贸易中使用的语言和许多国家的第二语言，而在以前，这些位置上是被法语或德语占据的。（李建军 用例）

译文二：此外，英语是商业贸易中的常用语言，还取代了法语和德语而成为许多国家的第二语言。（李建军 用例）

译文三：此外，英语成了商业交往中使用的语言，也成了许多国家的第二语言，而这些国家先前是以法语或德语为第二语言的。（李明 译）

【例 2】

原　文：Sleep is most graceful in an infant; soundest, in one who has been tired in the open air; completest, to the seaman after a hard voyage; most welcome, to the mind haunted with one idea; most touching to look at, in the parent that has wept; lightest, in the playful child; proudest, in the bride adored. (Leigh Hunt, *A Few Thoughts on Sleep*)

译文一：婴儿的睡眠，最为优美；疲劳的人在户外睡眠，最为酣畅；水手在艰苦航程之后的睡眠，最为圆满；为某种意念所苦的人，对睡眠最为欢迎；哭泣后的母亲的睡眠，最动人心弦；一个顽皮小孩的睡眠，最为轻松；一个深受爱慕的新娘的睡眠，最为骄傲。（刘炳善 译）

译文二：睡眠，于婴儿，最为优美；于户外疲劳之人，最为酣畅；于远行回家之水手，最为完满；于思虑问题之人，最受欢迎；于哭泣过后之父母，最令人同情；于顽皮之小孩，最为轻松；于人见人爱之新娘，最为骄傲。（李明 译）

【例3】

原　文：Several canals were built to facilitate world commerce, the most important being the Suez (1869), which shortened the route between Western Europe and India by 4,000 miles, and the Panama (1914), which reduced the distance between New York and San Francisco by almost 8,000 miles.

译文一：几条运河的开凿便利了世界贸易，其中最重要的是将西欧到印度的航程缩短了4 000英里的苏伊士运河（1869年）和将纽约到旧金山的距离减少了近8 000英里的巴拿马运河（1914年）。（傅敬民等 用例）

译文二：几条运河的开凿便利了世界贸易，其中最重要的是苏伊士运河（1869年）和巴拿马运河（1914年）；前者将西欧到印度的航程缩短了4 000英里，后者将纽约到旧金山的距离减少了近8 000英里。（傅敬民等 用例，稍有改动）

译文三：所开凿的几条运河给世界贸易带来了便利。在这几条运河中，最重要的是苏伊士运河（1869年）和巴拿马运河（1914年）。苏伊士运河将西欧到印度的航程缩短了4 000英里，而巴拿马运河则将纽约到旧金山的距离缩短了近8 000英里。（李明 译）

【例4】

原　文：Man for the field and woman for the hearth;

Man for the sword and for the needle she.

Man with the head and woman with the heart;

Man to command and woman to obey. (Alfred Tennyson)

译文一：男人适于农耕，女人适于家务；

男人宜于征战，女人宜于缝纫；

男人善于深思，女人富于感情；

男人发号施令，女人唯有服从。（傅晓玲等 用例）

译文二：丈夫劳作在田野，女子持家炉台边。

丈夫挥舞刀枪剑，女子织补拿针线。

丈夫威武智勇全，女子贤德真心善。

丈夫统率声令下，女子遵命垂手间。（丁树德 用例）

译文三：夫外妇内，

夫勇妇慧。

夫聪妇情，

夫唱妇随。（丁树德 用例）

译文四：男人长于耕作，女人长于家务；

男人嗜好动武，女人喜欢针活；

男人惯于分析，女人巧于心计；

男人好发命令，女人惟命是从。（李明 译）

四、翻 译 练 习

句子翻译

1. A writer's work is a constant struggle to get the right word in the right place, to find that particular word **that will convey his meaning exactly, that will persuade the reader or soothe him or amuse him**.

2. The mice **which haunted my house** were not the common ones **which are said to have been introduced into the country**, but a wild native kind not found in the village.

3. While there are almost as many definitions of history as there are historians, modern practice most closely conforms to one **that sees history as the attempt to recreate and explain the significant events of the past**.

4. He liked his sister, **who was warm and pleasant**, but he did not like his brother, **who was aloof and arrogant**.

5. You, whose predecessors scored initial success in astronomical research, have acquired a greater accomplishment in this respect.

6. I have met children **who not only are growing emotionally and intellectually but also are trying to make sense of the world morally**.

7. The traders wanted safe access to large quantities of oriental spices, which the European world had come to like, and which people needed for presenting food in days before the introduction of cold storage.

8. I should like to see in her eyes that strength of character which has enabled her to stand firm in the face of difficulties, and that compassion for all humanity which she has revealed to me so often.

9. True, not everyone sees me as you saw me or even as I see myself; but deep down inside I have that marvelous feeling **that** comes from being an integrated whole person, not afraid of being just what I am.

10. I consider my letter to you of October twenty-seventh and your reply of today as firm undertakings on the part of both our governments which should be promptly carried out.

11. Our aim is to establish in Ghana a strong and progressive society … where poverty and illiteracy no longer exist and disease is brought under control; and where our educational facilities provide all the children of Ghana with the best possible opportunities for the development of their potentialities.

12. The idea that the President of the United States, **who had important business to take care of**, would spend five minutes relaxing in laughter was more than Stanton could endure.

13. The agricultural industry in New Zealand has developed a comprehensive extension service, which allows for new ideas to be disseminated widely to the farming community.

14. It was a strange opposition, of the like of which she had never dreamed—an opposition in which the vital principle of one was a thing of contempt to the other.

15. He sat in fascinated contemplation of the way in which her hands went up and down above the strip of stuff, just as he had seen a pair of birds make short perpendicular flights over a nest they were building.

16. Emergency measures must be taken to eliminate the air pollution of a city, which, as reported by the control center, exceeds tolerance limits and endangers the safety of the inhabitants.
17. There are few circumstances among those which make up the present condition of human knowledge, more significant of the backward state in which speculation on the most important subjects still lingers, than the little progress which has been made in the decision of the controversy respecting the criterion of right and wrong.

篇章翻译

篇章翻译 1

In some societies people want children for what might be called familial reasons: to extend the family line or the family name, to propitiate the ancestors; to enable the proper functioning of religious rituals involving the family. Such reasons may seem thin in the modern, secularized society but they have been and are powerful indeed in other places.

In addition, one class of family reasons shares a border with the following category, namely, having children in order to maintain or improve a marriage: to hold the husband or occupy the wife; to repair or rejuvenate the marriage; to increase the number of children on the assumption that family happiness lies that way. The point is underlined by its converse: in some societies the failure to bear children (or males) is a threat to the marriage and a ready cause for divorce.

Beyond all that is the profound significance of children to the very institution of the family itself. To many people, husband and wife alone do not seem a proper family—they need children to enrich the circle, to validate its family character, to gather the redemptive influence of offspring. Children need the family, but the family seems also to need children, as the social institution uniquely available, at least in principle, for security, comfort, assurance, and direction in a changing, often hostile, world. To most people, such a home base, in the literal sense, needs more than one person for sustenance and in generational

extension. (1999 年高等院校英语专业八级考试英译汉试题)

篇章翻译 2

I lost my sight when I was four years old by falling off a box car in a freight yard in Atlanta City and landing on my head. Now I am thirty-two, I can vaguely remember the brightness of sunshine and what color red is. It would be wonderful to see again, but a calamity can do strange things to people. It occurred to me the other day that I might not have come to love life as I do if I hadn't been blind. I believe in life now. I am not so sure that I would have believed in it so deeply, otherwise. I don't mean that I would prefer to go without my eyes. I simply mean that the loss of them made me appreciate more what I had left.

Life, I believe, asks a continuous series of adjustments to reality. The more readily a person is able to make these adjustments, the more meaningful his own private world becomes. The adjustment is never easy. I was bewildered and afraid. But I was lucky. My parents and my teachers saw something in me—a potential to live, you might call it—which I didn't see, and they made me want to fight it out with blindness.

The hardest lesson I had to learn was to believe in myself. That was basic. If I hadn't been able to do that, I would have collapsed and become a chair rocker on the front porch for the rest of my life. When I say belief in myself I am not talking about simply the kind of self-confidence that helps me down an unfamiliar staircase alone. That is part of it. But I mean something bigger than that: an assurance that I am, despite imperfections, a real, positive person; that somewhere in the sweeping, intricate pattern of people there is a special place where I can make myself fit.

It took me years to discover and strengthen this assurance. It had to start with the most elementary things. Once a man gave me an indoor baseball. I thought he was mocking me and I was hurt. "I can't use this," I said. "Take it with you," he urged me, "and roll around." The words stuck in my head. "Roll it around!" By rolling the ball I could hear where it went. This gave me an idea how to achieve a goal I had thought impossible: playing baseball. At

Philadelphia's Overbrook School for the Blind I invented a successful variation of baseball. We called it ground ball.

All my life, I have set ahead of me a series of goals and then tried to reach them, one at a time. I had to learn my limitations. It was no good to try for something I knew at the start was wildly out of reach because that only invited the bitterness of failure. I would fail sometimes anyway but on the average I made progress. (Robert G. Allman, "A Ball to Roll Around")

第十七章 英语特殊句式的翻译

> 翻译可能是宇宙进化史上到目前为止所出现的最为复杂的一种活动。
>
> ——I.A.里查兹

一、理论探讨

英语中存在着一些特殊句式,他们之所以被认为特殊,是因为它们的结构属于英语这种语言所独有的惯用结构,因此我们也可以将它们称之为"惯用法"。既然这种惯用结构为英语这种语言所独有,在汉语中就要谨慎小心,努力找到与之相对应的表达法。在翻译过程中,对于英语中的这类特殊句式,除了对其中某些句式可根据已形成的固定译法进行翻译之外,对其他还未形成固定译法的句式,必须结合其所出现的上下文和语境,通过综合分析,进行逻辑推理,充分而又地道地将原文信息再现到译文当中。

由于英语特殊句式较多,这里只列举其中一些最为常见、较为容易引起误解的特殊句式,通过对它们的翻译,让读者从中得到启示,并在自己的翻译实践中学会关注这类特殊的结构或句式,并尝试运用其中一些翻译技巧。

二、译例举隅及翻译点评

【例1】

原　文：It is not supposed to be easy for women to rise to the height of taking the large free view of anything—anything that calls for action.

译　　文：人们认为，妇女们对任何事情，尤其是需要采取行动的事情，都心怀广阔，要达到这个境界是很难的。

【点评】it 在英语中使用得非常广泛，它除了可以作"它"，用以指代表示动物或物体的名词之外，很多时候是用作先行词作主语或宾语。汉语中就缺乏先行词作主语或宾语的情况。这种差异给我们翻译这类含有先行词作主语或宾语的英语句子带来了困难。但只要仔细斟酌、善于分析，就可以用意义相当的汉语句子表达其意。再如：1) Make it the first object to be able to fix and hold your attention upon your studies. 要把专心致志于学业并在学业上持之以恒作为首要目标。2) I have heard it remarked by a statesman of high reputation that most great men have died of overeating themselves. 我曾听到一位有名望的政治家说过：大多数伟人都是因吃得过多而命归黄泉的。

【例2】

原　　文：George Washington was discretion itself in the use of speech, never taking advantage of an opponent, or seeking a short-lived triumph in a debate.

译　　文：乔治·华盛顿措辞非常谨慎，在辩论中从不欺骗他的对手，也不贪求一时的胜利。

【点评】翻译此句的难度就在于对 discretion itself 该作如何理解。英语中有一种特殊的表达，即"all + 名词（抽象名词或名词复数）"或"抽象名词 + itself"，这种表达所传达的意思就等于"very + 该名词所转换的形容词"。所以，本例中的 discretion itself 就被翻译成"非常谨慎"。再如：1) The winner was **all smiles** as he heard the results of the voting. 听到投票结果，获胜者兴高采烈。2) He was **all gentleness** to her. 他对她非常温存。3) To his superiors, he is **humility itself**. 他对长辈非常谦恭。

【例3】

原　　文：They say that he had no university education, but he seems to be something of a scholar.

译　文：据说他并没有受过大学教育，但他看上去却有点儿学者的派头。

【点评】英语中有一些表示不同程度的短语使用频率很高，它们主要由不定代词 something、anything、nothing 以及 little、much 等再加上 of 构成。比如 something of 的意思是"在某种程度上"，anything of 的意思是"有点""略微"，nothing of 的意思是"毫无""全无"，much of 的意思是"大有"，not much of 的意思是"算不上""称不上"，little of 的意思是"几乎无"，something like 的意思是"有点像""略似"。由于这类表达的丰富多彩性，它们很容易为中国学生混淆。通过翻译来弄清它们之间的区别是一条有效的途径。再如：1) He was very much of a gentleman. 他颇有绅士风度。2) He is more of a scholar than a teacher. 与其说他是教师，不如说他是学者。

【例4】

原　文：So vast and so pervasive is the sea that if the earth's crust were made level, ocean water would form a blanket over 8,000 feet deep.

译文一：海洋如此广大浩瀚，如此分布辽阔，地球表层如果使之平整起来，那么海水可以形成深 8 000 多英尺的覆盖层。（陈文伯 译）

译文二：海洋浩瀚无边、分布辽阔，如果将地球表层平整起来，海水就会以 8 000 多英尺的深度覆盖着地球。（李明 译）

【点评】这里的英语原文是一个倒装句。这种倒装句可以有两种功能，其一是可以突出放在句首的这部分内容，即 so vast and so pervasive；其二是由于主语之后接了一个较长的从句，如果按照正常语序排列，就会主语太长，从而使得整个句子显得头重脚轻，因此倒装是为了使得整个句子平衡。在将这类英语句子翻译成汉语时，由于汉语语言的特点，完全可以按照英语的语序进行翻译。再如：Particularly remarkable, Mr. Holton said in an interview, is the extent to which their interest in physics dominates the correspondence despite their personal difficulties.（尤其难能可贵的是，霍尔顿先生在一次会见中说，尽管他们各自都有困难，但他们在通信中对物理学的兴趣竟然占着最重要的位置。）

【例 5】

原　文：They are all too satisfied to take the opinions of others without the pain of thought for themselves.

译　文：他们都非常满足于接受别人的意见，而自己懒得动脑筋去思考问题。

【点评】英语中的 too... to 结构是非常常用的结构，意思是"太……而不……"，但当其前面加上了诸如 only、all、but、never、not 等的时候，其由 to 引出的不定式就失去了否定的意义。这时，在 too 与 to 之间所使用的形容词往往为 ready、eager、apt、inclined 等表示主语的心理状态、心理活动或感情态度的词语。另外，在 too ready/apt to do something 的结构中，不定式也没有否定的意义。比如：1) You know but too well to hold your tongue. 你最知道应该住嘴。2) They are too apt to keep their inferiors at a distance. 他们对部下总爱抱着高高在上的态度。3) I shall be only too pleased to do my best in that line of work. 做那方面的工作，我会很高兴地去尽我的最大努力。4) English is not too difficult a language to learn as long as you make up your mind to learn it. 只要你下决心学习，英语是很容易学好的一种语言。

【例 6】

原　文：Success in life does not depend so much on one's school record as on one's honesty and diligence.

译　文：一个人一生中能否取得成功并不取决于他在学校时的成绩，而是取决于他是否有诚信，是否勤奋。

【点评】翻译这个句子的难点在于对 not so much... as 的理解。英语中的 not so much... as 的意思相当于 rather than，其中的 as 有时还可以换成 but rather，其汉语对等语是"与其说是……毋宁说是……"。在关注 not so much... as 的同时，还必须将其同 not so much as 区分开来。这四个词中间没有被其他成分隔开时，其意思相当于 without/not even，即汉语里的"甚至……还没有"。如：1) She is a society woman, but strange to say, she

cannot so much as write her own name. 她非常善于社交，但说来也怪，她甚至连自己的名字都写不出。2) Law, in its true notion, is not so much the limitation as the direction of a free and intelligent man to his proper interest. 法律，从真正意义上说，并不是限制一个自由而有智慧的公民的正当权益，而是引导他们享用其正当权益。

【例7】

原　文：In the Middle Ages widespread use was made of arguments from analogy, on the belief that the universe formed an ordered structure and that the macrocosmic pattern of the whole is reproduced in the microcosmic pattern of parts so that it is possible to draw inferences by analogy from one to the other.

译　文：在中世纪，广泛采用了类推法的各种论点，这些论点基于这样的观念：宇宙形成了一个有次序的结构，整体的宏观格局是部分微观格局的再现，这样，就有可能通过类推法来作出由此及彼的推断。

【点评】本例中的英语原文采用了分割结构。分割结构是英语表达中经常出现的一种比较特别的句法，其作用是保持句子平衡，避免头重脚轻或为了语义严密、结构紧凑，将语法关系密切的两个句子成分（如主语和谓语）用其他句子成分分隔开来。英语的分隔必须遵循两点：1) 尾重原则，即把长而复杂的成分放在句末；2) 句尾信息焦点原则，即把新信息、语义重点放在句尾。

　　本例中的这个句子虽然较长，但若首先挑出了其中的主、谓、宾三个成分，意思就一目了然。英语原文中的谓语非常短，只有 was made 两个词。of arguments from analogy 是 use 的定语。正因为谓语短，定语长，为使句子保持平衡，was made 便插在 use 和它的定语之间，形成分隔结构。on the belief... other 是介词短语，作状语。belief 后面有两个以 that 引导的同位语从句：that the universe... structure 和 that the microcosmic... of parts。so that 引导的是状语从句，表结果。从结构来讲，该句可按原文顺序翻译。分隔部分可以不管，只要把 use 转换成动词，把被动的 was made 转译成主动，即译成汉语的无主语句就文从字顺了。

三、翻译比较与欣赏

【例 1】

原　　文：It was very neatly written, and except that "friend" was written "freind" and one of the "S's" was the wrong way round, the spelling was correct all the way through.

译文一：字写得很整齐，除了 Friend（友）写成了 Freind 其中有一个 S 写成相反的形状 2，此外拼写完全无误。（李启纯 译）

译文二：字写得很整齐，除了把 Friend 写成了 Freind 所有的 S 都写成了 2 之外，对于拼写都没有错误。（耕雨 译）

译文三：字体很干净。除去字母有两处颠倒外，拼字也没错误。（孔繁云 译）

译文四：它们是被很整齐的写出来的；除了"朋友"被写成了"用友"，以及一个"平"字被写倒了之外，也完全没有错误。（任稚羽 译）

译文五：字迹写得非常整洁，除了把"朋友"写成了"明友"，把"卍"字写成了"卐"字之外，拼写都没有错误。（李明 译）

注　　释：这里的翻译所涉及的是因语言文字的差异而产生的翻译问题，李启纯和耕雨在这里就没有恰当地解决好因为语言文化差异而产生的翻译问题。孔繁云的翻译属于意译，同任稚羽和李明的翻译相比，孔的翻译就没有在语言文字的对比上下功夫。

【例 2】

原　　文：Algernon: How are you, my dear Ernest? What brings you up to town?

　　　　　Jack: Oh, pleasure, pleasure! What else should bring one anywhere? (Oscar Wilde, "The Importance of Being Earnest")

译文一：阿尔杰农：亲爱的埃纳斯特，你好。什么风把你吹进城来的?

　　　　杰克：寻欢作乐，寻欢作乐！一个人出门无非是为了寻欢作乐，是吗?（钱之德 译）

译文二：亚：哎哟，我的好任真。什么事进城来了？

杰：寻欢作乐呀！一个人出门，还为了别的吗？（余光中 译）

译文三：奥：你好哇，任真。什么风把你吹进城里来啦？

杰：当然是风流快活的风啦！别的风吹得动人吗？（张南峰 译）

【例3】

原　文：All day long they lie in the sun, and when the sun goes down, they lie some more! (K. Kelly, *His Way: The Unauthorized Biography of Frank Sinatra*)

译文一：在太阳下躺着，两人一整天说鬼话，到太阳下山，他们说鬼话越发起劲。（郑雅丽 译）

译文二：整个大白天，他们都在说黑话，而当黑夜来临，他们越发黑话连篇。（李明 译）

译文三：整个大白天，他们躺在太阳底下谎话连篇，而当太阳下山，他们更要躺到床上谎话不断。（李明 译）

【例4】

原　文：Perhaps from some vague rumor of his college honors, which had been whispered abroad on his first arrival, perhaps because he was an unmarried, unencumbered gentleman, he had been called the bachelor.

译文一：也许是因为他初来乍到就有关于他在国外大学求学的种种流言蜚语，也许是因为他是一位没有结婚、无拘无束的绅士，他便被称为光棍。（傅敬民等 用例）

译文二：也许是因为他初来时大家交头接耳传说他在大学里有过学位，也许是因为他是一位没有结婚、无拘无束的绅士，他便被称为光棍学士。（傅敬民等 用例）

译文三：也许是有人谣传他读过大学，这在他刚刚到达国外时就被谣传开了，也许是因为他谦谦君子，单身一人，无拘无束，因此，人们当时称他为光棍儿学士。（李明 译）

第十七章 英语特殊句式的翻译

四、翻译练习

句子翻译

1. He is an interpreter, one whose duty it is to act as a bridge or channel between the minds of his readers.

2. No less obvious is the fact there are great numbers of people so constituted or so brought up that they cannot get so much pleasure out of processes and experiences which result in a rich, significant life, as they can get out of processes and experiences resulting in a poorer life less full of meaning.

3. While she was waiting for the tinkling of the bell, all nerves, suddenly he stood before her.

4. If he is anything of a gentleman, he will keep his promise, I should think.

5. There was nothing of the student about him, but very much of the miner.

6. Science moves forward, they say, not so much through the insights of great men of genius as because of more ordinary things like improved techniques and tools.

7. You have all heard it repeated that men of science work by means of induction and deduction, that by the help of these operations, they, in a sort of sense, manage to extract from Nature certain natural laws, and that out of these, by some special skill of their own, they build up their theories.

8. And numerous experiments have shown once the concept of self is changed, other things consistent with the new concept of self are accomplished easily and without strain.

9. Philosophers have been too ready to suppose that question of fact can be settled by verbal considerations.

10. I soon perceived that she possessed in combination the qualities which in all other persons whom I had known I had been only too happy to find singly.

11. The great use of a school education is not so much to teach you things as to teach you the

art of learning.

12. Knowledge about the most powerful problem-solving tool man has ever developed is too valuable not to share.

篇章翻译

篇章翻译 1

Possession for its own sake or in competition with the rest of the neighborhood would have been Thoreau's idea of the low levels. The active discipline of heightening one's perception of what is enduring in nature would have been his idea of the high. What he saved from the low was time and effort he could spend on the high. Thoreau certainly disapproved of starvation, but he would put into feeding himself only as much effort as would keep him functioning for more important efforts.

Effort is the gist of it. There is no happiness except as we take on life-engaging difficulties. Short of the impossible, as Yeats put it, the satisfaction we get from a lifetime depends on how high we choose our difficulties. Robert Frost was thinking in something like the same terms when he spoke of "the pleasure of taking pains". The mortal flaw in the advertised version of happiness is in the fact that it purports to be effortless.

We demand difficulty even in our games. We demand it because without difficulty there can be no game. A game is a way of making something hard for the fun of it. The rules of the game are an arbitrary imposition of difficulty. When someone ruins the fun, he always does so by refusing to play by the rules. It is easier to win at chess if you are free, at your pleasure, to change the wholly arbitrary rules, but the fun is in winning within the rules. No difficulty, no fun. (2001 年全国高等院校英语专业八级考试试题)

篇章翻译 2

1) This reputation for incorruptibility is the greatest of our advantages in administering the Empire. 2) Its rarity among nearly all the other peoples I have known raises our officials

almost to the level of divine superiority, and without it we could not hold the Empire together, nor would it be worth the pains. 3) A business man who has worked long under the system of concessions in Russia tells me that it is now impossible to bribe the Commissar or other high officials there. 4) That is an immense advance, for under Tsarism one had only to signify the chance of a good bribe and one got what one wanted. But nowadays on the suspicion of bribery both parties are shot off-hand. 5) It is a drastic way of teaching what we have somehow learnt so smoothly that we are scarcely conscious of the lesson or of our need of it. 6) Yet there was need. 7) The change is remarkable, and I think it may be traced to an unconscious sense of honor somehow instilled among the boys.

第十八章 隐喻的翻译

> 语言文字是有机的、动态的、发展的，是随不同语言环境的改变而变化的。
>
> ——阎德胜

一、理 论 探 讨

隐喻（metaphor）是"一种语义变化的过程，这种过程从语义角度看是迅猛的，即在两个语义域之间通过某种抽象图式类比的方式，将一个词从一个语义域（始源语义域）应用到另一个语义域（目标语义域）"（Lakoff & Johnson, 1980）。

从以上定义可以看出，这里所谈的隐喻是一个非常宽泛的概念，它不同于传统修辞中所谈到的暗喻。非常宽泛意义上的隐喻在日常生活中随处可见。哲学家们认为，隐喻性是语言的根本特性，人类语言从总体上、从根本上讲都具有隐喻性。过去近四十年，哲学家、心理学家和语言学家们已经达成共识，认为隐喻是人类语言和思维不可或缺的基础（Goatly, 1997: 1）。英国语言学家 I. A. Richards 曾说，人们时刻都在运用隐喻，如果不使用隐喻，就不可能流畅连贯地说上三句话（詹蓓，2003: 33）；如果不使用隐喻，要描写日常生活中所发生的一切是难以想象的。

试看下面例子：

1. Jo gave Kim a book.

2. Jo gave Kim a push.

3. Jo gave Kim a hearing test.

4. Jo gave Kim an opportunity to speak.

5. Jo gave Kim some good advice.

第十八章　隐喻的翻译

6. Jo gave Kim a lot of help.

7. Jo gave Kim a strange look. (Lee, 1992: 67）

上面七个例子中，give一词覆盖了非常宽泛的语义范围。第一句中give一词之意是"对拥有权的转让"，这是其字面义，非隐喻义。第二、三句中give一词的意义已经发生变化，隐喻为"执行"之意。第四、五、六句中give隐喻为"提供"。第七句中give隐喻为"传递"。这样，从第二句开始，give一词的意义已经从字面义向隐喻义方向转化。所以，give一词就从原来的字面义——对拥有权的转让——跨越到新的语义域，从而形成隐喻义。这种形式的隐喻在日常使用的语言中具有无比威力。难怪西班牙哲学家Jose Ortega y Gasset对隐喻作过如此评论："隐喻是人类所拥有的最具语言生成力的力量"[18]。

Lee（1992: 66）也认为，我们的世界是通过我们在不同情景之间以近似的感知方式所建立起的各种关系来建构的。正是由这些所建立起的各种关系而形成的网络组成了我们认知系统的构架，使得我们这个世界"可以想象"。然而，这些近似的各种感知都是通过语言来运作的。Lakoff和Johnson（1980）也认为，我们的概念系统的构建具有隐喻性：在他们看来，日常生活中经常使用的隐喻性短语就是佐证，它证明我们在平时理解事件和经历时就已经具有隐喻性。他们还举例阐明,有关建筑(buildings)的语言就常常用于谈论理论建构，比如语言学家们和经济学家们在讨论自己的理论时，往往要谈到模型（models）、构架（constructs），这些模型和构架又需要有一个结构（structure），其中的各种组成部分又要结合（bonded）或者粘合（cemented）在一起，这样它们就不会根基不稳或者倒塌（shaky/crumbling），还可能需要有证据来支撑（support）它们。因此完全可以说，隐喻是日常谈话中的一个普遍方面，它在语言（包括学术语言）使用的各个方面扮演着重要角色。

对英语中的隐喻进行汉译要充分考虑到英语隐喻的特点和汉语隐喻的特点。英语中的隐喻有些在汉语中已经有了固定译法，但有些隐喻则没有汉语对等语，需要译者依据原文创造性地将它们翻译到汉语中来。对英语中隐喻的汉译，一般认为可以采取三种办法：一是运用同原文隐喻一模一样的对应语进行翻译；二是寻找另一个表达相似意义的隐喻性短语进行翻译；三是用最近似的字面解释来替换原文中无法翻译的隐喻。

18　原文为：The metaphor is the most fertile power possessed by man.

二、译例举隅及翻译点评

【例1】

原　文：An organization is a machine that occasionally **breaks down**, and requires the services of an external expert to fix it. When that happens, it needs to be **retooled** to become more efficient and may even require periodic **reengineering** in order to remain "cutting edge".

译　文：一个组织机构就是一台偶尔会出毛病的机器，它需要外部专家经常进行**维护和修理**。在进行维护和修理时，它需要**更换零件**，以便更为有效地运转；它甚至还需要进行定期**重新装配**，以保持其"犀利"。

【点评】英语原文明显使用了隐喻，汉语译文运用了同原文一模一样的隐喻进行了完全对应的翻译。由于英语和汉语均可采用相同的隐喻方式来描写组织机构，故汉语译文中可以采取同原文一模一样的隐喻进行完全对应的翻译。再如：Many people fear inflation, even moderate inflation rates of 6 or 9 percent, because they begin to worry that **prices will begin to gallop upwards**, or perhaps that the moderate inflation will degenerate into a hyperinflation. Is this concern warranted? **Does creeping inflation inevitably become a trot? A trot become a canter? A canter become a gallop**?（许多人都担心通货膨胀，哪怕是只有百分之六或百分之九的适度通货膨胀率，因为他们这时就开始担心价格会急速上升，要么也许会担心适度的通货膨胀会演变成恶性通货膨胀。这种担心是否有道理？是不是潜行通货膨胀一定会变成"快步小跑"，"快步小跑"一定会变成"慢跑"，"慢跑"一定会变成"大步疾驰"呢？）

【例2】

原　文：Fat reserves are **like bank accounts** to be drawn on in the winter when food supplies are limited and sometimes difficult to reach because of deep snow.

译　文：脂肪储备如同银行账户的存款，供冬天食物来源有限以及有时由于大雪深得难以获得的时候使用。

【点评】传统修辞中的明喻，即使用诸如 as、like 等之类的比喻词的比喻属于隐喻中的一种。对于这类隐喻的翻译，通常采用同原文隐喻一模一样的对应语来进行翻译。但如果碰到原文中的喻体形象同目的语中的喻体形象不一致，而该喻体形象对于目的语读者来说难以理解，在翻译时就可以舍弃源语中的喻体形象而采用目的语中的喻体现象进行翻译，如通常将 as timid as a chicken/hare 翻译成汉语的"胆小如鼠"而不将它翻译成"胆小如鸡/兔"。再如：1) Every tree and every branch was encrusted with bright and delicate hoarfrost, white pure **as snow**, delicate and refined **as carved ivory**. 每棵树、每个树枝都裹上了一层晶莹剔透的白霜，洁白得像雪，精致得像雕刻完美的象牙。2) It is a vitreous greenish blue, as I remember it, **like those patches of the winter sky seen through cloud vistas in the west before sundown**. 我还记得，那是一种蓝中透绿的晶莹色彩，就像冬季日落之前透过云层西望时所见到的一片片的天空。

【例3】

原　文：He is **as poor as a church mouse**.

译　文：他一贫如洗。

【点评】这里的翻译是用最近似的字面解释替换了原文中无法翻译的隐喻。这是因为，有时候英语原文中的喻体若在译文中保留下来要么意义不清，要么会使人产生误解或者令人不知所云。比如，如果将 I can read his mind like a book 这句话翻译成"我可以像读一本书一样来读他的心思"，译文所表达的意义就非常不清楚，这时就要考虑采用意译方法，舍弃原文形象，直接表达其比喻意义即可。将这句话翻译成"我对他的心思了如指掌"就清楚明了了。再如：1) These politicians are **as slippery as an eel**. 这些政客个个油嘴滑舌。2) This method of measurement is **as easy as ABC**. 这种测量方法非常简单。3) The hall was packed **as close as herrings**. 大厅里拥挤不堪。

以上这些情况多出现在以 as... as 构成的比喻性短语中，汉译时往往只能将它们用最近似的字面解释来替换原文中无法翻译的形象。再如：

as bold as brass	厚颜无耻
as clear as noon	一清二楚的
as cheerful as a lark	兴高采烈的
as clean as pin	非常整洁的
as cool as a cucumber	非常冷静的
as cross as two sticks	非常生气的
as deep as a well	高深莫测的
as drunk as a lord	酩酊大醉的
as dry as a chip	干燥的
as dull as ditch water	枯燥无味的
as dumb as a fish	一声不吭的
as easy as winking	非常容易的
as fat as an alderman	大腹便便的
as fine as silk	柔软的，身体健康的
as flat as a board	直挺的，极平的
as free as wind	自由自在的
as fresh as a rose	精力充沛的
as good as a feast	绰绰有余的
as good as gold	规规矩矩的
as good as a play	很有趣味的
as greedy as a wolf	贪得无厌的
as happy as a king	非常快乐的

【例 4】

原　文：His father compared that couple's new life together to **a railroad train on a long, unknown track, "there may be curves and dark tunnels ahead,"** he

228

told them, "but we wish you **a safe journey**."

【译　文】：他父亲将这对伴侣在一起的新生活比作一列在漫长而不知其终点的轨道上奔驰的火车，"在前进的道路上可能有许多曲折，也可能有许多阴暗的隧道。"他告诫他们说，"但我们预祝你们一生平安。"

【点评】：在英语中，我们经常会发现英美人以与汉语同样的方式作隐喻。这时，我们可以以英语相同的隐喻方式进行翻译，即不改变英语中的隐喻形象，照英语原文的字面进行翻译。在翻译本例时，尽管将原文中比较虚的 a safe journey 翻译成了汉语中比较实的"一生平安"，但其他的隐喻方式均没有改变。再如：1) **Wild horses** could not drag me down to Cape Horn and that sinister southern Ocean again. 即使是**野马**也休想能够再把我拖回到合恩角和那个凶险莫测的南部海洋去了。2) Jane's uncle is **an old fox**, up to all kinds of evils. 珍妮的叔叔是一只**老狐狸**，他什么勾当都能干得出来。

【例 5】

原　文：I never anticipated that my case would **snowball** into one of the most famous trials in the US history.

译　文：我绝没有料到我的案子会像**滚雪球**般越滚越大，成为美国历史上最出名的审判之一。

【点评】：对于英语中的隐喻，有时汉语中不使用相同或者相似的形象；有时汉语中有相同或者相似的形象，但不用于相似的隐喻当中。在将英语中的这种隐喻进行翻译时，就需要对英语中所使用的隐喻进行引申或者进行解释，以便将原文中使用的形象所传达的意义再现出来。再如：1) With determination, with luck, and with the help from lots of good people, I was able to **rise from the ashes**. 凭着自己的决心和运气，凭着许许多多的善良的人们的帮助，我终于可以**东山再起了**。2) He has not even "a nodding acquaintance", because he is **an iceberg**. 他甚至连点头之交的朋友也没有一个，因为他是一个冷酷无情的人。

【例6】

原　文：Yes, young boys are the same as lightening. They both dart around fast and you just can't tell what they are going to do. They both act unpredictably. They never stay still. Both are always darting around from place to place. They will shoot aimlessly, too. They will both shoot anywhere, not aiming away from people's camps, not caring what they hit. That is why they both cause damage.

译　文：是的，小男孩跟闪电一样。他们都到处乱窜，你搞不清他们要做什么。他们的行为都有点不可预测。他们从来不会静静地待在哪儿。他们总是从某处窜向另一处。他们还毫无目的地乱窜。他们都会到处乱跑，不是避开人们的营地，不管他们碰到了什么。那就是为什么他们都会造成破坏。（束定芳 译）

【点评】在讨论隐喻翻译时，不能忽视对延喻（extended metaphor）翻译的探讨。延喻是隐喻中的一种，其特点是先将某一物比作另一物，然后再对这种比较进行延伸（develop）和拓展（expand）。再如，1) Laws are like cobwebs, where the small flies are caught and the great break through. (Francis Bacon) 法律犹如蛛网，小的苍蝇被网住了而大苍蝇却冲破而过。2) A photographer is the cod, which produces a million eggs in order that one may reach maturity. (Bernard Shaw) 摄影师是豆荚，豆荚里蹦出百万个豆子，期望其中有一个能够成熟。

　　翻译延喻时，一定要考虑到喻体以及在该喻体基础上所作的延伸性描述。比如，本例中小男孩被喻为闪电，因此，闪电为喻体；接下来是对他们的行为进行延伸性描述，但这些描述均与闪电密切相关。在翻译成汉语时，必须选择与闪电相关的词语进行描述。这样才能在目的语中形成同英语原文一样的延喻。

【例7】

原　文：All the time the creeping fear that he would never come back to her grew strong within her.

译文一：那种一直令她毛骨悚然的恐惧愈来愈强烈——她感到他将永远离他而去。

译文二：他永远也不会回到她的身边。每时每刻，这种令她感到毛骨悚然的恐惧在她内心深处变得越来越强烈。（李明 译）

【点评】隐喻翻译可谓复杂多变。隐喻翻译给译者以多种选择的方式：要么传递其意义，要么重塑其形象，要么对其意义进行适度调整，要么对其意义和形象进行紧密结合。而这一切均与语境因素、文化因素及文本因素等密切相关。本例英语原文中的 the creeping fear 是隐喻表达，是 the fear that gives you a very strong feeling of horror 之意。英语原文中，充当整个句子主语的是名词短语 the creeping fear，紧跟其后，由 that 引导的从句是一个定语从句，因而整个句子是一个主从复合句，谓语由系表结构 grew strong 承担。类似这样的句子，看起来不是很长的句子，但翻译起来却特别棘手。译文一使用了破折号将原文的定语从句 that he would never come back to her 所表达的信息单独列出来，放在破折号后面，并凭空添加了"她感到"这一信息：她感到他将永远离他而去。但我们发现，尽管译者为翻译这句话做了极大努力，但译文仍缺乏关联性，而且在某种程度上篡改了原文之意。译文二作了新的尝试，尽可能摆脱原文束缚，将原文的定语从句译成独立的一个句子作为背景信息予以交代：他永远也不会回到她的身边。接着，译者再将整个主句翻译成：这种令她感到毛骨悚然的恐惧在她内心深处变得越来越强烈。这样，原文作者旨在表达的意思应该说是充分地传达出来了，而且汉语译文也比较自然和地道。

三、翻译比较与欣赏

【例1】

原　文：Some books are to be tasted, others to be swallowed and some few to be chewed and digested.

译文一：有些书只需浅尝，有些书可以狼吞，有些书要细嚼慢咽，漫漫消化。（廖运范 译）

译文二：一些书浅尝即可，另一些书却要囫囵吞下，只有少数的书才值得咀嚼和消化。（李鑫华 译）

译文三：书有可浅尝者，有可吞食者，少数则须咀嚼消化。（王佐良 译）

【例2】

原　　文：If beauty means something, yet we must not seek to interpret the meaning. If we glimpse the unutterable, it is unwise to try to utter it, nor should we seek to invest with significance that which we cannot grasp. Beauty in terms of our human meanings is meaningless.

译文一：如果美有某种意义的话，那我们切不可去阐明它。如果我们看到不可言传的东西而硬要把它说出来，这是不明智的，我们也不应该给我们所不了解的东西寻找一个意义。用人类的语言来解释美，美就成为毫无意义的了。

译文二：如果美即是美，那么我们则大可不必去诠释美为何物。只可意会的东西，又何必硬要去言传？又何必要牵强地去附会？其实，美之所以妙，妙就妙在不可言传。

【例3】

原　　文：A notion has taken hold in the United States to the effect that the only people who should be encouraged to bring children into the world are those who can afford them.

译文一：一种观点已经在美国站稳脚跟，即那些被鼓励把孩子带到这个世界的人是那些养得起孩子的人。（傅敬民等 用例）

译文二：在美国有一种根深蒂固的观点，说是只有那些抚养得起子女的人才应鼓励其生育。（傅敬民等 用例）

译文三：在美国一直有这样一种观念：只有那些能够供养得起孩子的人才应受到鼓励将孩子带到这个世界上来。（李明 译）

【例 4】

原　文：When I was a child I thought
　　　　The new moon was a cradle
　　　　The full moon was granny's round face

　　　　The new moon was a banana
　　　　The full moon was a big cake

　　　　When I was a child
　　　　I never saw the moon
　　　　I only saw what I wanted to see

　　　　And now I see the moon
　　　　It's the moon
　　　　Only the moon and nothing but the moon

译文一：我小时候想
　　　　新月是个摇篮
　　　　满月是奶奶的脸

　　　　新月是只香蕉
　　　　满月是块大饼

　　　　我还是个孩子时
　　　　我从未见过月亮
　　　　我只见到了我所想见的

现在我看到了月亮

月亮

除了月亮，还是月亮。（束定芳 译）

译文二：孩提时

我心中的新月是摇篮

满月是奶奶那圆圆的脸

我心中的新月是香蕉

满月是一块大大的蛋糕

少年时

我再也没有见到月亮

我只见到我想见到的东西

现在

我看到了月亮

就是那个月亮

除了月亮，再无其他（李明 译）

四、翻 译 练 习

句子翻译

1. Happiness is like a visitor, a genial, exotic Aunt Tilly who turns up when you lease expect her, orders an extravagant round of drinks and then disappears, trailing a lingering scent of gardenias.

2. Habit is cable; every day we weave thread, and soon we cannot break it.
3. His friends in the audience shout at him to read the plaque. Frozen on the stage, Bill cannot.
4. For us, all bets were off. These were uncharted waters.
5. Kind hearts are the gardens; kind thoughts are the roots; kind words are the flowers; kind deeds are the fruit.
6. Her knowledge of love was purely theoretical, and she conceived of it as lambent flame, gentle as the fall of dew or the ripple of quiet water, and cool as the velvet-dark of summer nights. (Jack London, *Martin Eden*)
7. They realized that stopping drinking was only the first step on a long and at times difficult road to recovery from alcoholism.
8. Middlesex, now a shadow of the side that dominated English county cricket in the early 1980s, were brushed aside at Southampton.
9. In the last fifteen years there has been increasing evidence of athletes using drugs to boost their performance, and this problem was brought to light dramatically at the Seoul Olympics in 1988.
10. It is a moving account of his early childhood, his work in the theater and Hollywood, spiced with encounters with stars.

篇章翻译

篇章翻译 1

Though fond of many acquaintances, I desire an intimacy only with a few. The Man in Black, whom I have often mentioned, is one whose friendship I could wish to acquire, because he possesses my esteem. His manners, it is true, are tinctured with some strange inconsistencies, and he may be justly termed a humorist in a nation of humorists. Though he is generous even to profusion, he affects to be thought a prodigy of parsimony and prudence; though his conversation be replete with the most sordid and selfish maxims, his heart is dilated with the most unbounded love. I have known him profess himself a man-hater, while his cheek was glowing with compassion; and, while his looks were softened into pity, I have heard him use the language of the most unbounded ill-nature. Some affect humanity and tenderness, others boast of having such dispositions from Nature; but he is the only man I ever knew who seemed ashamed of his natural benevolence. He takes as much pains to hide his feelings, as any hypocrite would to conceal his indifference; but on every unguarded moment the mask drops off, and reveals him to the most superficial observer.

篇章翻译 2

1) Our tragedy today is a general and universal physical fear so long sustained by now that we can even bear it. 2) There are no longer problems of the spirit. 3) There is only the question: 4) When will I be blown up? 5) Because of this, the young man or woman writing today has forgotten the problems of the human heart in conflict with itself which alone can make good writing because only that is worth writing about, worth the agony and the sweat. 6) He must learn them again. 7) He must teach himself that the basest of all things is to be afraid; and, teaching himself that, forget it forever, leaving no room in his workshop for anything but the old verities and truths of the heart, the universal truths lacking which any story is ephemeral and doomed—love and honor and pity and pride and compassion and sacrifice. 8) Until he does so, he labors under a curse. 9) He writes not of love but of lust, of defeats in which nobody loses anything of value, of victories without hope and, worst of all, without pity or compassion.

第十九章 英语长句的翻译（一）

> 就句子的结构而论，西洋语言是法治的，中国语言是人治的。
>
> ——王力

一、理 论 探 讨

英语和汉语不属于同一个语系，因而在遣词造句、句法结构和行文方式等方面存在着很大差异，其中最重要的差异就是英语重形合，汉语重意合。这主要表现在英语句子各成分的相互结合常常需要使用恰当的结构性词语，以明示其词与词之间的结构关系。英语句子之所以枝蔓横生、互相攀附而又不失严谨、缜密，完全得益于英语这种语言中句子的形合特点，因为形合句句子内部的逻辑推理关系（如：因果、目的、取舍、转折等）与逻辑非推理关系（如：并列、承接、递进、选择、假设、条件等）非常清晰可辨，同注重隐含的意合句相比，形合句透明的能见度理所当然地远远大于意合句含蓄的能见度。比如：

原文：It is flattering to believe **that** they are too profound to be expressed so clearly **that** all **who** run may read, **and** very naturally it does not occur to such writers **that** the fault is with their own minds **which** have not the faculty of precise reflection. (W. S. Maugham, *Lucidity, Simplicity, Euphony*)

译文：认为自己的思想深奥，不可能表达得很清楚，让任何人都能理解，这是一种虚荣的念头。这样的作家当然不会想到，问题还是出在自己脑子缺乏精确思考的能力。（连淑能，1993：50）

从以上英语句子和汉语译文可以看出，英语句子需要借助于不同的连接词以明示其内涵逻辑，而与之相对应的汉语译文却主要是较强地依赖上下文来展示复句内涵逻辑的表意功能，即完全凭语义的贯通来行文，这是英语重形合、汉语重意合的重要表现。

此外，英语重形合还体现在大量运用介词上，介词成为连接词语、语句和从句的重要纽带，离开了介词可以说英语就无法成句。我们信手拈来一个句子，假如去掉句子中的介词，整个句子往往会变得难以卒读。再者，英语中"其他连接手段，如形态变化形式，包括词缀变化，动词、名词、代词、形容词和副词的形态变化（如性、数、格、时、体、语态、语气、比较级、人称等）及其保持前后一致的关系，广泛使用代词以保持前呼后应的关系，以及使用 it 和 there 作替补词（expletives）起连接作用等等"（连淑能，1993：52）也都是英语中重形合的表现。另外根据 Eric Partridge 的观点，英语句子十句有九句按 SV 或 SVO 排列，实际上，任何英语句子都可以还原成主谓提挈全句的基本程式。这说明了英语语言的高度形式化和严密逻辑性（范红升，1996：52）。以上诸多形式手段规约着英语句子各成分之间的排列，使得句子内部的语义关系一目了然；与此同时，正因为英语句子具备这一特点，英语句子里的限制和修饰成分可以不断叠加，形成非常复杂的复合长句，但即使是最长的句子也能够借助句中的连接词和其他外形手段来发掘其中的信息和语义逻辑关系。

重意合的汉语同英语有很大差别，汉语话语之间的词与词、句与句等语言单位之间的结合少用甚至不用形式连接手段，而主要是凭借语意上的关联进行，即"注重隐性连贯，注重逻辑事理顺序，注重功能、意义，注重以神统形"（连淑能，1993：53），所以句法结构形式短小精悍、灵活多变。因为它的意合特点，汉语里就没有像英语中经常使用的那些关系代词、关系副词、连接代词、连接副词，介词的使用也很少见，名词和动词等都没有形态变化，代词的使用远没有英语那样频繁，"语法意义和逻辑联系常隐含在字里行间"（连淑能，1993：54）。汉语的意合法是通过语序、词语本身、词汇接应、结构平行、重叠形式、反复、排比、对偶、对照、推理、约定俗成的紧缩句以及历经千锤百炼、言简意赅的四字格成语等来实现的。比如汉语的意合特点可以很好地表现在下面的例子之中：

枯藤老树昏鸦，小桥流水人家，古道西风瘦马。夕阳西下，断肠人在天涯。（马致远《天净沙·秋思》）

该首散曲小令文字简短却意蕴丰富，前三句每句只有六字，却都写了三样不同的事物，表面上看好像彼此之间没有联系，但通过后两句，就可以将这些事物有机联系起来了。由此可见，汉语句中各成分之间的相互结合依靠的是语义贯通。

因此，在对英汉两种语言进行互译时，其一是非常有必要对目标语的形合程度和意合程度有很好的把握；其二是必须弄清楚源语复杂的主从结构能否移译到目标语当中（Fawcett, 1997: 97）。由于英语为形态语言，其连接手段丰富多彩，形合程度高，汉语为非形态语言，连接手段不发达，形合程度低而意合程度高，在将英语翻译成汉语时，往往需要在汉语中以词汇的形式再现出源语中的形态，如动词的时态、名词的复数形式等；至于连接手段，由于汉语里不惯于使用，在汉语译文当中就应该省略掉源语中的连接手段，代之以汉语的意合句来再现源语的形合句所再现的语义关系。

本章同第二十章所讨论的都是英语长句的翻译。对于英语长句的翻译，可以有几种方法。本章主要介绍拆分扩句翻译法，也有人叫做分句翻译法。这种翻译法就是将原文中的某个单词、短语或从句从原文句子中分离出来，并根据译文的语义结构，将这些单词、短语或从句扩展开来，分别译成短语、从句，甚至是独立的句子等来进行翻译，并将它们置于句首、句中或句尾，以利于句子的总体安排。换言之，在翻译英语的长句时，可以将原文中的单个词或词组扩成句子，或者将一个句子拆开为两个以上的单句，即将句子成分前后加上的某些修饰语（如定语、状语、定语从句、状语从句）、多级短语、多级从句等翻译成句子。

1. 词的扩展

The Chinese seemed **justifiably** proud of their economic achievements.

中国人似乎为他们在经济上所取得的成就而自豪，**这是合乎情理的**。

2. 短语的扩展

1) He arrived in Washington **at a ripe moment internationally**.

他来到华盛顿，**就国际形势来说，时机正合适**。

2) It all began in the mid-1850s, when **Lowe's experiments with balloons** led him to believe in the existence of an upper stream of air that moved in an easterly direction, no matter what direction the lower currents flowed.

这一切始于 19 世纪 50 年代中期。当时，**洛乘气球进行多次试验**，这些试验使他相信，不管低空中的气流往什么方向移动，高空中总是存在着一股向东移动的气流。

3. 句子的扩展

His failure to observe the safety regulations resulted in an accident to the machinery.
由于没有遵守安全规则，他把机器弄出故障了。

二、译例举隅及翻译点评

【例1】

原　文：The senior leaders' departure could **curiously** help the two parties sink an age-long party feud.

译文一：**说也奇怪**，老一代领导人的离去竟然使这两个党陷入了长期的政党之间的不和。

译文二：老一代领导人的离去竟然使这两个政党陷入了长期的不和，**这确实让人百思不得其解**。

【点评】英语很多句子中的某个词语，尤其是副词，看上去是修饰与其相邻的某个成分，但实际上是对整个句子所陈述的内容进行描述、评述或评价，例如，本句中 curiously 是评述整个句子所描述的情况。在将该句翻译成汉语时，采用了两种处理办法：第一种是将该副词的意思先翻译出来，放到句首，即先将对整个句子的评述放到句首，造成一种悬念，然后再将句子所陈述的内容呈现出来。译文一就采用了这种表达方式。第二种是将句子所讲述的内容先呈现出来，然后再将副词翻译出来，作为对整个句子的评述。这两种翻译方法都叫做拆分扩句法。译文二就是这种处理方式。再如：1) He was **wisely** determined to give up smoking. 译文一：他很明智，下决心戒烟了。译文二：他下决心戒烟了，**这很明智**。2) Months of air-raids and a hundred-hour campaign turned Saddam into a permanent and professional anti-American who of course had the **joys** of schadenfreude at the news that Bush lost the election. 几个月以来的空袭和一场旷日持久的地面战使得萨达姆变成了一个以反美为终身职业的人，听到布什没有当选上总统的消息，他自然幸灾乐祸，**欣喜无比**。3) The prisoners are permitted to receive Red Cross food parcels and write **censored letters**. 那些战俘得到允许，可以领取由红十字会提供的食品包裹，也可以写信，不过所写信件要接受检查。

【例2】

原　文：The Congressman tends to be very interested in public works—such as new government buildings, water projects, military bases—**that will bring money to the area or improve living conditions there**.

译　文：那位国会议员往往对于公共建设工程，比如政府办公大楼、水利工程、军事基地等非常感兴趣。这些公共建设工程要么会为本地区开辟财路，要么会为本地区改善生活条件。（李明 译）

【点评】拆分是将英语的长句翻译成汉语时常用的翻译技巧。这是因为，英语的长句可以盘根错节，从句套从句，但在汉语中，尽管可以存在流水句，但汉语的行文方式同英语的行文方式却不尽相同。因此，在将英语的长句翻译成汉语时，必须根据汉语的地道表达方式进行适度调整。调整的方式之一就是根据英语原文，按照层次将原文所表达的意思在汉语中用不同的句子表达出来。本例句中原文只有一个句子，其中含有一个定语从句。但在汉语译文中，将其翻译成了两个句子，非常符合汉语的表达。这里的拆分是依据原文的语序来进行的。再如，1) Moreover, in China, government subsidies for housing and other necessities reduced household spending on these items to a mere 5%, **compared with 20%-40% in other Asian countries**. 此外，在中国，政府对住房和其他日用品进行补贴，使家庭在这些项目的支出上降到只占整个家庭支出的百分之五。在亚洲其他国家，这方面的支出却要占整个家庭支出的百分之二十至百分之四十。2) All members, **in order to ensure to all of them the rights and benefits resulting from membership**, shall fulfill in good faith the obligations assumed by them in accordance with the present Charter. 各会员国须依据本宪章真心实意地履行其所应承担之义务，以保证全体会员国享有作为会

员国资格而得到的各项权利和利益。3) Citibank, which often leads the way on reductions in the banking industry's lending rate, **today became the first major bank to cut its rate by a quarter point to 15%**. 花旗银行在降低银行业的借款利率方面往往走在前头。如今，它成为第一家将借款利率由零点二五降低到零点一五的主要银行。

【例3】

原　文：With a view to successfully maintaining a balanced system implemented by a basically even distribution of Federal resources, Federal financial aid is given only if a state has acceptable standards of administration.

译文一：一个州只有制定了合乎要求的管理标准，联邦政府才会给予财政援助，这样就可以通过实施基本上平均地分配联邦政府资源的办法，来确保维持一种平衡的财政制度。

译文二：考虑到要通过实施基本上平均地分配联邦政府的资源的办法来确保维持一种平衡的财政制度，联邦政府只有在一个州具备合乎要求的管理标准的情况下才给予财政援助。

【点评】这里的译文一采取了逆序翻译法，译文二采取了顺序翻译法。对于英语长句的汉译，采取逆序翻译法和顺序翻译法都是常见的做法。到底采取逆序翻译法还是顺序翻译法取决于所翻译的句子在整个篇章中与上下文的关系以及整个篇章的侧重点。比如在这里，使用译文一就着重表明了美国各州的所为与联邦政府给予财政援助的关系；使用译文二的行文方式则体现了联邦政府为维持平衡的财政制度而采取的办法。有时因英汉两种语言在行文方式上存在差异，对于长句的翻译只能采取逆序翻译法，如：1) A great number of graduate students were driven into the intellectual slum when in the United States the intellectual poor became the classic poor, the poor under the rather romantic guise of the Beat Generation, a real phenomenon in the late fifties. 美国在五十年代末期的一个重大社会现象是，贫穷的知识分子已经成为真正意义上的穷人，成为在"垮掉的一代"这个颇为浪漫的外衣掩护下的穷人，正是在这个时期，一大批大学毕业生被赶进了知识分子聚集的贫民窟。2) American business is much freer than most competitors—which are often restrained by unions, social policies, and regulations—to hire and fire, reorganize and deploy resources where they will be most productive. 在雇佣和解聘员工、配置和重组资源以发挥最大效用方面，美国企业享有较大自主权，而与其竞争的大多数外国企业则往往要受到各自的工会、各国的社会政策及规章制度的约束。

【例4】

原　文：Behaviorists suggest that the child who is raised in an environment where there are many stimuli which develop his or her capacity for appropriate responses will experience greater intellectual development.

译　文：行为主义者的看法是，如果一个儿童在有许多刺激物的环境里长大，而这些刺激物能够发展其作出适当反应的能力，那么，这个儿童将会有更高的智力发展。

【点评】根据上下文的逻辑关系可以看出，本句中 suggest 的词义不是 propose，而是 bring an idea into the mind，故译为"……的看法是"。译文中把 who 引导的定语从句译为条件句，这是翻译技巧允许的，因为定语从句有时从原因、结果、目的或条件等方面对被修饰词加以限定，为了更确切地表明这种逻辑关系，可译成相应的状语从句。这样处理的前提是对语法结构、上下文的逻辑关系有深刻的理解。此外，译文对 where 引导的定语从句采用合译法，而对 which 引导的定语从句采用分译法，使译文在表达原意的前提下，读起来更为通顺。

【例5】

原　文：A book, tight shut, is but a block of paper.
译文一：一本书，紧紧合上，只是一叠纸。
译文二：一本书，如果紧紧合上不读，只是一叠纸。

译文三：一本书，如果紧紧合上不读，只是一叠废纸。

译文四：闲置之书只是一叠废纸。

【点评】 上面同一个句子的四个译文，可以体现翻译的不同层次。译文一，与原文似乎丝丝入扣，但却显得支离破碎、关系不清、语意不足；译文二，增加了"如果……不读"，意思明白无误，只是觉得"言犹未尽"；译文三，又增加了一个"废"字，这可是点睛之举。能否译出这个"废"字，是翻译这个句子的关键，也是判断这个译文优劣的一个重要标准。不读的书，不仅是一叠纸，而且是叠废纸。因为如果是叠白纸，还可画出最新最美的图画，只有废纸才是无价值的东西。一个"废"字，说话者的语意才得以充分表达。译文三的不足之处，就是行文拖沓累赘；而译文四则简明扼要，笔酣墨浓了。

【例6】

原　文：It was a day as fresh as grass growing up and clouds going over and butterflies coming down can make it. It was a day compounded from silences of bee and flower and ocean and land, which were not silences at all, but motions, stirs, flutters, risings, fallings, each in its own time and matchless rhythm.

译文一：绿草萋萋，白云冉冉，彩蝶翩翩，这日子是如此清新；蜜蜂无言，春花不语，海波声歇，大地音寂，这日子是如此安静。然而并非安静，因为万物各以其独特的节奏，或动，或摇，或震，或起，或伏。

译文二：绿草萋萋，白云飘飘，蝴蝶翩翩，那天就是那么让人心旷神怡；蜜蜂无言，花儿不语，海浪歇息，大地静默，那天就是那么寂静无声，但实际上，万事万物根本毫不静止，而是按照各自的时间和独特的节奏不停地运动着、不停地摇动着、不停地摆动着、不停地上升着、不停地下降着。（李明译）

【点评】 对于词语的选择，第四章已经讲过。对于较长句子的翻译，词语的选择就显得更为重要，因为词语不仅体现意义，而且体现语体、节奏、音像效果以及语义连贯。译文一之所以读来佶屈聱牙，就是因为在词语的选择上没有考虑到词语所体现的意义、语体、节奏、音像效果以及语义连贯。文字的长短并不能决定语义的优劣。换言之，译文一在文字的数量上比译文二要短，但由于选词的不甚恰当，译文一读来非常不顺。译文二则对词语进行了精心选择，不仅考虑到词语的意义，还考虑到它们的语体、节奏、音像效果及语义连贯，因而译文读来文从字顺。

【例7】

原　文：Hopeful renters may be feeling the heat this summer as mounting temperatures are matched by mounting prices—and seemingly surpassed by the growing number of New Yorkers and soon-to-be New Yorkers looking for a place to call home.

译文一：当不断攀升的气温与不断攀升的价格互相媲美的时候，满怀希望的出租人可能会感觉到今年夏天的热度——而这一热度似乎已被寻房为家的现成纽约客和即成纽约客之增长数字所超越。（宋德利，2014：120）

译文二：气温在不断上升，其速度似乎远不及那些正在寻找称之为"家"的住所的纽约本地居民的人数以及纽约未来居民的人数的增长速度，价格也因此在不断上涨。这样，充满希望的出租人算是感受到今年夏天的热度了。（李明 译）

【点评】原文是一个主句在前、由 as 引导的从句在后的主从复合句。要翻译好该英语句子，关键的关键就是要把握英语句子的结构，充分理解原文作者所要表达的意思，尤其是要充分理解原文中 and seemingly surpassed by the growing number of New Yorkers and soon-to-be New Yorkers looking for a place to call home 这部分同整个句子之间的关系。从译文一的汉语行文来看，译者似乎将这部分看做是 the heat 的定语从句了。这样理解显然是错误的。正是这一理解上的错误，导致译文完全不通。根据我们的理解，该部分同前面的 are matched by mounting prices 应理解为并列成分才符合整个句子的逻辑。而在翻译 surpassed 这个词语时，如果缺少灵活和变通，也会导致汉语译文不顺畅。我们通过转换视角的方式，将 surpassed 一词翻译成了"远不及"似乎能够使得整个段落的汉语译文通顺畅达。

三、翻译比较与欣赏

【例 1】

原　文：There are times when computers seem to operate like a mechanical "brain", but their achievements are not very spectacular when compared to what the minds of men can do.

译文一：计算机像机械"脑"进行运算的那个时代将会到来，但是如果把它们的成就和人脑所能做的事相比拟，其成就并不惊人。

译文二：有时计算机的运算看来好像机械"脑"一样，但它们的成就如与人脑所能做到的相比，并不非常出色。（黄汉生 译）

译文三：计算机运算起来有时像机械"脑"，但与人脑相比，其成就就要略微逊色。（黄忠廉、李亚舒 译）

译文四：有时计算机运算起来俨然就像一个机械"大脑"，但同人脑的处事能力相比，计算机所能做到的事情就非常有限了。（李明 译）

【例 2】

原　文：Success is often just an idea away.
译文一：成功往往只是一个念头的距离。
译文二：成功往往只是一念之差。
译文三：成功与否往往只是一念之差。

【例 3】

原　文：The big problem of comprehension of the English text and the bigger problem of how to express it in rich, present-day Chinese which ranges from the classical to the colloquial both have to be solved in the course of translation.

译文一：理解英语的内容是一个大问题，更大的问题是如何用丰富现代的、古典口语的中文来表达，这两个问题都在翻译中得到了解决。（傅敬民等 用例）

译文二：了解英文原意是一个大问题，现代汉语既然是文言口语，兼收并蓄，怎么用这样一个丰富多彩的文字来表达英文原文是一个更大的问题，这两个问题在翻译中都得解决。（傅敬民等 用例）

译文三：理解英语原文就是一个大问题，而要使用融古文和口语于一体的丰富多彩的现代汉语来表达英语原文则是一个更大的问题。但这两个问题都必须在翻译的过程中得到解决。（李明 译）

【例4】

原　文：**Stopping by Woods on a Snowy Evening**

　　　　Whose woods these are I think I know,

　　　　His house is in the village though;

　　　　He will not see me stopping here

　　　　To watch his woods fill up with snow.

　　　　My little horse must think it queer

　　　　To stop without a farmhouse near

　　　　Between the woods and the frozen lake

　　　　The darkest evening of the year.

　　　　He gives his harness bells a shake

　　　　To ask if there is some mistake.

　　　　The only other sound's the sweep

　　　　Of easy wind and downy flake.

The woods are lovely, dark and deep.

But I have promises to keep,

And miles to go before I sleep,

And miles to go before I sleep.

译　文：　雪夜林边停

　　　　 树林属谁我自明,
　　　　 他家住在那村中;
　　　　 安能料到我来此,
　　　　 赏观大雪漫林丛。

　　　　 小小马儿显疑情,
　　　　 为何偏在这儿停?
　　　　 冰湖林间无农舍,
　　　　 又逢雪夜黑蒙蒙。

　　　　 马儿甩动缰绳铃,
　　　　 欲告主人迷路径。
　　　　 只闻轻风簌簌语,
　　　　 鹅毛雪片渐渐生。

　　　　 夜林深沉尤可爱,
　　　　 信守诺言难久停。
　　　　 找店尚早需赶路,
　　　　 投宿之前再远行。（秦秀白 译）

四、翻译练习

> 句子翻译

1. Others are luckier they have prepared themselves for the change in their lives or they may be temperamentally suited to retirement.

2. I would like to point particularly to the last paragraph in which there is an admirable degree of pragmatism which I think is typical of that country in the present day.

3. He found a book especially useful and relaxing during the periods of waiting which all of us experience daily-waiting for meals, buses, doctors, hair-cuts, telephone calls, dates, performances to begin, or something to happen.

4. The boy, who was crying as if his heart would break, said, when I spoke to him, that he was very hungry, because he had had no food for two days.

5. The assertion that it was difficult, if not impossible, for a people to enjoy its basic rights unless it was able to determine freely its political status and to ensure freely its economic, social and cultural development was now scarcely contested.

6. While there are almost as many definitions of history as there are historians, modern practice most closely conforms to one that sees history as the attempt to recreate and explain the significant events of the past.

7. It is the insistence, as a first consideration, upon the interdependence of the various elements in, and parts of, the United States—a recognition of the old and permanently important manifestation of the American spirit of the pioneer.

8. Abraham Lincoln is the most famous instance of the claim that Americans often made that in their country a man may rise from the lowest to the highest position.

9. There was the growing realization that for all their vastness, the resources to be found in the oceans and seas were not inexhaustible. One could not hunt whales at will without risking their extermination or catch herring limitlessly without threatening survival of the stock.

10. There have been attempts to explain these taboos in terms of inappropriate social relationships either between those who are involved and those who are not simultaneously involved in the satisfaction of a bodily need, or between those already satiated and those who appear to be shamelessly gorging.

篇章翻译

篇章翻译 1

The Method of Scientific Research

1) The method of scientific investigation is nothing but the expression of the necessary mode of working of the human mind; it is simply the mode at which all phenomena are reasoned about, rendered precise and exact. 2) There is no more difference, but there is just the same kind of difference, between the mental operations of a man of science and those of an ordinary person, as there is between the operations and methods of a baker or of a butcher weighing out his goods in common scales, and the operations of a chemist in performing a difficult and complex analysis by means of his balance and finely graded weights. 3) It is not that the scales in the one case, and the balance in the other, differ in the principles of their construction or manner of working; but that the latter is a much finer apparatus and of course much more accurate in its measurement than the former.

篇章翻译 2

1) Since a particular bookstore happens to resemble a supermarket anyway, the inescapable, though perhaps unintended, message is that books are consumable items, meant to be devoured and forgotten, like potatoes or pizza. 2) The implied inclusion of books among the world's perishable goods is hardly made more agreeable by the reflection that increasing numbers of books these days do seem to be written with just such consumption in mind, and that most bookstores have become little more than news stands for hard cover publications of this sort, which are merchandised for a few weeks—sometimes only as long as they remain

on the best-seller lists—and are then retired to discount store (those jumbled graveyards of books, so saddening to the hearts of authors) shortly before dropping out of print altogether. 3) Books that are planned for rapid oblivion probably make some kind of economic sense to publishing houses, but as contribution to literature they amount to a contradiction in terms.

第二十章 英语长句的翻译（二）

> 英国人写文章常化零为整，而中国人写文章则往往化整为零。
>
> ——王力

一、理 论 探 讨

上一章的内容已经涉及英语长句的翻译。英语长句的翻译往往令英汉翻译者费尽心机。英语长句之所以难以翻译，主要是其中包含多个短语或从句，使得句子结构变得十分复杂，而要将这种复杂的句子结构翻译成汉语，则更是需要斟酌良久才能理顺。我们认为，要翻译好英语的长句，必须解决好对原文的理解和对原文的翻译问题。

根据孟庆升（2003：305-306）的分析，理解英语长句常常应采取以下步骤：

1. 通读全句，根据主语和谓语动词的数目以及有无连词来确定句子的类型，是简单句、并列复合句、主从复合句或由多个从句和分句组成的复杂句。

2. 找出长句中每个从句或分句的主要成分（主语和谓语），并进一步判明各次要成分（定、状、补、同位、插入语）与主要成分之间的关系。

3. 判断各从句或分句之间的并列或主从关系，并注意它们的时态、语气和语态以及是否有强调或省略等。

对于英语长句的汉译，除了第十九章中所讲到的拆分扩展翻译法或分句翻译法之外，还有顺序翻译法、逆序翻译法、插入翻译法和重新组合翻译法。现分类介绍如下：

1. 顺序翻译法

所谓顺序翻译法就是，基本上按英语句子的语序把英语长句"化整为零"，就是在英语原句的连接处，如使用关联词语处、并列或转接处、后续成分与主体连接处等按意群将英语的长句断开翻译成若干汉语分句（赵桂华，2002：112-113）。如：The problem is that in the last generation or so we've come to assume that women should be able, and should want, to do everything that by tradition men have done at the same time as pretty well everything that by tradition women have done.（问题是，在过去的二三十年时间里，我们已经认定，妇女们应该能够且应该想做男人们传统上所做的一切，而同时也能够且想做得跟妇人们传统上所做的一切同样好。）

顺序翻译法是在翻译英语长句时最经常使用，也是最便利的翻译方法。在遇到英语长句时，译者应首先考虑能否将此长句化整为零，在采用顺序翻译法时，要注意的一个问题是，适当运用汉语的关联词。因为英语长句往往是由各种不同的从句和短语构成的。这些附加成分可以通过词形变化或从属连词的应用，使他们自己在句中所起的功能十分明显，而当这种长句被分割成几个汉语分句时，各分句之间的这种关系就要靠巧妙地运用汉语关联词来体现，有时候则要运用重复手段（如在处理定语从句中的关系代词等时）。

2. 逆序翻译法

逆序翻译法是指在翻译英语长句时，将英语长句中所传达的信息在译文中分割成若干短句，然后再按照汉语习惯表达法进行重新安排，很多时候，汉语译文中各分句的顺序同原文中信息铺陈的顺序恰好相反，比如汉语复合句中往往是次要信息前置，主要信息后置（少数情况除外），而英语复合句则往往将主要信息前置，次要信息后置。也就是说，将英语句子信息前重心移向汉语句子后重心的翻译方法，我们往往称之为逆序翻译法。本书第十三章"翻译中句子结构的调整"中对此做了大量介绍。再如：A great number of graduate students were driven into the intellectual slum when in the United States the intellectual poor became the classic poor, the poor under the rather romantic guise of the Beat Generation, a real phenomenon in the late fifties.（这是50年代后期在美国出现的一个真实现象：贫穷的知识分子在"垮掉的一代"这种颇为浪漫的姿态掩护下成为美国典型的穷人，正是在这个时候，一大批大学毕业生被赶进了"知识分子的贫民窟"。）

3. 插入翻译法

插入翻译法就是利用破折号、括号将原文句子中的某部分信息以插入成分的方式插入到译文当中。在英译汉中采用插入语往往有两种情况：一是将英语原文中已有的插入语直接翻译成汉语中的插入成分放到汉语译文当中；二是英语原文中没有插入语，但由于其附加成分很多，且结构复杂。这时，汉语译文中就不得不采用插入法将其中的某部分信息用插入语的方式置于译文当中。英语中含有同位语从句的句子在汉译时常常采用这种方法。如：1) Although fluent in English, he uses—and sometimes nitpicks with translators, a ploy that gives him time to ponder his answers. 尽管他英语很流利，但他仍然要，——有时还要挑译员的毛病——运用一种策略来给自己争取时间思考如何回答问题。2) The snow falls on every wood and field, and no crevice is forgotten: by the river and the pond, on the hill and in the valley. 雪，飘落在每一片森林、每一片田野上：河边、湖畔、山上、谷底等到处都是——就连岩石上的裂缝中也都盖满了雪。

4. 重新组合翻译法

在汉译英语长句过程中纯粹运用顺序翻译法、逆序翻译法、插入翻译法或第十九章中所讲到的分句翻译法的时候并不多见，更多时候则是需要将以上几种或各种翻译法进行综合运用，这便是重新组合翻译法，或曰综合翻译法。重新组合翻译法又分抽叙翻译法和插叙翻译法两类（王宏印，2002：220）。前者是指在句首、句尾不便起译的情况下，从句子的中间选取一个便于起译且能带动全句的起点，以便统领译文全句，使其他部分依次跟上。插叙翻译法是指在分析原句时发现句子中存在某一相对游离的成分，或者在安排译句时存在暂时安排不上合适位置的成分，这时，可以先将这一部分搁置一旁，待全句译文基本上安排妥当之后，再插入句中某个适当的位置，必要时也可以用括号或者破折号将其与其他部分隔开来行文（出处同上），使译文行文流畅自然，符合汉语表达习惯。比如：

原文：In that same village, and in one of these very houses (which, to tell you the precise truth, was sadly time-worn and weather-beaten), there lived many years since, while the country was yet a province of Great Britain, a simple good-natured fellow of the name of Rip Van Winkle.

译文：许多年前（那时这片土地还属于大不列颠），就在这同样的一座村庄里，就在这同样的一所房子里（这类房子，说实话，因年深月久、风吹雨打而破烂不堪），一直住着一个淳朴善良的伙计，他叫瑞普·凡·温克尔。（李明 译）

这里的英语原文主句采用的是 there be 的变体结构 there lived，这属于英语的倒装结构。整个句子的句首是两个状语短语 In that same village 和 in one of these very houses，在谓语动词 lived 和主语 a simple good-natured fellow 之间插入了状语 many years since, while the country was yet a province of Great Britain。如果在汉语译文中按照英语原文的语序行文，汉语译文就会因地点状语过长以及汉语习惯于时间状语先于地点状语的表达方式而显得不通畅，故译文从原句中的时间状语开始翻译，接着安排地点状语，再接着谓语跟上，最后是原文中的主语。与此同时，在翻译原句中的时间状语 many years since, while the country was yet a province of Great Britain 时，又采取了插叙翻译法，即将 while the country was yet a province of Great Britain 用括号"（那时这片土地还属于大不列颠）"置于"许多年前"之后。因此，这里的汉语译文采用了抽叙翻译法和插叙翻译法的组合。译文符合汉语表达习惯，通顺、地道、流畅。

下面再看一个运用插叙翻译法的例子：

原文：These new observational capabilities would result in simply a mass of details were it not for the fact that theoretical understanding has reached the stage at which it is becoming possible to indicate the kind of measurements required for reliable weather forecasting.

译文：理论上的认识现在已经达到了逐渐能够指明各种测量（这类测量对于天气预报的可靠性不可或缺）类型的阶段，如果没有达到这个阶段，即使有了这些新型的各种观察能力，所收集到的仍然只能是一堆杂乱无章的数据。

重新组合翻译法的关键就在于透彻理解原文的意思，抓住原文的精神实质，在汉语表达时求得神似而不求形似。翻译的情况是千变万化的，作为译者，要充分领会和把握各种翻译技巧的精神实质，做到在翻译过程中以不变应万变，大胆运用灵活多变的翻译方法，不断锤炼，最终达到至善至美的境界。

二、译例举隅及翻译点评

【例1】

原　文：The days of his youth appeared like dreams before him, and he recalled the serious moment when his father placed him at the entrance of the two roads—one leading to a peaceful, sunny place, covered with flowers, fruits and resounding with soft, sweet songs; the other leading to a deep, dark cave, which was endless, where poison flowed instead of water and where devils and poisonous snakes hissed and crawled.

原文一：年轻时代的美好时光梦幻般地浮现在他的眼前。他会想起早年的严肃时刻——父亲将他放在人生的岔路口上，摆在他面前有两条道路，供他挑选：一条路是通向和平宁静、阳光灿烂的胜境，那里缀满了鲜花、硕果，到处回荡着柔和、甜美的歌声；另一条路则通向黑暗的永无止境的深窟，那里的河流流淌的不是清水而是毒汁，在那里，恶魔肆虐，毒蛇嘶嘶爬动。

译文二：青年时代的时光如梦一般浮现在他眼前。他回忆起当年那个严肃的时刻——父亲将他放在人生的岔路口上：一条路通向和平宁静、阳光灿烂的佳境，那里百花齐放、果实累累，到处回荡着柔和、甜美的歌声；另一条路通向没有尽头的黑暗的深渊，那里流淌的不是清水，而是毒液，那里魔鬼肆虐、毒蛇咝咝。（李明 译）

【点评】原文为并列句，由两个分句组成。第二个分句带一个由 when 引导的定语从句，定语从句中在名词短语 the two roads 之后有两个同位语 one leading to… 和 the other leading to…。在后一个同位语中有三个定语从句，均修饰名词 cave。可见，原文是非常复杂的句子。翻译此句子首先是要弄清原文句子结构和所传达的意义，接着在表达阶段要选择恰当方式传达原文信息，译文一和译文二均选用破折号"——"来翻译 the serious moment 之后由 when 引导的定语从句不失为最佳办法。另外，在同位语"一条路……"之前均使用冒号"："也很好地再现了原文句子结构信息。接下来就要斟酌所选择的词语，使得译文既要准确，又要简洁。译文一在选词上有以下不恰当之处：1) 说"缀满了鲜花"通顺，但说"缀满了硕果"似不妥，汉语中多说"挂满了硕果"；且将 fruits 翻译成"硕果"属超额翻译，翻译成"果实"足矣；2) 用"永无止境的"来修饰"深窟"欠妥当，"永无止境"多用于修饰或说明抽象概念的东西，如"学习永无止境"等；3) 将 where poison flowed instead of water 翻译成"那里的河流流淌的不是清水而是毒汁"亦属超额翻译,原文中没有出现"河流",将 poison 翻译成"毒汁"在文字上欠练达,"毒汁"给人的印象是量很小,和"流淌"不能搭配使用;4) 拟声词 hiss 表示蛇向前爬行的声音,一般翻译成"咝咝"而不是"嘶嘶"。译文总共使用了 157 个字,译文二只用了 133 个字。译文二更简洁、通顺、达意。

【例 2】

原　文:For whether the change is temporary and tactical, or lasting and basic, our task is essentially the same to transform that change into a permanent condition devoted to the purpose of a secure peace and mankind's aspiration for a better life.

译　文:因为不管这种变化是暂时性的、策略性的,抑或是持久性的、根本性的,我们的任务从本质上讲都一样,那就是,要把这种变化转换成一种长久局面——这种局面致力于实现牢靠的和平,致力于满足人类追求更加美好生活的愿望。(李明 译)

【点评】对于英语长句的翻译,在汉语中所应采取的最好办法之一便是使用短句并依据原文的顺序进行翻译。汉语主要重意合,多使用短句表达,短句不断叠加,娓娓道来,说话人或写作者的意思就渐渐传达出来。在英汉翻译中也可以采用汉语的这种使用短句的表述方式对原文所传达的意思进行表达,这样做不仅可以使译文忠实于原文,更可以使译文符合地道的汉语表达。再如:My parents insisted upon college instead of a conservatory of music, and to college I went—quite happily, as I remember, for although I loved my violin and spent most of my spare time practicing, I had many other interests.(我的父母坚持要我上大学,而不是进音乐学院,于是我就上了大学——在我的记忆中,我当时上大学还是挺高兴的,因为,虽说我酷爱小提琴,也花费了大量业余时间练习小提琴,但我还有许多其他爱好。)(李明 译)

【例3】

原　文：From **what is stated above**, it is learned **that** the sun's heat can pass through the empty space between the sun and the atmosphere **that** surrounds the earth, and **that** most of the heat is dispersed through the atmosphere and lost, **which is really what happens** in the practical case, **but to what extent it is lost** has not been found out.

译　文：由上述可知，太阳的热量可以穿过太阳与地球大气层之间的真空，而大多热量在通过大气层时都扩散消耗了。实际发生的情况正是如此。但是热量的损失究竟达到什么程度，目前尚未弄清楚。（郭富强 用例）

【点评】原文是一个含有多个从句的主从复合句。具体说来，主干部分有两个并列的主语从句，分别由 that 引导，在第一个主语从句中有一个限定性定语从句 that surrounds the earth，在第二个主语从句中有一个非限定性定语从句 which is really what happens in the practical case，该非限定性定语从句中又含有一个表语从句 what happens，最后一个分句由 but 引出，同 it is learned that... 并列。在句首的介词 from 之后是宾语从句。在翻译长句时，弄清楚长句中各个分句之间和从句之间的关系至关重要。这是正确翻译长句的基础，不管采用什么样的方法对长句进行翻译都是如此。

【例4】

原　文：On the whole such a conclusion can be drawn with a certain degree of confidence but only if the child can be assumed to have had the same attitude towards the test as the other with whom he is compared, and only if he was not punished by lack of relevant information which they possessed.

译文一：总的来说，得出这样的一个结论是有一定程度把握的，但是必须具备两个条件：能够假定这个孩子对测试的态度和与他相比的另一个孩子的态度相同；他也没有因缺乏别的孩子已掌握的有关知识而被扣分。

译文二：总的来说，得出这样的结论一定要在一定程度上有所把握，但必须具备两个条件，一是要假定这个孩子对测试的态度与同他相比照的另一个孩

子的态度一直相同，二是即使他缺乏相关知识，也不应扣分。（李明 译）

【点评】原文中两个 only if 引导的从句显然使整个句子变得复杂，可是由于有并列连词 but 和 and，整句话的逻辑关系十分清楚，即：……能够得出结论……但是只要……而且只要……。从上面的译文我们可以看出，为了使中文表达更加清楚，对 but only if... and only if... 的翻译，译文首先提纲挈领地表述为：但是必须具备两个条件……，这样的翻译处理方法给读者的感觉是：译文中没有从句，有的只是一些不同的分句。这样，读者读起来就轻松易懂，因为这样表达符合汉语的习惯，符合汉语作为意合语言的特征。

【例5】

原　文：Four milestones can be identified in the slow process by which the meteorology has been transformed from the beginning stages when it embraced most of sciences, on through an era of narrow concern with local weather conditions to the present, when its subject matter is so broadened and changed that it has even acquired a new name—the atmospheric science.

译文一：气象学已从包罗科学大部分内容的萌芽阶段经过只涉及当地气候条件的阶段而发展到目前阶段——这一缓慢的发展过程中曾出现了四个里程碑。由于这门学科的题材如此之广，变化如此之大，而今获得了一个新的名称——大气科学。（王宏印 用例）

译文二：气象学现在已经从包罗大部分科学的初始阶段，途经仅仅关注当地气候条件的视野狭窄的时期，进入到现代这个其主题变得非常宽泛，并已发生巨大变化，从而获得"气象科学"这个名称的时代。这一缓慢进程可以划分出四个里程碑式的阶段。（李明 译）

【点评】英语原文是一个长句，它以 Four milestones 开头总领 meteorology 的整个发展过程，继而以十分严密的连接手段和修饰成分列举了三个发展阶段，最后落脚到现代这个阶段，而这一阶段又通过由 when 所引导的非限定性定语从句对 meteorology 所获得的"气象科学"这一名称提供背景介绍。

因此，英文原文是先总括，后分述，在分述中是以时间的先后顺序进行铺排。在将该句翻译成汉语时，考虑到汉语的惯常表达方式，须将语序进行调整，即先分述，后总括。全句所讨论的话题为气象学，故将这一术语放在句首作主语。接着是对所提到的三个阶段——初始阶段、视野狭窄的时期和现代——进行铺陈。要正确理解原文的意思，还必须弄明白在 the present 之后由 when 所引导的从句的性质。我们认为，这是一个非限定性定语从句，the present 的意思就是 the present era，只有这样理解才符合原文之意。译文一显然是错误地理解了原文的意思，导致所给译文的前后两句之间缺乏语义连接和逻辑连贯。译文二在充分理解原文的情况之下，采用了合乎原文句意和汉语表达习惯的句子结构，尽最大努力再现了原文句子的信息。

【例6】

原　　文：As a righteous intellectual, I'm ashamed of the outrageous policy of intimidation employed by the die-hard conservatives who control the government to try to strangle social reform and to prevent the people from carrying forward their praiseworthy efforts towards building an ideal society.

译文一：作为一名具有正义感的知识分子，我对操纵着我国政府的顽固保守分子实行旨在扼杀社会改革并阻止人民为建立理想社会而做出的令人称道的努力的残暴威吓政策感到耻辱。

译文二：操纵着我国政府的顽固保守分子，实行残暴的威吓政策，企图扼杀社会改革并阻止人民为建立理想社会而做出的令人称道的努力。作为一名具有正义感的知识分子，我对此感到耻辱。

译文三：作为一名具有正义感的知识分子，我对操纵我国政府的顽固保守分子实行残暴的威吓政策感到耻辱，因为这个政策企图扼杀社会改革并阻止人民为建立理想社会而做出的令人称道的努力。

【点评】对于英语长句的翻译，要视具体情况而采取灵活多变的处理方式。通常对英语长句汉译的方法是化整为零，分散解决。对于译者来说，最要紧的是怎样把握好译文所要传达的信息要点，安排好译文的句子结构，从而生成通顺地道的译文。本例中的英语原文可谓是多枝共干的复合句，比如仅修饰 policy 这个词的定语就有五个：1) outrageous；2) of intimidation；3) employed by…；4) to try to strangle…；5) to prevent…。其中第 3 个定语 employed by… 之后又带一个定语从句 which control…，如果依照原文词序进行翻译，并用"的"结构进行翻译，则势必使得汉语译文中"政策"之前的定语过多（一共六个），造成"政策"这个名词不堪重负，整个译文也必然累赘不堪，从而难以让人接受。

造成译文一读来不通顺的原因是：第一，译者太过拘泥于英语原文的定语结构。其二，译者没有按照汉语民族逻辑思维方式进行意义的传达，因而无法为以汉语为母语的人所接受。这样，译文的可读性当然就很差。译文二就避免了译文一所出现的问题，对译文的句式进行了变化，且把长句拆成若干个短句，同时将词序进行了调整，比如把表态部分放置句尾，这就是所谓的"倒译法"。

译文三所采用的是"顺译法"，译文对句子结构做了部分改变，并增加"因为"这一连词，使得前后两个句子在意义上连贯得通顺流畅。

【例 7】

原　文：Few mountains anywhere in the world are more aptly named than the Great Smokies. Rank upon rank of smoothly rounded ridges recede toward the horizon like shadowy silhouettes, their contours blurred during the summer months by an ever-present haze—the product of incalculable quantities of vapor exhaled into the air by the luxuriant mantle of forest that covers these well-watered slopes.

译文一：世界上任何地方都没有什么山的命名比大烟山更贴切了。光溜溜、圆乎乎的山岭，就像隐隐约约的剪影，一道一道地朝着地平线的方向下降，它们的轮廓在夏季里，被必不可少的烟雾弄得模糊不清——而这些烟雾就是覆盖这些潮湿的山坡的森林所形成的丰富的覆盖物所发散到空中的大量的水蒸气的产物。（宋德利，2014：118-119）

译文二：堪称名实相符之山者，大烟山为世间绝无仅有。线条圆柔的道道山岭透迤不绝，酷似朦朦胧胧的剪影被赋予了生命，朝地平线缓缓蠕动。夏季，潮湿的山坡透过茂密的森林，把夏季必有的大量水蒸气源源不断地发散到空中，致使此地终日烟雾缭绕，山影憧憧。此时的大烟山，迷迷蒙蒙，虚无缥缈，宛若仙境。（宋德利，2014：118-119）

译文三：世界上哪个地方的山的命名都没有比大烟山的命名更为贴切的了。那连绵不断、平滑而浑圆的山脊，犹如朦朦胧胧的影子，朝着地平线的方向渐渐隐去；它们的轮廓被夏季那永不消散的迷雾给罩住，一片模糊。茂密的森林覆盖着水分充足的山坡，那迷雾正是由这茂密的森林散发到空气中的大量水蒸气形成的。（李明 译）

【点评】原文出自美国出版的《我们的国家公园·大烟山》(*Our National Parks: Great Smoky Mountains*) 一书中的第一自然段。破折号后面的短语是同位语短语，与前面的名词 haze 同位，是对该词语的进一步说明。该同位语短语的名词短语是 the product of incalculable quantities of vapor，其中有两个由 of 引导的介词短语修饰中心名词 the product；其后面的过去分词短语 exhaled into the air by the luxuriant mantle of forest that covers these well-watered slopes 作前面名词短语的定语，该过去分词短语中又有一个定语从句 that covers these well-watered slopes，修饰前面的名词短语 the luxuriant mantle of forest。尽管破折号后面的这个短语是一个同位语短语，但由于它的修饰语较多，翻译起来就比较复杂，处理起来也比较棘手。

　　宋德利提供的两种译文中，译文一是字对字的硬译。据宋德利（2014：118-119）说，译文二是他根据汉语的惯常表达而凝练成的译文。他对自己所给出的译文二是这样点评的：这一段译文与原文相比就有点模糊哲学，因为译文虽然不是原来的语序，但原文包含的意思，一个也不少，在这里都朦朦胧胧地依稀可见。

　　但笔者读完译文二的感觉是，整个译文语篇性不足，而且最后的"此时的大烟山，迷迷蒙蒙，虚无缥缈，宛若仙境"这句话是原文中根本上就没有的，这是译者凭着自己的理解额外添加的文字。这在翻译中叫做"超额翻译"(overtranslation)。作为严肃的译者，应该尽量避免这样的翻译处理方式。原文固然结构复杂，在译文当中比较难以处理，但只要译者冥思苦想、绞尽脑汁，最终一定是可以找到解决方案的。

译文三观照到了原文的语篇性。原文谈的是"山"，接着谈的是"山脊"，谈完"山脊"再引出"迷雾"。我们认为，译文也应该按照这样的路径进行翻译，才能够将原文作者的意图充分传达出来。至于原文破折号后面的同位语短语 the product of incalculable quantities of vapor exhaled into the air by the luxuriant mantle of forest that covers these well-watered slopes，我也尝试过将它翻译成"覆盖着水分充足的山坡的茂密森林把大量水蒸气散发到空中，形成了这般迷雾"，但最终还是觉得这样表述与上面的行文搭配不够妥帖，故最终还是觉得应翻译成"茂密的森林覆盖着水分充足的山坡，那迷雾正是由这茂密的森林散发到空气中的大量水蒸气形成的"才读来文从字顺、一目了然。

三、翻译比较与欣赏

【例1】

原　文：There is nothing more disappointing to a hostess who has gone to a lot of trouble or expense than to have her guest so interested in talking politics or business with her husband that he fails to notice the flavor of the coffee, the lightness of the cake, or the attractiveness of the house, which may be her chief interest and pride. ("Western Manners")

译文一：最令女主人失望的是，她花了许多心神或费用来招待客人，可是这位客人只顾津津有味地与她的丈夫谈政治、谈生意，却没注意到香喷喷的咖啡，松软的糕点，或房间内讲究的陈设，而这些却可能是她感兴趣并引以自豪的主要所在。(连淑能 用例)

译文二：对于一个劳心费力、颇费资财地款待客人的女主人来说，如果客人只津津乐道于同自己的丈夫大谈政治和生意而忽视了咖啡的浓香、蛋糕的松软或房屋内考究的陈设等这些女主人可能更感兴趣和更感骄傲的所在，

那么，没有什么比这更令她失望的了。（李明 译）

【例2】

原　　文：There are swift rivers, slow, sluggish rivers, mighty rivers with several mouths, rivers that carry vast loads of alluvium to the sea, clear limpid rivers, rivers that at some seasons of the year have very much more water than at others, rivers that are made to generate vast quantities of electricity by their power, and rivers that carry great volumes of traffic.

译文一：河流多种多样。有的河水湍急，有的河流速缓慢，有的大河出海口有好几处，有的河带着大量冲积土入海，有的河清澈见底，有的河的水量在一年中的某些季节较少，而在某些季节里却很多，有的河利用其动力大量发电，有的河所负担的运输量很大。（李建军 用例）

译文二：江河有多种多样：有的江河水流湍急，有的江河水流缓慢，有的江河汹涌澎湃、多处入海，有的江河挟带泥沙、冲向大海，有的江河清澈见底，有的江河依不同季节而流量大小不一，有的江河充满威力，被用于发电，有的江河水深岸阔，适于大量行船。（李明 译）

【例3】

原　　文：One of my best speeches was delivered in Hyde Park in torrents of rain to six policemen sent to watch me, plus only the secretary of the society that had asked me to speak, who held an umbrella over me.

译文一：我最精彩的一次讲话是在海德公园讲的。那一天大雨倾盆，听讲的是派来监视我的六名警察，另外还有邀请我讲话的那个团体的秘书，他给我打着伞。（宋天锡等 用例）

译文二：我最精彩的一次讲话是在海德公园的暴雨中讲的。我的话是讲给六名派来监视我的警察听的，另外还有邀请我讲话的那个团体的唯一秘书，他给我打着伞。（宋天锡等 用例）

译文三：我最精彩的一次讲演是在海德公园。当时大雨倾盆，听众只有六名被指

派来监视我的警察。邀请我讲演的那个团体仅仅派来一个秘书,他替我打着伞。(宋天锡等 用例)

译文四:我最精彩的一次演讲是在海德公园进行的。当时正下着倾盆大雨,听我演讲的只有受人指派前来监视我的六名警察,再加上邀请我发表演讲的那个团体中的秘书一个人,当时他替我打着伞。(李明 译)

【例4】

原　文:There are several reasons why Kissinger no longer appears to be the magician the world press had made him out to be, an illusion which he failed to discourage because, as he would admit himself, he has a tendency toward megalomania.

译文一:有几个原因可以说明为什么基辛格不再看起来像全世界报界渲染的那样是个魔术师,他不愿打破这样的幻觉,因为,他自己也承认,他有一种自大狂的倾向。(傅敬民等 用例)

译文二:全世界报界曾经把基辛格渲染成魔术师一般的人物,他也没有阻止人们制造这种错误印象,因为正如他自己愿意承认的,他有一种自大狂的倾向。现在他不再像是这样的人物了,这有几个原因。(傅敬民等 用例)

译文三:基辛格曾被全世界报界渲染成魔术师般的人物,他当时也没能阻止人们所进行的这种虚幻的渲染,但现在,他似乎不再是这样的人物了。这有几个原因,因为,正如他自己所承认的,他有妄自尊大的倾向。(李明 译)

四、翻译练习

句子翻译

1. The moon, one day short of fullness, rode with me, first gliding smoothly, then bouncing over the bumpy stretches, now on my right, then straight ahead, finally disappearing as the road wound its way through the hills. (Mary E. Potter, "When the Moon Follows

Me")

2. But now it is realized that supplies of some of these resources are limited, and it is even possible to give a reasonable estimate of their "expectation of life", the time it will take to exhaust all known sources and reserves of these materials.

3. The court shall be composed of a body of independent judges, elected regardless of their nationality from among persons of high moral character, who possess the qualifications required in their respective countries for appointment to the highest judicial offices.

4. A singular disadvantage of the sea lies in the fact that after successfully surmounting one wave you discover that there is another behind it just as important and just as nervously anxious to do something effective in the way of swamping boats.

5. It has been recently shown that the increasingly complex technologies of today need nearly as much mathematics for their effective utilization as was required for their initial creation.

6. Americans who would be patriots must try to learn what it is that they have in common, what it is in the public that is worth cherishing and preserving; until they know that, their patriotism will have no more content than a bright, loud afternoon parade.

7. He needs to feel challenged, admired, put upon, despised, loved; he needs to feel cornered so he can outperform everyone, almost as though he enjoys overcoming adversity and showing off his brilliance and subtlety.

8. During the first three rounds of the talks, the Chinese side made it plain that as the two sides had agreed upon the three principles as the basis for the talks, it believed it is important for the British side to first of all confirm the agreements and understandings previously reached between the two sides, for this was the only way to enable the talks to move on the right track.

9. Then we are faced with a choice between using technology to provide and fulfill needs which have hitherto been regarded as unnecessary or, on the other hand, using technology to reduce the number of hours of work which a man must do in order to earn a given

standard of living.

10. Some people, tired out after all exhausting yet satisfying life revolving around work, are anxious to relax in retirement with all the strains relieved; others resent the prospect of being put on the "scrapheap", and seek alternative outlets for their energies and alternative sources of satisfaction or joy.

11. What the New Yorker would find missing is what many outsiders find oppressive and distasteful about New York—its rawness, tension, urgency; its bracing competitiveness; the rigor of its judgments; and the congested, democratic presence of so many other New Yorkers encased in their own world.

篇章翻译

篇章翻译 1

He was a man of fifty, and some, seeing that he had gone both bald and grey, thought he looked older. But the first physical impression was deceptive. He was tall and thick about the body, with something of a paunch, but he was also small-boned, active, light on his feet. In the same way, his head was massive, his forehead high and broad between the fringes of fair hair; but no one's face changed its expression quicker, and his smile was brilliant. Behind the thick lenses, his eyes were small and intensely bright, the eyes of a young and lively man. At a first glance, people might think he looked like a senator, it did not take them long to discover how mercurial he was. His temper was as quick as his smile, in everything he did his nerves seemed on the surface. In fact, people forgot all about the senator and began to complain that sympathy and emotion flowed too easily. Many of them disliked his love of display. Yet they were affected by the depth of his feeling. Nearly everyone recognized that, though it took some insight to perceive that he was not only a man of deep feeling, but also one of passionate pride.

篇章翻译 2

1) But owing to the constant presence of air currents, arranging both the dust and

vapor in strata of varying extent and density, and of high or low clouds which both absorb and reflect the light in varying degree, we see produced all those wondrous combinations of tints and those gorgeous ever-changing colors which are a constant source of admiration and delight to all who have the advantage of an uninterrupted view to the west and who are accustomed to watch for those not infrequent exhibitions of nature's kaleidoscopic color painting. 2) With every change in the altitude of the sun the display changes its characters; and most of all when it has sunk below the horizon, and owing to the more favorable angle a larger quantity of the colored light is reflected toward us. 3) These, as long as the sun was above the horizon, intercepted much of the light and color; but when the great luminary has passed away from our direct vision, its light shines more directly on the under sides of all the clouds and air strata of different densities.

附　录

附录一：中国翻译简史

　　中国的翻译事业历史悠久，约有两千余年光辉灿烂的历史，已经形成自己独树一帜的体系。中国的翻译活动最初是从佛经翻译开始的。译界许多学者均认为，中国的翻译事业迄今已经历五次大高潮（five peaks of translation activity），它们分别是：1) 东汉至唐宋时期的佛经翻译；2) 明末至清代"科学时期"的翻译；3) 五四运动时期的西学翻译；4) 建国初期至文革之前的东西方文学翻译；5) 二十世纪七十年代末至今翻译在各个领域繁荣发展的时期。

第一次高潮

东汉至唐宋时期的佛经翻译

　　中国最初的翻译始于佛经翻译，时间是东汉桓帝建和二年（即公元148年），译者为安世高，其人为安息（即波斯人）译了《安般守意经》等30多部佛经。

　　后来，支娄迦谶也来到中国翻译佛经。他同自己的学生支亮以及支亮的弟子支谦，号称"三支"，在当时佛经翻译方面享有盛名。其时，月支派里有一个叫竺法护的人，是一个大翻译家，译了175部佛经，对佛法的流传贡献甚大。

　　上述活动仅为民间私人事业，只是到符秦时代在释道安主持下设置了译场，从此，翻译才真正成为有组织的活动。道安（Dao'an）在此期间请来了天竺（即现在的印度）人鸠摩罗什（Kumârajîva, 344-413），略称"罗什"。罗什同其弟子僧肇一道翻译了《金刚经》《法华经》《维摩经》《中观论》和《百论》等共74部、384卷佛经，为佛教在中国的发展奠定了基础。其译文妙趣盎然，"有天然西域之语趣"，较好地再现了原作的精神和神韵，为我国翻译文学奠定了基础。他所翻译的经论后来成为中国佛教宗派依据的重要著作。

　　真谛（Paramartha, 499-569），南朝梁、陈时代来华的僧人。他是应梁武帝之邀（原本是西天竺人）来到中国，翻译佛经并传教。他与弟子一道翻译佛经共计49部，所译《摄大乘论》对中国佛教思想影响最大。

玄奘（Xuan Zang, 602-644），俗称"唐三藏""唐僧"，在我国家喻户晓。他与鸠摩罗什、真谛一起号称我国佛教三大翻译家或"译经三大家"。贞观二年（公元 826 年），玄奘去印度求经，17 年后归国，带回佛经 657 部。他还主持了更大规模的译场，用 19 年时间译经 75 部共 1 335 卷。玄奘深通佛学，精通梵文，汉语造诣精深，因而翻译出来的经论非常精确，在他主持下还纠正了旧译的许多错误，后人通常称玄奘主译的经论为"新译"。他不仅把佛经由梵文译成汉文，而且还把老子著作的一部分译成梵文，因而成为我国历史上第一个把汉文著作向国外介绍的中国人。

把玄奘称为我国古代翻译界巨星毫不为过，他在世界翻译史上也占有很高地位。现代印度学者柏乐天（P Prodham）曾说，玄奘是"有史以来翻译家中的第一人，他的业绩将永远被全世界的人们深深牢记"。

这一时期的佛经翻译不仅为我国的佛教作出了重大贡献，由佛经翻译而演绎出的有关翻译方法的论说构筑出中国早期翻译理论的雏形。比如释道安主张严格的直译，译文不增不减，以便忠实于原文的内容。鸠摩罗什则主张意译，主张对译文进行改动以便适应汉语的表达和文体，同时他还提倡译者署名。玄奘则主张灵活采用直译和意译的翻译方法，他提出了"既须求真，又须喻俗"的翻译标准，亦即今天所谓的"忠实，通顺"。他们三人关于翻译方法的主张，对我国后世翻译理论均产生了深远影响。

在佛经翻译取得辉煌成就的同时，当时我国其他领域的翻译工作方兴未艾。例如，服务于政治、外交的翻译古已有之。从周代开始，历代中央政府都没有接待外宾的机构。西汉张骞出使西域，沟通了汉朝和中亚各国的友好关系，促进了经济文化的交流与合作。在这类活动中，离开翻译是不行的。唐代末年，因无人赴印度求经，佛经翻译事业逐渐衰微。

➡ 第二次高潮
明末至清代"科学时期"的翻译

从明代万历年间到清代"科学时期"，在佛经翻译呈现一片衰落景象的同时，出现了徐光启、林纾（林琴南）、严复（严又陵）等为代表的介绍西欧各国科学、文学、哲学的翻译家。

第一个把西方近代科学思潮和方法引进我国的是徐光启（1562-1633）。他是明末科学家，十分重视当时科学技术事业的发展。他从意大利人（罗马天主教耶稣会会士）利玛窦（M. Ricci）那里学习天文、算法、火器等，跟他合译了古希腊人欧几里得（Euclid）的《几何原本》。两人又合写了《天学实义》，介绍天文知识。他还与利玛窦合作翻译过《测量法义》一卷，我国经纬度的精确概念，当始于此。他不懂外文，但经他勘定的术语，其中不少沿用至今。

林纾（1852-1924）是我国近代著名的文学家、文论家、诗人和画家，也是一位杰出的翻译家。他和他的合作者以口述笔记的方式翻译了 160 多部文学作品，其中最著名的有《巴黎茶花女遗事》(*La Dame au Camelias*)、《黑奴吁天录》(*Uncle Tom's Cabin*)、《块肉余生述》(*David Copperfield*)、《王子复仇记》(*Hamlet*) 等。林纾本人不懂外文，故他的译作删减、遗漏之处甚多，但可读性却很强，对介绍西方文学起了一定作用。这些译作第一次使中国读者接触到西方文学作品，尤其是英美文学作品，培养了他们对西方文学作品的兴趣，同时也打破了中国旧式章回小说的旧格式，对中国的文学创作也产生了很大影响。

严复（1853-1922）在我国翻译史上占有突出地位。他 13 岁入船政学堂，23 岁受派留学于英国海军学校。学成回国后钻研古文，因此他在外文和科学技术以及社会科学方面的造诣很深。他的翻译活动除涉及科技外，如他翻译了赫胥黎（T. H. Huxley）的《天演论》(*Evolution and Ethics and Other Essays*)，还涉及政治，如他翻译了甄克思（E. Jenks）的《社会通诠》(*A History of Politics*)，涉及经济，如翻译了亚当·斯密（A. Smith）的《原富》(*An Inquiry into the Nature and Causes of the Wealth of Nations*)，涉及法律，如翻译了孟德斯鸠（C. L. S. Montesquieu）的《法意》(*L'esprit des Lois*) 等。

严复每翻译一部书，都有一定的目的和意义。他常常借西方名著资产阶级思想家的著作表达自己的思想。他译书往往加上许多按语，发表自己的见解。

严复的另一巨大贡献是，他参照古代翻译佛经的经验，根据自己的翻译实践，在《天演论》(1898 年出版) 卷首的《译例言》中提出了著名的"信、达、雅"三字翻译标准。这一翻译标准近百年来一直为翻译界所普遍遵循。

第三次高潮

五四运动时期的西学翻译

五四运动是我国近代翻译史的分水岭。五四运动前后直至新中国建立的一段时期是我国翻译史上的重要时期,其翻译活动的规模和影响都超过了近代任何一个时期。

标志是:

1. 1915年《新青年》杂志一创刊,就开始译介西方文化思潮和文学作品。《新青年》高举批判封建旧文化、发展中国新文化的旗帜,提倡民主和科学。屠格涅夫、王尔德、莫泊桑、易卜生、泰戈尔、安德生等外国作家的作品相继在《新青年》上译载。

当时《新青年》社的成员既是新文化运动、新文学运动的成员,又是外国文化思潮的翻译者和介绍者。如陈独秀、胡适、刘半农、周作人等,都十分重视翻译介绍外国文学和外国文化思潮。

2. 1917年十月革命在俄国取得胜利之后,马克思主义随即传入中国。1920年陈独秀、陈望道在上海组织起第一个马克思主义研究会。同年陈望道从日文翻译的《共产党宣言》问世。郑次川翻译的《科学的社会主义》也问世,由李达负责编辑的《共产党宣言》《工钱、劳动与资本》《资本论入门》等也相继出版。此外,在当时的《晨报》副刊、《民国日报》副刊《党悟》上也不断有翻译和介绍马克思主义的文章发表。

此后,180万字的《资本论》三卷本于1938年第一次在上海翻译出版,译者为郭大力、王亚南。恩格斯、斯大林的著作也分别译介到中国。

在解放区延安,中共中央马列学院组织翻译了《列宁选集》20卷本。这样,马列主义在中国得到进一步传播。

不仅如此,1937年抗日战争开始后,我党成立了直属南方局领导的对外宣传小组,由周恩来领导,王炳南具体负责,任务是向国外翻译介绍毛泽东著作、八路军战报以及抗日文章,译者有许孟雄等人。这些有关抗战的报道在国外产生了巨大影响。

3. 鲁迅:中国现代翻译史上杰出的翻译家和披荆斩棘的开拓者。据统计,他一生中创作与翻译各半。其译作的特点是思想性强、涉及面广、体裁多样。他一生翻译介绍了大量作家的作品。据不完全统计,他翻译介绍了俄国、法国、英国、西班牙、荷兰、奥地利、芬兰、匈牙利、波兰、保加利亚、罗马尼亚、捷克、日本等14个国家近百位作家的 200 多种作品。鲁迅的文学生涯可以说是从翻译开始,又以翻译结束的。对于翻译事业,他表现了始终一贯的高度革命责任感和明确的目的性。

鲁迅和瞿秋白两人关于翻译问题的通信,为我们提供了一些应遵循的基本翻译原则。他同瞿秋白通过翻译实践,总结了许多宝贵的经验,在翻译标准问题上鲁迅的主要观点是:"凡是翻译,必须兼顾着两面,一当然力求其易解,一则保存原作的丰姿。"

4. 30 年代后期至 40 年代,楼适夷译介了高尔基的《老板》、斯诺的《西行漫记》;梅益翻译了《钢铁是怎样炼成的》,这些译作在抗日战争时期、解放战争时期以及解放后都曾经鼓舞教育了许许多多的中国读者。

5. 令国内外读者大为震惊的是,1947 年秋,我国第一次由世界书局出版了由朱生豪翻译的《莎士比亚戏剧全集》。

6. "左联"从 1930 年成立到 1936 年解散。虽然历时仅六年,但它对我国翻译文学的贡献非常巨大。当时许多作家在创作的同时,致力于翻译介绍外国文学,尤其是鲁迅、瞿秋白、茅盾、郭沫若、冯雪峰、周杨、夏衍等人,对翻译并传播马克思主义文艺理论和当时苏联社会主义现实主义作品作出了杰出的贡献。

总之,从五四运动至新中国成立这一时期,特别是 30 年代以后的进步翻译者,无论翻译哪方面的著作,都有一定的政治目的。他们或是直接输入马列主义以鼓动革命,或是借西方著名思想家、科学家的著作,来表达自己的思想和主张,以推动社会改革和社会进步。

➡ 第四次高潮
建国初期至文革之前的东西方文学翻译

第四次高潮可分为三个时期,其一是 1949 年至 1956 年上半年我国翻译队伍初具规模的时期;其二是 1956 年下半年至 1966 年上半年我国翻译事业有组织、有计划地发展时期;其三是 1966 年下半年至 1977 年我国翻译事业的停滞时期。

1949 年新中国成立后,我国翻译事业取得的巨大成就超过了历史上任何一个时期。这主要体现在我国有组织、有计划、有系统地翻译了《马克思恩格斯全集》和《毛泽东选集》。我们在翻译理论方面的研究成果令人瞩目,翻译水平大大提高,对翻译的标准也达成了共识。我们既把外国的文化和先进科学技术译介到中国来,同时也把中

国的国情和发展情况介绍到国外。（孟庆升，2003：6）

从建国之初到"文革"之前，只有短短的十七年时间。但50年代的十年时间是我国在这一阶段翻译最繁荣的时期。当时的重点放在译介东西方的文学作品上，尽管所译作品的数量远远比不上今天，但由于当时的组织得力，狠抓了计划译书和提高翻译质量两个环节，当时的译者也没有功利思想，因而译文质量普遍较高，所译作品堪称译文典范，成为中国不朽的名著名译，为后世翻译树立了榜样。

这一时期的翻译工作有以下几个特点（张培基，1980：5）：

1. 翻译工作者在党的领导下，有组织、有计划、有系统地进行工作，逐渐取代了抢译、乱译和重复浪费现象；

2. 翻译作品质量大大提高，逐渐克服了粗枝大叶、不负责任的风气；

3. 翻译工作者为了更好地服务于社会主义建设，开展了批评与自我批评，逐渐消除了过去各种不良现象和无人过问的状况；

4. 翻译工作者不仅肩负着外译汉的任务，同时也肩负着汉译外的任务，以便更好地宣传马列主义、毛泽东思想、介绍我国社会主义革命和建设的经验和我国的优秀文化遗产；

5. 对翻译标准的认识日趋统一，有效地推动了我国的翻译工作。

第五次高潮
20世纪70年代末至今翻译在各个领域繁荣发展的时期

1978年至今为我国翻译事业蓬勃发展的时期。1978后，随着我国对外开放的深入，我国的职业翻译队伍迅速壮大。

1978年至1990年间，全国共出版翻译著作28 500多种，其中社科翻译著作占7 400多种。所译重要著作有：《简明不列颠百科全书》《汉译世界学术名著丛书》《现代西方学术文库》《二十世纪西方哲学译丛》《西方学术译丛》《外国著名思想家译丛》《当代西方美学名著译文丛书》等。

外国电影、电视和戏剧方面的翻译工作也成绩斐然。

我国古典名著如《红楼梦》《水浒传》《西游记》《三国演义》等以及唐诗宋词等

分别以不同外文出版。

我国是一个多民族的国家,少数民族语翻译在我国翻译工作中占有特殊的地位。

我国机器翻译的研究始于 1957 年,起步不晚,1978 年以后有更大发展。

中国翻译工作者协会于 1982 年在北京宣告成立,并于 1987 年被国际翻译工作者联盟接纳为团体会员。中国翻译工作者已步入世界翻译之林。现在全国各省市均有省市翻译工作者协会。各高校外语学院或者外语系均开设了翻译课程,一支生力军正在茁壮成长,长江后浪推前浪,老翻译家们将退出,后起之秀将取而代之。

随着改革开放的不断深入,与国外的经济文化交流与合作不断加强,我国许多方面的工作将实行与国际"接轨"。因此,我国的翻译所涉及的领域已经拓展到除文学艺术之外的社科、科技、军事、外交、贸易、法律、文教、卫生等各个方面。正如刘宓庆先生(1999:Ⅱ)所说,第五次翻译高潮同中国翻译史上的任何一次翻译高潮相比,"信息量更庞大,涵盖面更广泛,题材体裁更丰富多彩,操作方式更灵活便捷,技术装备更先进,从业人员更众多,受益者更普遍,理论研究更活跃,人才培训更具规模。"

面广量大的翻译实务以及随之而来的许多翻译理论和实践问题将有待解决。我们要继承并学习先辈们的经验与成就,发扬他们的优秀译德和译风,学习和钻研先进的翻译理论,为进一步繁荣我国的翻译事业而奋斗。

附录二:翻译标准的新思考

一谈到翻译标准,立刻就会让人想起一百多年前译学的开创者严复所提出的至今仍具生命力的"信、达、雅"三字标准。毫无疑问,严复因提出"信、达、雅"三字翻译标准,为我国翻译事业的发展和翻译水平的提高做出了有益贡献,但其历史局限性也是不言而喻的。但时至今日,翻译界人士在考虑制定翻译标准也好,在具体所制定出的翻译标准也好,似乎都没有跳出严复所厘定的"信、达、雅"三字翻译标准的框框。比如,自严复之后,许多译家们根据自己的经验体会提出了各自的翻译标准,如林语堂的"忠实、通顺、美",瞿秋白的"信顺统一",朱生豪的"神韵"说,傅雷

的"神似"说,钱钟书的"化境"说,刘重德的"信、达、切"等,但这些翻译标准同严复所厘定的翻译标准没有本质上的区别。

我们认为,严复所提出的"信、达、雅"三字翻译标准存在三大缺陷:一是纯粹基于个人的翻译经验而提出,感性的成分较多;二是只注重追求译作同原作在语言层面上的相似或对等,而没有将作为社会交往行为的翻译活动置于社会文化大背景下进行考察,因而用此翻译标准评价译文很容易失之偏颇;三是具有单向度静态性的特点。这不仅表现在所使用的三个汉字都是形容词,因而具有静态性,还表现在这三个词的顺序始终如一,因而缺乏有效的动态性。我们认为,翻译时不可能总是"信、达、雅",有时因不同文本的特点而应达到"达、信、雅""雅、信、达"或"雅、达、信"的标准。这三大问题不仅在严复等人所提出的翻译标准中存在,在泰特勒所提出的翻译三原则中也多多少少地存在着。这是在结构主义语言学翻译观指导下所提出的翻译标准中易于出现的问题。

自20世纪80年代以来所引入的西方译论为我国翻译研究提供了有力借鉴,我国翻译理论界以此为契机对我国传统的翻译标准进行了重新审视,同时也引进了西方的诸如"等值""等效""等同""对等"等翻译新概念。但西方的翻译标准或准则均是基于语文习惯非常接近的西方语言文字之间的翻译而提出,若将它们直接用作语言文化差异较大的汉语同西方语言之间的翻译标准显然不合适。另外,西方的"所有这些提法,不管字面上如何不同,其实都与'忠实'的说法一脉相承"(辜正坤,2003:342)。机械地"把外国的译论'照搬'进来并力图取代中国传统译论的做法是无效的,行不通的……我们的任务就是要在严复开辟的道路上继续前进,去创立和发展一个完整的理论体系。在这样做的时候,我们必须从外国已有的译论研究成果中去吸取营养。"(沈苏儒,1998:147,148)这里,沈苏儒强调了从外国译学研究成果中吸取营养的重要性,但同时我们认为,我们还要从西方较为发达的研究语言性质的语言学和语言哲学中吸取营养。只有这样,我们才有可能具备更为宽阔的、更为科学的学术视野,真正把握翻译的本质,从而提出具有我国特色的翻译标准,为我国的译学建设服务。

哈蒂姆和梅森(Hatim & Mason, 2001: 3)认为,翻译是一定社会语境下发生的交际过程。沈苏儒(1998:156)也认为,翻译是一种跨语言、跨文化的交流。换言之,翻译是一种社会交往行为,其过程具有动态性。因此,要制定翻译标准,必须既要关注其"社会"和"行为"这两个属性,又要关注其动态的特性。"信、达、雅"三字翻译标准较多地关注原文和译文在语言层面上的忠实与通顺,而未将原文作者的写作意图、译者的主体创造性、译文在目的语中的效果等放入其中进行考察。因而它所关注的是两种语言之间的静态状态。再者,它主要是针对文学翻译而提出,而对如今广泛用于社会生活的内容繁复、形式多样、目的不一的非文学翻译或曰应用翻译却没有关注。这样,该翻译标准就不能较好地指导和服务于翻译实践。对翻译标准的探讨应关注语言同个体主体、自然世界以及社会世界这三者之间的关系。只有将对翻译活动发生影响的各种因素都考虑其中,所制定出的翻译标准才有可能具备充分的解释力。

当代哲学的发展既为我们提供了看待语言的新方式,也为我们提供了从事翻译研究的新视角。德国著名思想家和哲学家哈贝马斯的交往行为理论正是这样一种哲学。哈贝马斯认为,结构主义语言学只关注语言的系统(langue),而忽视言语(parole)的问题;结构主义认为,语言是有规律性的结构系统,而言语则仅仅是个人现象,不受规律制约,不可进行规律分析。哈贝马斯刚好持相反的观点。他认为,言语才是实际交往中所使用的,其单位是言语行为,该言语行为不仅受语言规律的制约,还受社会规范的制约。换言之,人们要合理地进行交往,其言语行为必须按照一定的社会规范和准则进行。(吕俊,2001:10)据此提出了普遍语用学的思想。

他的普遍语用学不再强调主观对客观的认识问题,而将重心放在主体与主体交往的主体间性上,并从中去寻找交际中所存在的合理性,即取得一种共识性。这样,他就将语言学在传统上仅重视句法与语义学的研究转向了语用研究上,即注重研究在主体间的交往中如何取得相互理解的内在规律,重视对语境条件和有能力言说的主体所建构的适合语境的语句并取得共识的有效性条件的研究。其普遍语用学理论不仅增加了在结构主义语言学中被排斥在外的言说主体与语境的内容,同时也关注起了社会世界对言语行动的接受与理解的准则与规范,把语言同个体主体、自然世界以及社会世界这三者的关系作了全面的理解和合理的解释。(吕俊,2001:10)

在哈贝马斯看来,交往行为就是以符号、语言、意识和文化等方式表现出来的人与人之间的相互关系和相互作用,或者说是主体之间借助语言符号、通过对话而达到相互理解、信任与和谐的过程(李彬,2003:204-205)。哈贝马斯认为,普遍语用学的功能有三项:"呈示世界中的某种东西、表达言说者的意向、建立合法的人际关系。"(哈贝马斯,1989:33)交往行为理论的重点在第三方面,即建立合理的人际关系。他认为,语言的意义不仅在于日常语言学派所主张的行为上面,而且在于它所体现的特定的人际关系方面。他说:"一个句子在被言说时,就被嵌入特定的人际关系中,通过一定的方式,每一个清晰的施行性话语既建立又呈示了某种人际关系"。(哈贝马斯,1989:35)所以,看待"以言行事"就不能只局限于行为本身,还需看到它所衍生的外在关系。为什么有的言语行为成功了而有的却失败了呢?个中原因就在人际关系上面:"只有当接受者不仅懂得被言说句子的意义,而且实际进入了言说者所欲求的关系时,一个言语行为才能是成功的。"(哈贝马斯,1989:60)

针对语用学的三项功能即呈现事实、建立关系和表达意向,哈贝马斯提出了三点要求,即相应于事实的真实性、相应于关系的正确性和相应于表达的真诚性:

1)在语言的认识式运用中,陈述内容的真实性就居于显著地位;2)在语言的相互作用式运用中,人际关系的正确性(或适宜性)就居于显著地位;3)在语言的表达式运用中,则是言说者的真诚性居于显著地位。但是在每一个交往行为的实际场合,所有有效性要求系统都将投入运作。它们必须并总是同时被提出,尽管它们并非同时被强调。(哈贝马斯,1989:67)

他认为,每一个言说的话语都可以依据这三个标准进行检验,"看它是真实的还是不真实的,正确的还是不正确的,真诚的还是不真诚的。"(哈贝马斯,1989:69)举例来说,凡是办得成功的电视节目,其叙述的事情都是真实的,表达的态度都是真诚的,与观众的关系都是得当的。相反,凡是不成功的电视节目,则问题往往出在这三个方面的某一个或两个或所有方面。

上文谈到,翻译是一种社会交往行为,制定翻译标准,必须既要关注其"社会"和"行为"这两个属性,又要关注其动态性。根据哈贝马斯的普遍语用学理论,我们将文学翻译的标准定为"达意"(conveyance of semantic meaning)、"达旨"(conveyance of intention)、"达趣"(conveyance of charm)、"达效"(conveyance of effects)的"四达"翻译标准,非文学翻译的标准定为"达意""达旨""达效"的"三达"翻译标准。所谓"达意"就是指译文必须传达源语文本的语义;"达旨"就是指译文必须传达原文作者的写作意图;"达趣"是指译文必须传达源语文本的神韵;"达效"是指译文必须取得同原文一样的效果。

在以上所列出的"四达"或"三达"翻译标准中，它们的顺序可以根据不同文本及其翻译目的的不同而有所变化。这种顺序的变化正可以体现出翻译的动态性，因为对不同文本的翻译应有不同的要求。比如，非文学翻译中广告的翻译标准应为"达效""达旨"和"达意"而非通常情况之下的"达意""达旨""达效"这种顺序。

附录三：金隄建议的翻译的步骤

金隄先生在其专著《等效翻译探索》（1998年）第225页至227页中提出了翻译过程的三个阶段、九个步骤。因金先生当时写的有些情况与现在略有出入（如现在从事翻译主要借助电脑而非金先生所说的用手誊抄的方式进行），故对此文作者略有改动。

金先生认为，翻译共分三个阶段、九个步骤。

第一阶段为准备阶段：以理解原文为主，基本上单纯使用原语思维，其中以下第一、三两步尤其要避免使用译入语思维。

第一步：仔细阅读原文，以求对原文从内容到形式都有相当清楚的认识；避免使用自己的母语去思索词句的意义，不试图进行翻译。这一步非常重要，因为任何文字都有上下文关系。对原文先有一个清晰的整体概念，便可以在具体翻译过程中左右逢源。

第二步：研究作者，研究同一作者的其他著作，研究有关对作者进行研究和评论的背景材料。（这一步可利用译入语资料。以外译中而言，外文、中文资料都要看）。

第三步：对即将动手翻译的原文（一章或一节）进行彻底研究，务求对其中的内容、形象、细节、暗藏涵义（包括双关语之类复杂词语的多层涵义等）取得尽可能充分的理解，对原文的艺术风格及其韵味心领神会，产生共鸣。在这一过程中，力求逐个解决原文中各种疑难问题，做到尽可能全面掌握原文。为避免受到译入语（往往是译者母语）"对等词"和语言习惯的干扰，在不知不觉之间误入歧途，这一掌握原文的步骤要坚持用原语思维，特别是在解决文字难点时更是如此。在该过程中，要尽可能不用双语词典，充分利用描述性的原语词典和其他原语参考资料。

若要请教以原语为母语的人帮助，要在这一阶段进行。

第二阶段为双语双轨工作的具体翻译阶段。

第四步：在明确掌握原文基础上，运用译入语创造自己的译文。创造译文过程中要摆脱原语词汇、语法规律和各种语言习惯的约束，充分发挥自己在译入语中的写作才能，利用一切可利用的文字艺术手段，尽量做到恰到好处，以求获得最接近原文意境和情调的效果。头脑一方面要吸收原文，一方面要创造译文，处于一种双轨并行的工作状态，既要彼此不受对方语言规律的干扰，又要切切实实反映对方的精神内容和风格神态。这时有可能在原文中发现一些原来没有充分理解的深意，便须暂停双语工作，重返原语单语工作，以便深入准确掌握新意。

第五步：译稿完成后逐句核对原文，确保没有遗漏、节外生枝和歪曲。

第六步：将译稿放置一个时期以便"冷却"，目的是使自己的印象淡漠下去（在此期间可进行其他部分工作）。

第三阶段为基本上单纯使用译入语的复核阶段。

第七步：用"冷却"后的新眼光审阅译稿，使自己的眼光尽可能接近客观的读者，不要参考原文。（如有不看原文不明白处，可以肯定此处译文有问题，须重新加工。）最好朗诵，以便调动更多官能参与，因为口、耳往往能发觉眼睛漏掉的问题。审阅修改译文时，慎重考虑某些特别巧妙的译文，至少做到读者经过咀嚼能够吸收。这一步完成后便可打印定稿。

第八步：请不懂原语的读者阅读基本定稿，或为他们朗诵，请他们指出不易理解或感到别扭的地方。（其中一部分有可能在讨论之后就被接受，但此时的讨论决不能以原语规律为理由。）如为他们朗诵，注意观察他们的表情。如译文中有涉及某种专业知识处，应向懂行的读者请教。

第九步：仔细考虑读者意见，对译稿作最后润色。并非单纯从文采着眼，而是着眼作品的效果，力求恰如其分。有时可能需要反复核对原文，但看原文应采用第一阶段第三步的办法。本第三阶段的第七、八、九步，基本上都是使用译入语的单语工作，排除原语规律的干扰，但对于两种文本所传递的信息则力求一致，重点注意其中的事实、思想、形象和情趣。

参考文献

[1] 蔡基刚. 大学英语翻译教程 [M]. 上海：上海外语教育出版社，2003.

[2] 蔡宗源. 翻译 [M]. 上海：上海教育出版社，2000.

[3] 常春藤英语考试研究组. 英语专业八级翻译指南 [M]. 上海：上海交通大学出版社，2004.

[4] 陈宏薇. 新实用汉译英教程 [M]. 武汉：湖北教育出版社，1996.

[5] 陈宏薇. 汉英翻译基础 [M]. 上海：上海外语教育出版社，1998.

[6] 陈文伯. 译艺 [M]. 北京：世界知识出版社，2004.

[7] 陈新. 英汉文体翻译教程 [M]. 北京：北京大学出版社，1999.

[8] 丁树德. 翻译技法详论 [M]. 天津：天津大学出版社，2005.

[9] 范红升. 英语形合与汉语意合的特点对翻译的启示 [J]. 解放军外语学院学报，1996（6）：52-56.

[10] 范仲英. 实用翻译教程 [M]. 北京：外语教学与研究出版社，1994.

[11] 方梦之. 英语汉译实践与技巧 [M]. 天津：天津科技翻译出版公司，1994.

[12] 方梦之. 翻译新论与实践 [M]. 青岛：青岛出版社，2002.

[13] 冯庆华. 实用翻译教程 [M]. 上海：上海外语教育出版社，1995.

[14] 傅敬民，张顺梅，薛清. 英汉翻译辨析 [M]. 北京：中国对外翻译出版公司，2005.

[15] 傅晓玲，尚媛媛，曾春莲. 英汉互译高级教程 [M]. 广州：中山大学出版社，2004.

[16] 高等外语教学指导委员会英语组. 高等学校英语专业英语教学大纲 [M]. 上海：上海外语教育出版社，2000.

[17] 辜正坤. 中西诗比较鉴赏与翻译理论 [M]. 北京：清华大学出版社，2003.

[18] 古今明. 英汉翻译基础 [M]. 上海：上海外语教育出版社，1997.

[19] 顾子欣. 英诗三百首 [M]. 北京：线装书局出版社，2015.

[20] 郭富强. 英汉翻译理论与实践 [M]. 北京：机械工业出版社，2004.

[21] 郭著章. 英汉互译实用教程 [M]. 武汉：武汉大学出版社，1988.

[22] 郭著章，李庆生. 英汉互译实用教程 [M]. 武汉：武汉大学出版社，1996.

[23] 哈贝马斯. 交往与社会进化 [M]. 重庆：重庆出版社，1989.

[24] 黄德新. 英汉双向翻译教程 [M]. 济南：山东教育出版社，1996.

[25] 黄国文. 语篇分析概要 [M]. 长沙：湖南教育出版社，1998.

[26] 姜秋霞，张柏然. 整体概念与翻译 [J]. 中国翻译，1996（6）：15-18.

[27] 金隄. 等效翻译探索 [M]. 北京：中国对外翻译出版公司，1998.

[28] 金惠康. 跨文化交际翻译 [M]. 北京：中国对外翻译出版公司，2002.

[29] 金微. 知其然，亦应知其所以然——论英语关系分句（定语从句）及其汉译 [J]. 中国翻译，1991（5）：14-16.

[30] 柯飞. 翻译中的隐和显 [J]. 外语教学与研究，2005（4）：303-307.

[31] 柯平. 英汉与汉英翻译教程 [M]. 北京：北京大学出版社，1993.

[32] 孔子. 论语 [M]. WALEY A，译. 北京：外语教学与研究出版社，1998.

[33] 李彬. 符号透视：传播内容的本体诠释 [M]. 上海：复旦大学出版社，2003.

[34] 李建军. 新编英汉翻译 [M]. 上海：东华大学出版社，2004.

[35] 李鑫华. 英语修辞格详论 [M]. 上海：上海外语教育出版社，2000.

[36] 李运兴. 英汉语篇翻译 [M]. 北京：清华大学出版社，1998.

[37] 连淑能. 英汉对比研究 [M]. 北京：高等教育出版社，1993.

[38] 林煌天. 中国翻译词典 [Z]. 武汉：湖北教育出版社，1997.

[39] 刘重德. 文学翻译十讲 [M]. 北京：中国对外翻译出版公司，1991.

[40] 刘宓庆. 文体与翻译 [M]. 北京：中国对外翻译出版公司，1986.

[41] 刘宓庆. 当代翻译理论 [M]. 北京：中国对外翻译出版公司，1999.

[42] 刘宓庆. 翻译美学导论 [M]. 北京：中国对外翻译出版公司，2005.

[43] 陆谷孙. 英汉大词典 [Z]. 上海：上海译文出版社，1993.

[44] 罗素. 西方哲学史 [M]. 何兆武，李约瑟，译. 北京：商务印书馆，1980.

[45] 吕俊. 对翻译学构建中几个问题的思考 [J]. 中国翻译，2001（4）：6-9.

[46] 吕俊. 结构·解构·建构——我国翻译研究的回顾与展望 [J]. 中国翻译，2001（6）：8-11.

[47] 吕俊. 翻译学：解构与重建——论哈贝马斯交往行动理论对翻译学的建构性意义 [J]. 外语学刊，2002（1）：87-92.

[48] 吕俊，侯向群. 英汉翻译教程 [M]. 上海：上海外语教育出版社，2001.

[49] 马红军. 翻译批评散论 [M]. 北京：中国对外翻译出版公司，2000.

[50] 毛荣贵. 英译汉技巧新编 [M]. 北京：外文出版社，2001.

[51] 毛荣贵. 翻译美学 [M]. 上海：上海交通大学出版社，2005.

[52] 孟庆升. 新编英汉翻译教程 [M]. 沈阳：辽宁大学出版社，2003.

[53] 穆凤良. 逻辑比较与英汉翻译 [M]. 北京：国防工业出版社，2009.

[54] 普特博. 天堂不可承受之亡 [J]. 孙建成，译. 中国翻译，2013（5）：116-118.

[55] 乔海清. 论隐译 [J]. 上海科技翻译，1999（1）：44-47.

[56] 乔萍，瞿淑蓉，宋洪玮. 散文佳作108篇 [C]. 南京：译林出版社，2011.

[57] 秦秀白. 当代英语习语大词典 [Z]. 北京：外语教学与研究出版社，2000.

[58] 沈苏儒. 论信达雅——严复翻译理论研究 [M]. 北京：商务印书馆，1998.

[59] 束定芳. 隐喻学研究 [M]. 上海：上海外语教育出版社，2000.

[60] 司显柱. 对我国传统译论的反思——关于翻译技巧研究的思考 [J]. 中国翻译，2002（3）：39-41.

[61] 宋德利. 译心——我的翻译三宗罪 [M]. 北京：金城出版社，2014.

[62] 宋天锡，袁江，袁冬娥. 英汉互译实用教程 [M]. 北京：国防工业出版社，2000.

[63] 隋荣谊. 英汉翻译新教程 [M]. 北京：中国电力出版社，2004.

[64] 孙迎春. 汉英双向翻译学语林 [M]. 济南：山东大学出版社，2001.

[65] 孙致礼. 译者的克己意识与创造意识 [J]. 上海科技翻译，2000（1）：1-5.

[66] 孙致礼. 新编英汉翻译教程 [M]. 上海：上海外语教育出版社，2003.

[67] 倜西，董乐山，张今. 英译汉理论与实例 [M]. 北京：北京大学出版社，1984.

[68] 汪涛. 实用英汉互译技巧 [M]. 武汉：武汉大学出版社，2001.

[69] 王东风. 中国译学研究：世纪末的思考 [C]// 张柏然，许均. 面向21世纪的译学研究. 北京：商务印书馆，2002：52-72.

[70] 王东风，章于炎. 英汉语序的比较和翻译 [J]. 外语教学与研究，1993（4）：36-44.

[71] 王宏印. 英汉翻译综合教程 [M]. 沈阳：辽宁师范大学出版社，2002.

[72] 王寅. 英译汉：句法结构比较 [J]. 中国翻译，1993（5）：10-13.

[73] 王治奎. 大学英汉翻译教程 [M]. 济南：山东大学出版社，1999.

[74] 王佐良. 英国诗文选译集 [M]. 北京：外语教学与研究出版社，1980.

[75] 王佐良. 英国诗选 [M]. 上海：上海译文出版社，2012.

[76] 吴群. 调整句界，整合语序——充分把握原文，有效落实译文 [J]. 中国翻译，2003（2）：79-84.

[77] 夏力力. 文学翻译与节奏美学 [J]. 中国翻译，1996（6）：19-21.

[78] 夏立新. 浅谈英汉翻译中的音韵和节奏美 [J]. 天津外国语学院学报，2003（6）：7-9.

[79] 徐莉娜. 英译汉中引申依据初探 [J]. 中国翻译，1996（4）：36-39.

[80] 徐志刚. 论语通译 [M]. 北京：人民文学出版社，1997.

[81] 许国璋. 许国璋论语言 [C]. 北京：外语教学与研究出版社，1991.

[82] 许建平. 英汉互译实践与技巧 [M]. 北京：清华大学出版社，2000.

[83] 杨莉黎. 英汉互译教程（上册）[M]. 开封：河南大学出版社，1993.

[84] 杨立民，徐克容. 大学英语教程 3（修订本）[M]. 北京：外语教学与研究出版社，1996.

[85] 叶子南. 高级英汉翻译理论与实践 [M]. 北京：清华大学出版社，2001.

[86] 殷宝书. 英语定语从句的译法 [J]. 外语教学与研究，1963（1）：12-19.

[87] 曾利沙. 论翻译艺术创造性的本质特征——从译者主体思维特征看艺术再现与艺术表现的典型性 [J]. 四川外语学院学报，2005（5）：114-118.

[88] 詹蓓. 英汉动物喻体喻用含义的对比分析 [J]. 外语研究，2003（3）：33-36.

[89] 张柏然，许均. 面向 21 世纪的译学研究 [C]. 北京：商务印书馆，2002.

[90] 张培基，喻云根，李宗杰，等. 英汉翻译教程 [M]. 上海：上海外语教育出版社，1980.

[91] 张泽乾. 翻译经纬 [M]. 武汉：武汉大学出版社，1994.

[92] 赵桂华. 翻译理论与技巧 [M]. 哈尔滨：哈尔滨工业大学出版社，2002.

[93] 赵前洋. 名利场 [M]. 成都：四川文艺出版社，1997.

[94] 郑军荣. 翻译中译者的开放与细节处理 [J]. 中国翻译，2013（5）：49-51.

[95] 仲伟合. 西方翻译理论 [M]. 广州：广州外语音像出版社，2001.

[96] 周方珠. 英汉翻译教程 [M]. 合肥：安徽大学出版社，1997.

[97] 朱佩芬. 实用英汉口译技巧 [M]. 上海：华东理工大学出版社，1995.

[98] Bell, R. T. (1991). *Translation and Translating: Theory and Practice*. Essex, UK: Longman Group UK Ltd.

[99] Bradbury, R. (1953). *Fahrenheit 451*. New York, NY: Ballantine Books.

[100] Fawcett, P. (1997). *Translation and Language: Linguistic Theories Explained*. Manchester, UK: St. Jerome Publishing.

[101] Goatly, A. (1997). *The Language of Metaphors*: *Literal Metaphorical*. London, UK: Routledge.

[102] Hatim, B., & Mason, I. (2001). *Discourse and the Translator*. Shanghai, China: Shanghai Foreign Language Education Press.

[103] Hervey, S., Higgins, I., & Loughridge, M. (1995). *Thinking German Translation*: *A Course in Translation Method*: *German to English*. London, UK: Routledge.

[104] Lakoff, G., & Johnson, M. (1980). *Metaphors We Live By*. Chicago, IL: University of Chicago Press.

[105] Lee, D. (1992). *Competing Discourse*: *Perspective and Ideology in Language*. Essex, UK: Longman Group UK Ltd.

[106] Levinson, S. C. (2001). *Pragmatics*. Beijing, China: Foreign Language Teaching and Research Press.

[107] Nida, E. A. (1959). Principles of translation as exemplified by Bible translating. In Brower, R. A. (Ed.) *On Translation* (pp. 323-342). Oxford, UK: Oxford University Press.

[108] Procter, P. (1978). *Longman Dictionary of Contemporary English* [Z]. Essex, UK: Longman Group UK Ltd.